Disaffections

Disaffections

Complete Poems 1930–1950

Cesare Pavese

Translated by Geoffrey Brock

COPPER CANYON PRESS
A Kage-an Book

Poems by Cesare Pavese copyright 1998 by Giulio Einaudi editore s.p.a., Torino

Translation copyright 2002 by Geoffrey Brock
"Walking with Pavese" copyright 2002 by Geoffrey Brock

Printed in the United States of America.

Cover art: *Wheat*, 1967, oil on wood, by Thomas Hart Benton. Courtesy of Smithsonian American Art Museum, gift of Mr. and Mrs. James A. Mitchell and museum purchase.

Copper Canyon Press is in residence under the auspices of the Centrum Foundation at Fort Worden State Park in Port Townsend, Washington. Centrum sponsors artist residencies, education workshops for Washington State students and teachers, Blues, Jazz, and Fiddle Tunes Festivals, classical music performances, and The Port Townsend Writers' Conference.

LIBRARY OF CONGRESS CATALOGING-IN-PUBLICATION DATA

Pavese, Cesare.
Disaffections: complete poems 1930–1950 / Cesare Pavese; translated by Geoffrey Brock.
    p. cm.
ISBN 1-55659-174-8
1. Pavese, Cesare — Translations into English.
1. Brock, Geoffrey, 1964–   II. Title.

PQ4835.A846 A23 2002
851'.912 — DC21   2001007425
9 8 7 6 5

Kage-an Books (from the Japanese, meaning "shadow hermitage" and representing the shadow work of the translator) present the world's great poetic traditions, ancient and modern, in vivid translations edited for Copper Canyon Press by Sam Hamill.

COPPER CANYON PRESS
Post Office Box 271
Port Townsend, Washington 98368

www.coppercanyonpress.org

ACKNOWLEDGMENTS

Warm thanks to the editors of the following journals, in which many of these translations first appeared:

Five Points: "Work's Tiring (I)," "Indian Summer," "Song," "Grappa in September," "Atlantic Oil," "City in the Country," and "People Who Don't Understand"

Gradiva: International Journal of Italian Literature: "Words for a Girlfriend"

International Quarterly: "Earth and Death"

Italian Americana: "Imagination's End"

Literary Review: "South Seas" and "Passion for Solitude"

Modern Poetry in Translation: "Death will come and will have your eyes"

New England Review: "The Boy Who Was in Me," "Deola's Return," and "Sleeping Friend"

New Letters: "Fallen Women"

The New Republic: "Two Poems for T."

Pequod: "Sand-Diggers' Twilight," "Tolerance," and "Two Cigarettes"

TriQuarterly: "Creation," "Habits" and "Sad Wine (II)"

Two Lines: "Alter Ego" and "Poggio Reale"

Yale Italian Poetry: "Street Song," "The House," "Betrayal," "Sad Wine (I)," "Landholders," and "Idleness"

I'm also grateful to the Academy of American Poets, which awarded me the Raiziss/de Palchi Translation Fellowship, and to the American Academy in Rome, where much of this work was completed. This book would not exist in its present form without the generosity of these organizations. Finally, my thanks to the many individuals who provided assistance and advice along the way, especially Anna Botta, Judith Moffett, Anthony Molino, Alessandra Osti, and Mark Pietralunga. They have contributed substantially to whatever virtues this volume possesses. Its vices, of course, are Pavese's and mine. — G.B.

Contents

3   Introduction: Walking with Pavese

PART ONE **Work's Tiring** (1936)

17   South Seas

25   Ancestors

29   Landscape (I)

33   Displaced People

35   Deola Thinking

39   Street Song

41   Two Cigarettes

43   Idleness

47   Landholders

51   Landscape (II)

53   Landscape (III)

55   A Season

59   Dina Thinking

61   Betrayal

65   Passion for Solitude

67   The Billy-Goat God

71   Time Passes

75   Grappa in September

77   Atlantic Oil

81   City in the Country

85   People Who Don't Understand

89   House under Construction

93   Ancient Civilization

97   Bad Company

99   Nocturnal Pleasures

101 Ballet

103 Fatherhood (I)

105 Ancient Discipline

107 Indiscipline

109 Landscape (V)

111 Discipline

113 Green Wood

115 Revolt

117 Outside

119 Work's Tiring (II)

121 Portrait of the Author

125 Mediterraneans

129 Sad Supper

133 Landscape (IV)

135 Motherhood

137 A Generation

139 Ulysses

141 Atavism

143 Affairs

145 Passionate Women

147 August Moon

149 Burnt Lands

151 Poggio Reale

153 Landscape (VI)

PART TWO Work's Tiring (1943)

157 The Widow's Son

161 People Who've Been There

163 The Night

165 Meeting

167 Revelation

169   Morning

171   Summer (I)

173   Nocturne

175   Agony

177   Landscape (VII)

179   Tolerance

181   The Country Whore

185   Afterwards

189   Sand-Diggers' Twilight

193   The Wagoner

195   A Memory

197   The Voice

199   The Boatman's Wife

203   The Drunk Old Woman

205   Landscape (VIII)

207   Smokers of Paper

211   Words from Confinement

213   Myth

215   Paradise above the Roofs

217   Simplicity

219   Instinct

221   Fatherhood (II)

223   Morning Star over Calabria

PART THREE   Poems of Disaffection

227   Words for a Girlfriend

231   The Schoolmistresses

237   Fallen Women

241   The Blues Blues

243   Song

245   Sad Wine (I)

249   The Boy Who Was in Me

253   Indian Summer

255   Work's Tiring (I)

259   The Unconvinced

261   Imagination's End

263   Jealousy (I)

267   Sad Wine (II)

269   Creation

271   Reigning Peace

273   Other Days

277   Poetics

279   Alter Ego

281   Sketch of a Landscape

283   Deola's Return

285   Habits

287   Summer (II)

289   Dream

291   Sleeping Friend

293   Indifference

295   Jealousy (II)

297   Awakening

299   Landscape (IX)

301   Two

303   The House

PART FOUR   Last Blues

Earth and Death

309   "Red earth black earth"

311   "You are like a land"

313   "You are also hill"

315　"Your face is sculpted stone"

317　"You do not know the hills"

319　"Your gaze is brine and earth"

323　"You always come from the sea"

327　"And then we cowards"

329　"You are earth and death"

Two Poems for T.

333　"The plants of the lake"

335　"You also are love"

Death Will Come and Will Have Your Eyes

339　To C. from C.

341　In the Morning You Always Come Back

343　"You have a blood, a breath"

347　"Death will come and will have your eyes"

349　You, Wind of March

353　I Will Pass through Piazza di Spagna

355　"The mornings pass clear"

357　The Night You Slept

359　The Cats Will Know

363　Last Blues, to Be Read Some Day

365　*Notes on the Text*

367　*About the Author*

367　*About the Translator*

369　*Index of English Titles*

371　*Index of Italian Titles*

Disaffections

Introduction: Walking with Pavese

On June 24, 1950, Cesare Pavese received the Strega Prize, Italy's most prestigious literary award. He wrote in his diary that it had "the appearance of being my greatest triumph," and indeed it marked the culmination of his rise to the forefront of postwar Italian letters. Yet he couldn't bring himself to care deeply about the award. "The trouble about these things," he told a friend, "is that they always come when one is already through with them and running after strange, different gods." The gods he ran after then, however, were the two he had always chased: love, which seemed always unattainable, and which was represented at this moment in his life by an American starlet who never matched his ardor; and death, which he had long considered love's most seductive alternative. He was continually torn between the desire to connect with the world ("I have a terrible thirst," he wrote in a January 1938 letter, "for friendship and community") and the desire to escape from it into radical solitude.

He had been profoundly drawn to suicide for most of his life, writing about it frequently in his diary, his letters, and his fiction. "I live with the idea of suicide always in my mind," he wrote when still not quite thirty. And when just eighteen, shortly after a friend had killed himself, Pavese foresaw and dramatized in a poem his own suicide, which would happen, he wrote, on "the night when the last illusion / and the terrors will have left me." In that early melodramatic fantasy, he put a gun to his temple and fired, but when the real night came, on August 26, 1950, just two months after his "greatest triumph," he chose sleeping pills, leaving a simple note: "I forgive everyone and ask everyone's forgiveness. OK? Don't gossip too much."

Though the note was brief, the timing speaks volumes about how little professional success sometimes matters in the face of personal unhappiness. Yet it is the fruit of his professional success—his *work*—that remains and that continues to matter. And though much of his life can be seen as a turning inward, away from the world and eventually toward death, his writing must be seen as arising from exactly the opposite impulse. Even when his subject is the turning inward, the work itself is a reaching out, an affirming gesture.

Pavese was born in 1908 on his parents' farm just outside Santo Stefano Belbo, a small rural town in the Langhe hills near the cosmopolitan city of Turin. Though he grew up mostly in Turin, he spent many summers, as well as his first year of elementary school, in Santo Stefano, and those hills and the people who lived in them and worked them marked him deeply. But Turin marked him too, and in his groundbreaking first collection of poems, *Lavorare stanca* (*Work's Tiring*), the division within himself between city and country developed into a major theme, as described in his diary:

> Chance made me begin and end *Work's Tiring* with
> poems about Turin—more precisely, about Turin as a
> place from which and to which one returns. You could
> call the book the spreading into and conquering of
> Turin by Santo Stefano Belbo.... The town becomes
> the city, nature becomes human life, boy becomes
> man. As I see it, "from Santo Stefano to Turin" is a
> myth of all the conceivable meanings of this book.
> (2/16/36)

The theme has broad cultural as well as personal significance, since Turin, like cities elsewhere, was a center of gravity whose pull grew stronger as the economy became increasingly industrialized. Many of Pavese's early poems are inhabited by characters who seem to have been drawn to the city by its economic promise, only to encounter varying degrees of disappointment and isolation: Masino, who spends his days in the city looking for work ("Idleness"); Gella, who works in the city but returns each evening to the family farm ("People Who Don't Understand"); a priest who lives and works in the city, having left his mother behind in their hometown, where she dies alone ("Landowners"), and others.

The tension between city and country life is just one aspect of the social dimension of Pavese's poetry, a dimension that is striking enough in itself but positively extraordinary when viewed in the context of the Hermeticism that dominated the Italian poetic landscape of the 1930s. *Work's Tiring*, published in 1936, consisted of poems written in accessible, rhythmic language that told the stories of farmers and factory workers, thieves and drunks, lonely prostitutes and lonelier men. This in a time when the work of many of the leading Italian poets, including Ungaretti, Montale, and Quasimodo, often dispensed with both the logical sequence of narrative and immediately apprehensible language. As Gian-Paolo Biasin wrote in *The Smile of the Gods,* his study of Pavese, Italian poetry had "rejected any contact with the political and social reality of its time (Fascism and the rise of the bourgeoisie), or else adopted only its most extreme and superficial aspects, such as the nationalism of F.T. Marinetti or of D'Annunzio." Pavese had no patience for such nationalisms, and he countered Hermeticism's deliberate obscurity (which to be fair may have been, in some cases, a response to Fascist censorship) with his own deliberate demotic, derived in part from his intensive study of American writers.

In the late 1920s, Pavese began to feel (as he described in an interview shortly before his death) that "the bold winds of the world," to which "the castle of the closed Italian literary culture remained impervious," were blowing strongest from America. By this time, he had for six years been steadily writing his own poetry, often with the results one would expect from a precocious teenager: formal experiments, satires of established styles, self-indulgent expressions of teenage lust and angst. (The vast majority of this juvenilia remained unpublished until 1998, when his Italian publisher released an expanded collection of his poems that contained more than a hundred pieces, not included in this volume, from the 1920s.) But in November of 1929, when Pavese was twenty-one, two things happened: he declared his resolve "to devote [him]self fully to the study of American literature," and, at the same time, he stopped writing his own poetry.

Over the next year, Pavese did indeed immerse himself in reading, translating, and writing about authors from across the Atlantic; within a few years he would be established as one of Italy's leading interpreters of American literature. Walt Whitman had earlier been the subject of Pavese's highly regarded thesis, and now he turned to American contemporaries including Sinclair Lewis (Nobel Prize, 1930), Sherwood Anderson, and Edgar Lee Masters, whose work had in common a social dimension he found lacking in the work of most of his

Italian contemporaries. His 1931 essay on *The Spoon River Anthology*, seems at times to describe the book of poems he himself was beginning to write:

> A book...where nearly everyone laments a wasted life might well seem, on casual reading, a survey of clinical cases. The difference lies only in the eye of the poet who views his dead not with a morbid or polemical satisfaction, nor with that pseudoscientific indifference that is now, unfortunately, so popular in the States, but rather with an austere yet sympathetic awareness of everyone's griefs and vanities. From each he elicits a confession, from each he extracts a definitive answer, not in order to produce a scientific or sociological document, but only out of a thirst for human truth.

Pavese is less likely than Masters to try to extract "definitive answers" from his characters, and that is an important difference between the two writers. But in general this passage, especially the final phrases, applies as well to many of the poems in *Work's Tiring*.

Nine months passed, after his immersion in American literature, before he wrote his next poem, "Words for a Girlfriend," in August of 1930, followed a month later by "South Seas." By this time a sea change had taken place in his style. "Words for a Girlfriend," the earliest of the poems included in this collection, may usefully be considered the first authentic Pavese poem; though still a youthful work, it is clearly more closely tied to what came next than to what had gone before. In it, he made two crucial discoveries that paved the way for all his poems of the 1930s. The first was the idea of the *poesia-racconto*, or "poem-story" —Pavese conceived of his poems as short stories in verse. The second was the idiosyncratic meter that he would later call "the rhythm of my imagination." As Pavese recognized, "South Seas" represents the first major success in achieving his new aims, and for that reason it became the opening poem in *Work's Tiring*.

Both these poems begin with two people walking together in silence, which is as good an emblem as any for the fraught relationship in Pavese's work (and life) between solitude and company. In both opening lines, we have the seeds of narratives and themes that will come to seem typically Pavesian, and in both we have also the distilled essence of his new prosody:

Vado a spasso in silenzio con una bambina
(I walk without saying a word with a girl)

from "Words for a Girlfriend"

Camminiamo una sera sul fianco di un colle
(We're walking one evening on the flank of a hill)

from "South Seas"

The two lines are, in the original, metrically identical, and though accentual-syllabic verse is rare in Italian poetry—the standard meters such as the *endecasillabo* and the *settenario* are primarily syllabic, without prescribed accentual patterns—Pavese in the 1930s is an accentual-syllabic poet, and a fairly strict one at that. His primary meter is (as in the lines above) anapestic, which is nearly as unusual in Italian as in English, and his usual line length is four feet, though he frequently extends lines to five or even six feet and occasionally shortens them to three.

In the essay "Il mestiere di poeta" ("The Poet's Craft"), which originally appeared as an appendix to the expanded 1943 edition of *Work's Tiring,* Pavese explains the origins of his new meter:

At that time, I knew only that free verse was ill-suited
to my spirit.... But I lacked faith in traditional meters....
And besides I had parodied them too often to take them
seriously now.... I knew of course that traditional
meters don't exist in any absolute sense, but are
remade according to the interior rhythms of each poet's
imagination. And one day I found myself muttering a
certain jumble of words (which turned into a pair of
lines from "South Seas") in a pronounced cadence that

I had used for emphasis ever since I was a child, when I would murmur over and over the phrases that obsessed me most in the novels I was reading. That's how, without knowing it, I found my verse, which was of course, for all of "South Seas" and several other poems as well, wholly instinctive.... Gradually I discovered the intrinsic laws of this meter..., but I was always careful not to let it tyrannize me and was ready to accept, when it seemed necessary, other stress patterns and line lengths. But I never again strayed far from my scheme, which I consider the rhythm of my imagination.

The prosodic change that followed his nine-month silence was dramatic. This "rhythm of his imagination," rarely present in his work of the 1920s, is rarely absent from his work of the 1930s.

Over the next few years, while writing the poems of *Work's Tiring*, Pavese translated American writers (Lewis, Melville, Anderson, Dos Passos, Steinbeck, and Gertrude Stein), helped build a publishing house, and, along with many of his friends and colleagues, ran afoul of the Fascist government. In 1933, Giulio Einaudi established his eponymous publishing house, now one of Italy's most prestigious, and surrounded himself with anti-Fascist intellectuals, including Leone Ginzburg, a brilliant activist later tortured to death in prison, and Augusto Monti, Pavese's college professor and mentor. This group drew the attention and ire of the government, and in 1935 Einaudi, Pavese, Monti, and many others were arrested in Turin for suspected anti-Fascist activities. Pavese spent several months in prison before being sentenced to three years of "confinement" in Brancaleone Calabro, a southern Italian coastal town that was about as remote as possible, both geographically and culturally, from Turin.

The irony of Pavese's arrest and confinement is that, despite the company he kept, he was not a political activist at all, at least not in any conventional sense. Indeed, he sometimes professed not to understand or even care about politics and often refrained from taking part in his friends' political discussions. It is not an exaggeration, however, to say that in the context of the time, when Fascism was making a religion of nationalism, Pavese's literary work, and particularly his translations of American writers, constituted an affront to, if not an assault on, the official culture. Davide Lajolo, in his biography of Pavese, *Il vizio assurdo* (*The Absurd Vice*), argues persuasively that Pavese's translations made not only a substantial literary contribution ("they opened the way to a new period in Italian fiction") but a political one as well, by countering the prevailing nationalistic rhetoric and presenting Italian readers with alternative cultural and social possibilities.

In his 1947 essay "Oggi e ieri" ("Yesterday and Today"), Pavese recalls that period as a kind of rediscovery of America, one which inspired outrage among Fascist officials and subversive joy among some readers:

> The air of scandal and easy heresy that surrounded the
> new books and their content, the passion for revolt
> and openness that even the most careless readers felt
> pulsating in those translated pages, were irresistible to
> a public not yet entirely stupefied by conformism and
> rhetoric. One can frankly say that at least in the fields
> of fashion and taste, the new trend helped more than a
> little to sustain and nourish the political opposition,
> however generic and futile, of the Italian reading pub-
> lic. For many people, the encounter with Caldwell,
> Steinbeck, Saroyan, and even old Lewis, provided the
> first glimmer of freedom, the first suspicion that not
> everything in the world's culture led to Fascism.

At the time, of course, his motives for undertaking such translations were primarily literary; it was only later that he came to understand the degree to which they harmonized with political ends.

We know from his letters and diary that Pavese's experience in Brancaleone proved more than even he, a connoisseur of solitude, could easily bear. In one of his many moving and often humorous letters from confinement ("my *Tristia*," he joked), Pavese reproached himself for having in the past actively sought to be alone:

> I remember my anger toward those three who wanted
> to come boating with me on the Po, and I mourn for
> my past unhappiness. What an utter fool I was to be-
> lieve, as I did then, that personal isolation, even for a
> moment, would be bliss. (3/2/36)

Days after writing these words, he learned that after eight months of confinement his sentence had been commuted and he was to be released. He had made good use of his time, completing *Work's Tiring* and beginning his diary, published posthumously to great acclaim as *Il mestiere di vivere* (*The Job of Living*). But his return to Turin was marked by twin disappointments that only deepened his sense of isolation: the woman he loved had just married someone else, and *Work's Tiring* appeared to general indifference.

He continued to believe strongly in the poems of *Work's Tiring*, and in 1943 he released a revised, restructured, and substantially expanded edition. (The second section of this volume contains the poems he added.) But by the late 1930s he had turned most of his creative energy toward fiction, and by the end of the 1940s had published, in addition to a collection of short stories, nine short novels that Italo Calvino, writing in *L'Europa letteraria* in 1960, called "the most dense, dramatic, and homogeneous narrative cycle of modern Italy" and "the richest in representing social ambiences, the human comedy, the chronicle of society."

Pavese returned to poetry only occasionally in the last years of his life, and his late poems (gathered here under the heading "Last Blues") mark an astonishing break from the *Work's Tiring* period. Gone are the long lines, the narrative structure, the ternary meter—in short, he has left behind both the poem-story and the rigorous rhythm that he first embraced in 1930 with "Words for a Girlfriend" and "South Seas." His new line is shorter and looser (primarily heptasyllabic), his style more lyrical, his subjects more darkly personal. And the mythic, Mediterranean atmosphere of much of this late poetry owes more to his fiction of this period, especially *Dialoghi con Leucò* (*Dialogues with Leucò*), than to *Work's Tiring*. The sequence of poems "Earth and Death," which originally appeared in a journal in 1945, were the last poems Pavese published during his lifetime. After his suicide, a new sequence, "Death Will Come and Will Have Your Eyes," was found in his desk, and it was published together with "Earth and Death" in a slim volume that remains extraordinarily popular in Italy.

Most of the late poems are addressed to a female "you," who, while inspired by particular real-life women, tends to blur into an archetypal figure who is by turns, and sometimes simultaneously, attractive and repulsive. She dominates the poems' mysterious and harrowing landscape of desire to such a degree that even the fresh specter of the war, present in several of these poems, seems overshadowed by her. These poems are the haunting coda of his career.

As a coda to this introduction, it seems appropriate to note the curiously circular relationship that Pavese has had with American literature. After pioneering (along with Elio Vittorini) the study of modern American writers in Italy through his translations and essays, he in turn has inspired new generations of American writers; Denise Levertov, Charles Wright, Philip Levine, and others have paid homage to him. Yet it has become difficult in this country to gain access to his work.

Most Americans who know Pavese's poetry at all know it primarily through *Hard Labor*, William Arrowsmith's 1976 translation of the 1943 edition of *Lavorare stanca*, and this translation is (like translations of his diary and novels) now unfortunately out of print. One of the strengths of the Arrowsmith versions is that they emerge into English with an undeniable energy and sensibility of their own. For my taste, such translations are nearly always preferable to blandly literal versions, which in their loyalty to the letter often betray the spirit. Still, Arrowsmith's versions sometimes betray the spirit of the Pavese poems in other ways. They are, for example, chattier and less *measured* (in all senses of that word) than Pavese's original poems, whose tight-lipped rhythm becomes an integral part of the experience of reading them, as it apparently was of the experience of writing them. I have felt obligated, in my translations, to try to create a similar rhythmic experience.

Of the American poets who have been influenced by him, I think Pavese himself would have felt the greatest admiration for the work of Philip Levine, who, in an interview about his 1999 collection *The Mercy,* called Pavese "the inspiration or maybe the trickster to whom I owe… whatever is worthy in the book." And in the poem "Cesare" from that volume, Levine conjures the Italian poet as an emblem for men confined to solitude:

> You too must know
> men like Cesare, still so young, brilliant,
> full of plans and tall tales. Then women
> enter their lives and the unfillable need
> for tenderness. They fall in love, then
> fall in love again and again and nothing
> comes of it but heartbreak. And they are men,
> so when you reach to touch them, to help them,
> they turn away because men must do that.

Certainly, much of Pavese's life and death was a turning away, but his work, it bears repeating, is a turning toward. It's my hope that this translation will help turn him and his poem-stories toward a new generation of American writers and readers.

— Geoffrey Brock

Part One

Work's Tiring

1936

I mari del Sud

a Monti

Camminiamo una sera sul fianco di un colle,
in silenzio. Nell'ombra del tardo crepuscolo
mio cugino è un gigante vestito di bianco,
che si muove pacato, abbronzato nel volto,
taciturno. Tacere è la nostra virtú.
Qualche nostro antenato dev'essere stato ben solo
—un grand'uomo tra idioti o un povero folle—
per insegnare ai suoi tanto silenzio.

Mio cugino ha parlato stasera. Mi ha chiesto
se salivo con lui: dalla vetta si scorge
nelle notti serene il riflesso del faro
lontano, di Torino. «Tu che abiti a Torino...»
mi ha detto «... ma hai ragione. La vita va vissuta
lontano dal paese: si profitta e si gode
e poi, quando si torna, come me, a quarant'anni,
si trova tutto nuovo. Le Langhe non si perdono».
Tutto questo mi ha detto e non parla italiano,
ma adopera lento il dialetto, che, come le pietre
di questo stesso colle, è scabro tanto
che vent'anni di idiomi e di oceani diversi
non gliel'hanno scalfito. E cammina per l'erta
con lo sguardo raccolto che ho visto, bambino,
usare ai contadini un poco stanchi.

Vent'anni è stato in giro per il mondo.
Se n'andò ch'io ero ancora un bambino portato da donne
e lo dissero morto. Sentii poi parlarne
da donne, come in favola, talvolta;
ma gli uomini, piú gravi, lo scordarono.
Un inverno a mio padre già morto arrivò un cartoncino
con un gran francobollo verdastro di navi in un porto

South Seas

to Monti

We're walking one evening on the flank of a hill
in silence. In the shadows of dusk
my cousin's a giant dressed all in white,
moving serenely, face bronzed by the sun,
not speaking. We have a talent for silence.
Some ancestor of ours must have been quite a loner—
a great man among fools or a crazy old bum—
to have taught his descendants such silence.

This evening he spoke. He asked if I'd join him to climb
to the top of the hill: from there you can see,
in the distance, on clear nights, the glow
of Turin. "You, living in Turin," he said,
"you've got the right idea. Life should be lived
far from here: make some money, have fun,
and then, when you come back, like me, at forty,
it all seems new. These hills will always be waiting."
He told me all this, not in Italian,
but in the slow dialect of these parts, which, like the rocks
right here on this hill, is so rugged and hard
that two decades of foreign tongues and oceans
never scratched its surface. And he climbs the steep path
with that self-contained look I saw as a boy
on the faces of farmers when they were tired.

For twenty years he wandered the world.
He left home when I was still being carried by women
and everyone figured he died. They spoke of him sometimes,
those women, as if his life were some fable,
but the men, more serious, simply forgot him.
One winter a card came for my dead father,
with a big green stamp showing ships in a port

e auguri di buona vendemmia. Fu un grande stupore,
ma il bambino cresciuto spiegò avidamente
che il biglietto veniva da un'isola detta Tasmania
circondata da un mare piú azzurro, feroce di squali,
nel Pacifico, a sud dell'Australia. E aggiunse che certo
il cugino pescava le perle. E staccò il francobollo.
Tutti diedero un loro parere, ma tutti conclusero
che, se non era morto, morirebbe.
Poi scordarono tutti e passò molto tempo.

Oh da quando ho giocato ai pirati malesi,
quanto tempo è trascorso. E dall'ultima volta
che son sceso a bagnarmi in un punto mortale
e ho inseguito un compagno di giochi su un albero
spaccandone i bei rami e ho rotto la testa
a un rivale e son stato picchiato,
quanta vita è trascorsa. Altri giorni, altri giochi,
altri squassi del sangue dinanzi a rivali
piú elusivi: i pensieri ed i sogni.
La città mi ha insegnato infinite paure:
una folla, una strada mi han fatto tremare,
un pensiero talvolta, spiato su un viso.
Sento ancora negli occhi la luce beffarda
dei lampioni a migliaia sul gran scalpiccío.

Mio cugino è tornato, finita la guerra,
gigantesco, fra i pochi. E aveva denaro.
I parenti dicevano piano: «Fra un anno a dir molto,
se li è mangiati tutti e torna in giro.
I disperati muoiono cosí».
Mio cugino ha una faccia recisa. Comprò un pianterreno
nel paese e ci fece riuscire un garage di cemento
con dinanzi fiammante la pila per dar la benzina
e sul ponte ben grossa alla curva una targa-réclame.
Poi ci mise un meccanico dentro a ricevere i soldi
e lui girò tutte le Langhe fumando.

and best wishes for the harvest. It was a shock,
but the boy, who had grown, explained with excitement
that it came from a place called Tasmania,
surrounded by the bluest waters, swarming with sharks,
in the Pacific, south of Australia. The cousin, he added,
was certainly fishing for pearls. And he peeled off the stamp.
Everyone had their opinion, but all were agreed
that if the cousin hadn't died yet, he would soon.
Then they forgot him again and many years passed.

Ah, so much time has gone by since we played
Malay pirates. And since the last time
I went down to swim in the dangerous waters
and followed a playmate up into a tree,
splitting its beautiful branches, and since
I bashed the head of a rival and got punched—
so much life has gone by. Other days, other games,
other spillings of blood in conflicts with rivals
of a more elusive kind: thoughts and dreams.
The city taught me an infinite number of fears:
a crowd or street could make me afraid,
or sometimes a thought, glimpsed on a face.
I still see the light from the thousands of streetlamps
that mocked the great shuffling beneath them.

After the war, my cousin, larger than life, came home,
he was one of the few. And now he had money.
Our relatives muttered: "A year, at the most,
he'll blow it all, and then take off again.
Bums live that way till the day they die."
My cousin's hardheaded. He bought a ground-floor place
in town, turning it into a concrete garage
with a gleaming red gas-pump out front
and over the bridge, at the curve, a big sign.
Then he hired a mechanic to handle the money
while he roamed the hills, smoking.

S'era intanto sposato, in paese. Pigliò una ragazza
esile e bionda come le straniere
che aveva certo un giorno incontrato nel mondo.
Ma uscí ancora da solo. Vestito di bianco,
con le mani alla schiena e il volto abbronzato,
al mattino batteva le fiere e con aria sorniona
contrattava i cavalli. Spiegò poi a me,
quando fallí il disegno, che il suo piano
era stato di togliere tutte le bestie alla valle
e obbligare la gente a comprargli i motori.
«Ma la bestia» diceva «piú grossa di tutte,
sono stato io a pensarlo. Dovevo sapere
che qui buoi e persone son tutta una razza».

Camminiamo da piú di mezz'ora. La vetta è vicina,
sempre aumenta d'intorno il frusciare e il fischiare del vento.
Mio cugino si ferma d'un tratto e si volge: «Quest'anno
scrivo sul manifesto:—*Santo Stefano*
è sempre stato il primo nelle feste
della valle del Belbo—e che la dicano
quei di Canelli». Poi riprende l'erta.
Un profumo di terra e di vento ci avvolge nel buio,
qualche lume in distanza: cascine, automobili
che si sentono appena: e io penso alla forza
che mi ha reso quest'uomo, strappandolo al mare
alle terre lontane, al silenzio che dura.
Mio cugino non parla dei viaggi compiuti.
Dice asciutto che è stato in quel luogo e in quell'altro
e pensa ai suoi motori.
                              Solo un sogno
gli è rimasto nel sangue: ha incrociato una volta
da fuochista su un legno olandese da pesca, il Cetaceo,
e ha veduto volare i ramponi pesanti nel sole,
ha veduto fuggire balene tra schiume di sangue
e inseguirle e innalzarsi le code e lottare alla lancia.
Me ne accenna talvolta.

Meanwhile he got married. He picked a girl
who was slender and blond like some of the women
he must have encountered during his travels.
But still he'd go out by himself. Dressed all in white,
hands clasped behind him, face bronzed by the sun,
he'd frequent the fairs in the morning, looking shrewd
and haggling over horses. He later explained,
when his scheme had failed, that he wanted to buy
every horse and ox in the valley, to force people
to replace them with things that had engines.
"But I was the real horse's ass," he said,
"to think it could ever have worked. I forgot
that folks around here are just like their oxen."

We've been walking for nearly an hour. Close to the peak
the wind begins rustling and whistling around us.
My cousin stops suddenly and turns: "This year
I'm making flyers saying: *Santo Stefano*
has always put on the best festivals
in the Belbo valley—even the guys in Canelli
should have to admit it." Then he keeps walking.
Around us in the dark the smell of earth and wind,
a few lights in the distance: farms, cars
you can barely hear. And I think of the strength
this man's given me, how it was wrenched from the sea,
from foreign lands, from silence that endures.
My cousin won't speak of the places he's been.
He says dryly that he was once here, or once there,
then he thinks of his engines.
                              Only one dream
has stayed in his blood: once, when he worked
as a stoker on a Dutch fishing boat, the *Cetacean*,
he saw the heavy harpoons sail in the sun,
and saw the whales as they fled in a frothing of blood
and the chase and the flukes lifting, fighting the launches.
Sometimes he mentions it.

Ma quando gli dico
ch'egli è tra i fortunati che han visto l'aurora
sulle isole piú belle della terra,
al ricordo sorride e risponde che il sole
si levava che il giorno era vecchio per loro.

But whenever I tell him
that he's one of the lucky ones to have seen the sun rise
over the loveliest islands in the world,
he smiles at the memory, then says that the sun
didn't rise till the day for them was already old.

Antenati

Stupefatto del mondo mi giunse un'età
che tiravo gran pugni nell'aria e piangevo da solo.
Ascoltare i discorsi di uomini e donne
non sapendo rispondere, è poca allegria.
Ma anche questa è passata: non sono piú solo
e, se non so rispondere, so farne a meno.
Ho trovato compagni trovando me stesso.

Ho scoperto che, prima di nascere, sono vissuto
sempre in uomini saldi, signori di sé,
e nessuno sapeva rispondere e tutti eran calmi.
Due cognati hanno aperto un negozio — la prima fortuna
della nostra famiglia — e l'estraneo era serio,
calcolante, spietato, meschino: una donna.
L'altro, il nostro, in negozio leggeva romanzi
— in paese era molto — e i clienti che entravano
si sentivan rispondere a brevi parole
che lo zucchero no, che il solfato neppure,
che era tutto esaurito. È accaduto piú tardi
che quest'ultimo ha dato una mano al cognato fallito.

A pensar questa gente mi sento piú forte
che a guardare lo specchio gonfiando le spalle
e atteggiando le labbra a un sorriso solenne.
È vissuto un mio nonno, remoto nei tempi,
che si fece truffare da un suo contadino
e allora zappò lui le vigne — d'estate —
per vedere un lavoro ben fatto. Cosí
sono sempre vissuto e ho sempre tenuto
una faccia sicura e pagato di mano.

E le donne non contano nella famiglia.
Voglio dire, le donne da noi stanno in casa

Ancestors

Stunned by the world, I reached an age
when I threw punches at air and cried to myself.
Listening to the speech of women and men,
not knowing how to respond, it's not fun.
But this too has passed: I'm not alone anymore,
and if I still don't know how to respond,
I don't need to. Finding myself, I found company.

I learned that before I was born I had lived
in men who were steady and firm, lords of themselves,
and none could respond and all remained calm.
Two brothers-in-law opened a store — our family's
first break. The outsider was serious,
scheming, ruthless, and mean — a woman.
The other one, ours, read novels at work,
which made people talk. When customers came,
they'd hear him say, in one or two words,
that no, there's no sugar, Epsom salts no,
we're all out of that. Later it happened
that this one lent a hand to the other, who'd gone broke.

Thinking of these folks makes me feel stronger
than looking in mirrors and sticking my chest out
or shaping my mouth into a humorless smile.
One of my grandfathers, ages ago,
was being cheated by one of his farmhands,
so he worked the vineyards himself, in the summer,
to make sure it was done right. That's how
I've always lived, too, always maintaining
a steady demeanor, and paying in cash.

And women don't count in this family.
I mean that our women stay home

e ci mettono al mondo e non dicono nulla
e non contano nulla e non le ricordiamo.
Ogni donna c'infonde nel sangue qualcosa di nuovo,
ma s'annullano tutte nell'opera e noi,
rinnovati cosí, siamo i soli a durare.
Siamo pieni di vizi, di ticchi e di orrori
—noi, gli uomini, i padri—qualcuno si è ucciso,
ma una sola vergogna non ci ha mai toccato,
non saremo mai donne, mai schiavi a nessuno.

Ho trovato una terra trovando i compagni,
una terra cattiva, dov'è un privilegio
non far nulla, pensando al futuro.
Perché il solo lavoro non basta a me e ai miei,
noi sappiamo schiantarci, ma il sogno piú grande
dei miei padri fu sempre un far nulla da bravi.
Siamo nati per girovagare su quelle colline,
senza donne e le mani tenercele dietro alla schiena.

and bring us into the world and say nothing
and count for nothing and we don't remember them.
Each of them adds something new to our blood,
but they kill themselves off in the process, while we,
renewed by them, are the ones to endure.
We're full of vices and horrors and whims—
us, the fathers, the men—one of us killed himself.
But there's one shame we won't ever suffer:
we'll never be women, never anyone's slaves.

Finding companions, I found my own land—
a hard-hearted land, where it's a privilege
to do nothing and think of the future.
Because work alone isn't enough for me and mine;
we know how to break our backs, but the great dream
of my fathers was to be good at doing nothing.
We are all of us born to wander these hills,
without women, clasping our hands at our backs.

Paesaggio (1)

Non è piú coltivata quassú la collina. Ci sono le felci
e la roccia scoperta e la sterilità.
Qui il lavoro non serve piú a niente. La vetta è bruciata
e la sola freschezza è il respiro. La grande fatica
è salire quassú: l'eremita ci venne una volta
e da allora è restato, a rifarsi le forze.
L'eremita si veste di pelle di capra
a ha un sentore muschioso di bestia e di pipa,
che ha impregnato la terra, i cespugli e la grotta.
Quando fuma la pipa in disparte nel sole,
se lo perdo non so rintracciarlo, perché è del colore
delle felci bruciate. Ci salgono visitatori
che si accasciano sopra una pietra, sudati e affannati,
e lo trovano steso, con gli occhi nel cielo,
che respira profondo. Un lavoro l'ha fatto:
sopra il volto annerito ha lasciato infoltirsi la barba,
pochi peli rossicci. E depone gli sterchi
su uno spiazzo scoperto, a seccarsi nel sole.

Coste e valli di questa collina son verdi e profonde.
Tra le vigne i sentieri conducono su folli gruppi
di ragazze, vestite a colori violenti,
a far feste alla capra e gridare di là alla pianura.
Qualche volta compaiono file di ceste di frutta,
ma non salgono in cima: i villani le portano a casa
sulla schiena, contorti, e riaffondano in mezzo alle foglie.
Hanno troppo da fare e non vanno a veder l'eremita
i villani, ma scendono, salgono e zappano forte.
Quando han sete, tracannano vino: piantandosi in bocca
la bottiglia, sollevano gli occhi alla vetta bruciata.
La mattina sul fresco son già di ritorno spossati
dal lavoro dell'alba e, se passa un pezzente,
tutta l'acqua che i pozzi riversano in mezzo ai raccolti

Landscape (1)

Up here the hill isn't worked anymore. It's all bracken,
and rocks on the ground, and sterility.
It's no place for work now. The peak is scorched
and the only cool thing is your breath. The real labor
is in reaching the top: one day the hermit climbed up
and has stayed ever since, to recover his strength.
The hermit wears nothing but goatskin,
and he gives off a musk of animal and pipe
that has soaked into the land, the bushes, the cave.
If he goes off to puff on his pipe in the sun,
I might not find him again, because he's the color
of scorched bracken. When visitors climb up here
and collapse on a rock, sweaty and breathless,
they find him stretched out, staring up at the sky,
breathing deeply. He's accomplished one thing:
he's managed to grow, over his sun-dark face, a beard
of sparse, reddish hair. He deposits his droppings
in a small clearing, where they dry in the sun.

The hill's slopes and valleys are green and steep.
The paths through the vineyards lead to crazed clusters
of girls, dressed up in loud colors,
celebrating the goats and yelling down to the plain.
Sometimes you'll see rows of fruit-baskets —
they're not going up: the peasants are taking them home
on their backs, bent double, sinking from sight among leaves.
They have too much to do, these peasants, they're not here
for the hermit: they go down, they go up, they work hard.
When thirsty they'll chug down some wine, planting the bottle
in their mouth, lifting their eyes to the scorched peak.
In the cool of morning they're already returning,
worn out with dawn's work. If a beggar appears,
they offer as much of the water from the wells in the fields

è per lui che la beva. Sogghignano ai gruppi di donne
o domandano quando, vestite di pelle di capra,
siederanno su tante colline a annerirsi nel sole.

as a person can drink. And they sneer at the clusters of girls,
or ask when they'll appear, dressed in their goatskins,
on top of these hills to sit and turn dark in the sun.

Gente spaesata

Troppo mare. Ne abbiamo veduto abbastanza di mare.
Alla sera, che l'acqua si stende slavata
e sfumata nel nulla, l'amico la fissa
e io fisso l'amico e non parla nessuno.
Nottetempo finiamo a rinchiuderci in fondo a una tampa,
isolati nel fumo, e beviamo. L'amico ha i suoi sogni
(sono un poco monotoni i sogni allo scroscio del mare)
dove l'acqua non è che lo specchio, tra un'isola e l'altra,
di colline, screziate di fiori selvaggi e cascate.
Il suo vino è cosí. Si contempla, guardando il bicchiere,
a innalzare colline di verde sul piano del mare.
Le colline mi vanno, e lo lascio parlare del mare
perché è un'acqua ben chiara, che mostra persino le pietre.

Vedo solo colline e mi riempiono il cielo e la terra
con le linee sicure dei fianchi, lontane o vicine.
Solamente, le mie sono scabre, e striate di vigne
faticose sul suolo bruciato. L'amico le accetta
e le vuole vestire di fiori e di frutti selvaggi
per scoprirvi ridendo ragazze piú nude dei frutti.
Non occorre: ai miei sogni piú scabri non manca un sorriso.
Se domani sul presto saremo in cammino
verso quelle colline, potremo incontrar per le vigne
qualche scura ragazza, annerita di sole,
e, attaccando discorso, mangiarle un po' d'uva.

Displaced People

Too much sea. We've had enough of the sea.
In the evening, pale water stretches away
and shades into nothing, my friend watching it,
and me watching him, and nobody speaking.
That night we end up finding a spot in the rear of a tavern,
an island in the smoke, and we drink. My friend has dreams
(one's dreams grow rather monotonous in the roar of the sea)
where the water is only a mirror, between islands,
of hills stippled with wildflowers and falls.
His wine is like that: he sees himself, as he looks in his glass,
raising hills of green on the plain of the sea.
Hills are fine things, and I let him go on about water,
because this water's so clear you can see down to the stones.

I see nothing but hills, close up and far off,
filling the sky and earth with the sure lines of their flanks.
But my hills are harsh, striped with vineyards
hard-won from scorched ground. My friend accepts this
but still wants to adorn them with flowers and wild fruit
and hidden girls laughing, more naked than fruit.
No need: even my harshest dreams can still manage a smile.
If early tomorrow we go out for a walk
through my hills, we might find, in those vineyards,
a couple of girls, made dark by the sun,
and we could make small talk and sample their grapes.

Pensieri di Deola

Deola passa il mattino seduta al caffè
e nessuno la guarda. A quest'ora in città corron tutti
sotto il sole ancor fresco dell'alba. Non cerca nessuno
neanche Deola, ma fuma pacata e respira il mattino.
Fin che è stata in pensione, ha dovuto dormire a quest'ora
per rifarsi le forze: la stuoia sul letto
la sporcavano con le scarpacce soldati e operai,
i clienti che fiaccan la schiena. Ma, sole, è diverso:
si può fare un lavoro piú fine, con poca fatica.
Il signore di ieri, svegliandola presto,
l'ha baciata e condotta (*mi fermerei, cara,*
a Torino con te, se potessi) con sé alla stazione
a augurargli buon viaggio.

                       È intontita, ma fresca, stavolta,
e le piace esser libera, Deola, e bere il suo latte
e mangiare brioches. Stamattina è una mezza signora
e, se guarda i passanti, fa solo per non annoiarsi.
A quest'ora in pensione si dorme e c'è puzza di chiuso
—la padrona va a spasso—è da stupide stare là dentro.
Per girare la sera i locali, ci vuole presenza
e in pensione, a trent'anni, quel po' che ne resta, si è perso.

Deola siede mostrando il profilo a uno specchio
e si guarda nel fresco del vetro. Un po' pallida in faccia:
non è il fumo che stagni. Corruga le ciglia.
Ci vorrebbe la voglia che aveva Marí, per durare
in pensione (*perché, cara donna, gli uomini*
vengon qui per cavarsi capricci che non glieli toglie
né la moglie né l'innamorata) e Marí lavorava
instancabile, piena di brio e godeva salute.
I passanti davanti al caffè non distraggono Deola
che lavora soltanto la sera, con lente conquiste
nella musica del suo locale. Gettando le occhiate

Deola Thinking

Deola passes her mornings sitting in a café,
and nobody looks at her. Everyone's rushing to work,
under a sun still fresh with the dawn. Even Deola
isn't looking for anyone: she smokes serenely, breathing
the morning. In years past, she slept at this hour
to recover her strength: the throw on her bed
was black with the boot-prints of soldiers and workers,
the backbreaking clients. But now, on her own,
it's different: the work's more refined, and it's easier.
Like the gentleman yesterday, who woke her up early,
kissed her, and took her (*I'd stay awhile, dear,*
in Turin with you, if I could) to the station
to tell him goodbye.

                   She's dazed this morning, but fresh—
Deola likes being free, likes drinking her milk
and eating brioches. This morning she's nearly a lady,
and if she looks at anyone now, it's just to pass time.
The girls at the house are still sleeping. The air stinks,
the madam goes out for a walk, it's crazy to stay there.
To work the bars in the evening you have to look good;
at that house, by thirty, you've lost what little looks you had left.

Deola sits with her profile turned toward a mirror
and looks at herself in the cool of the glass: her face pale,
and not from the smoke; her brow a bit furrowed.
To survive at that house, you'd need a will
like Marí used to have (*because, honey, these men*
come here to get something they can't get at home
from their wives or their lovers) and Marí used to work
tirelessly, full of good cheer and blessed with good health.
The people who pass the café aren't distracting Deola—
she only works evenings, making slow conquests
to music, in her usual bar. She'll make eyes

a un cliente o cercandogli il piede, le piaccion le orchestre
che la fanno parere un'attrice alla scena d'amore
con un giovane ricco. Le basta un cliente
ogni sera e ha da vivere. (*Forse il signore di ieri*
mi portava davvero con sé). Stare sola, se vuole,
al mattino, e sedersi al caffè. Non cercare nessuno.

at a client, or nudge his foot, while enjoying the band
that makes her seem like an actress doing a love scene
with a young millionaire. One client each evening
is enough to scrape by on. (*Maybe that gentleman from last night
really will take me with him.*) To be alone, if she wants,
in the morning. To sit in a café. To not look for anyone.

Canzone di strada

Perché vergogna? Quando uno ha pagato il suo tempo,
se lo lasciano uscire, è perché è come tutti
e ce n'è della gente per strada, che è stata in prigione.

Dal mattino alla sera giriamo sui corsi
e che piova o che faccia un bel sole, va sempre per noi.
È una gioia incontrare sui corsi la gente che parla
e parlare da soli, pigliando ragazze a spintoni.
È una gioia fischiar nei portoni aspettando ragazze
e abbracciarle per strada e portarle al cinema
e fumar di nascosto, appoggiati alle belle ginocchia.
È una gioia parlare con loro palpando e ridendo,
e di notte nel letto, sentendo buttarsi sul collo
le due braccia che attirano in basso, pensare al mattino
che si tornerà a uscir di prigione nel fresco del sole.

Dal mattino alla sera girare ubriachi
e guardare ridendo i passanti che vanno
e che godono tutti—anche i brutti—a sentirsi per strada.
Dal mattino alla sera cantare ubriachi
e incontrare ubriachi e attaccare discorsi
che ci durino a lungo e ci mettano sete.
Tutti questi individui che vanno parlando tra sé,
li vogliamo alla notte con noi, chiusi in fondo alla tampa,
e seguire con loro la nostra chitarra
che saltella ubriaca e non sta piú nel chiuso
ma spalanca le porte a echeggiare nell'aria—
fuori piòvano l'acqua o le stelle. Non conta se i corsi
a quest'ora non hanno piú belle ragazze a passeggio:
troveremo ben noi l'ubriaco che ride da solo
perché è uscito anche lui di prigione stanotte,
e con lui, strepitando e cantando, faremo il mattino.

Street Song

Why be ashamed? If a man's done his time
and they let him go, it means he's like anyone else
who's walking the streets after being in prison.

From morning till evening we wander the avenues,
and whether it's raining or sunny, it's fine with us.
It's a pleasure to see people talk in the street
and to talk to ourselves, bumping girls as we pass.
It's a pleasure to whistle in doorways, waiting for girls,
to embrace in the street and take them to movies,
to smoke in secret, leaning on beautiful knees.
It's a pleasure to speak with them, touching and laughing,
and at night in bed, to feel arms on your neck
pulling you down, and to think of the morning
when you'll get to trade prison again for fresh sun.

From morning till evening we drunkenly wander,
we laugh as we watch the people pass by,
all of them—even the ugly—enjoying the street.
From morning till evening we drunkenly sing
and meet other drunks and strike up the talk
that lasts a long time and makes us all thirsty.
All these people who wander and talk to themselves,
we want them to join us at night, in the back of the tavern,
to follow along with our guitar
that jumps like a drunk and can't be contained
but bursts through doors and resounds through the air—
whether it's raining water or stars. No matter
if by now the avenues are empty of beautiful girls:
we'll find the old drunkard who laughs to himself,
for he too was released from prison tonight,
and with him, shouting and singing, we'll make morning.

Due sigarette

Ogni notte è la liberazione. Si guarda i riflessi
dell'asfalto sui corsi che si aprono lucidi al vento.
Ogni rado passante ha una faccia e una storia.
Ma a quest'ora non c'è piú stanchezza: i lamponi a migliaia
sono tutti per chi si sofferma a sfregare un cerino.

La fiammella si spegne sul volto alla donna
che mi ha chiesto un cerino. Si spegne nel vento
e la donna delusa ne chiede un secondo
che si spegne: la donna ora ride sommessa.
Qui possiamo parlare a voce alta e gridare,
ché nessuno ci sente. Leviamo gli sguardi
alle tante finestre—occhi spenti che dormono—
e attendiamo. La donna si stringe le spalle
e si lagna che ha perso la sciarpa a colori
che la notte faceva da stufa. Ma basta appoggiarci
contro l'angolo e il vento non è piú che un soffio.
Sull'asfalto consunto c'è già un mozzicone.
Questa sciarpa veniva da Rio, ma dice la donna
che è contenta di averla perduta, perché mi ha incontrato.
Se la sciarpa veniva da Rio, è passata di notte
sull'oceano inondato di luce dal gran transatlantico.
Certo, notti di vento. È il regalo di un suo marinaio.
Non c'è piú il marinaio. La donna bisbiglia
che, se salgo con lei, me ne mostra il ritratto
ricciolino e abbronzato. Viaggiava su sporchi vapori
e puliva le macchine: io sono piú bello.

Sull'asfalto c'è due mozziconi. Guardiamo nel cielo:
la finestra là in alto—mi addita la donna—è la nostra.
Ma lassú non c'è stufa. La notte, i vapori sperduti
hanno pochi fanali o soltanto le stelle.
Traversiamo l'asfalto a braccetto, giocando a scaldarci.

Two Cigarettes

Each night's a liberation. You see light reflecting
on the asphalt avenues that open wide to the wind.
Each of the few passersby has a face and a story.
But nobody's tired at this time of night: thousands of streetlamps
just for people who pause to rummage for matches.

The small flame dies on the face of the woman
who's asked for a match. It dies in the wind,
and so, disappointed, she asks for another.
It too goes out, and now she laughs softly.
We could speak loud here, we could shout:
no one would hear. We turn our gaze
toward all the dark windows—eyes closed in sleep—
and we wait. The woman hunches her shoulders
and laments that she lost her colorful scarf,
as good as a heater at night. But leaning together
against a corner reduces the wind to a breath.
Already one cigarette butt lies on the worn asphalt.
The scarf was from Rio, she tells me, but now
she's glad to have lost it, because she's met me.
If the scarf came from Rio, it must have spent nights
on an ocean flooded with light by a great liner—
windy nights, certainly. It was a gift from a sailor;
one who's no longer around. She whispers to me
that, if I'd like to come up, she'll show me his picture—
curly-haired, bronzed. He worked on a dirty steamer,
cleaning the engines. She says I'm better-looking.

Two butts, now, on the asphalt. We look at the sky:
that window up there, she says pointing, is ours—
but the heater's not working. At night, lost steamers
have little to steer by, maybe only the stars.
We cross the street, arm in arm, playfully warming each other.

Ozio

Tutti i gran manifesti attaccati sui muri,
che presentano sopra uno sfondo di fabbriche
l'operaio robusto che si erge nel cielo,
vanno in pezzi, nel sole e nell'acqua. Masino bestemmia
a veder la sua faccia piú fiera, sui muri
delle vie, e doverle girare cercando lavoro.
Uno si alza al mattino e si ferma a guardare i giornali
nelle edicole vive di facce di donna a colori:
fa confronti con quelle che passano e perde il suo tempo,
ché ogni donna ha le occhiaie piú stracche. Compaiono a un tratto
coi cartelli dei cinematografi addosso alla testa
e con passi sostanti, vecchiotti vestiti di rosso
e Masino, fissando le facce deformi
e i colori, si tocca le guance e le sente piú vuote.

Ogni volta che mangia, Masino ritorna a girare,
perché è segno che ha già lavorato. Traversa le vie
e non guarda piú in faccia nessuno. La sera, ritorna
e si stende un momento nei prati con quella ragazza.
Quando è solo, gli piace restare nei prati
tra le case isolate e i rumori sommessi
e talvolta fa un sonno. Le donne non mancano,
come quando era ancora meccanico: adesso è Masino
a cercarne una sola e volerla fedele.
Una volta — da quando va in giro — ha atterrato un rivale
e i colleghi, che li hanno trovati in un fosso,
han dovuto bendargli una mano. Anche quelli non fanno piú nulla
e tre o quattro, affamati, han formato una banda
di clarino e chitarre — volevano averci Masino
che cantasse — e girare le vie a raccogliere i soldi.
Lui Masino ha risposto che canta per niente
ogni volta che ha voglia, ma andare a svegliare le serve
per le strade, è un lavoro da napoli. I giorni che mangia,

Idleness

All the big posters pasted up on the walls
with the muscular worker rising up toward the sky
above a factory background—they're shredding
in the sun and the rain. Masino curses
to see that face, prouder than his, on the walls
of the very streets he has to walk to look for a job.
You get up in the morning, you look at the papers
at newsstands alive with the full-color faces of women—
it's pointless to compare them to the women who walk by,
because real women have tired eyes. Then out of nowhere
the halting old men in red outfits appear
with cinema placards over their heads,
and Masino, seeing their misshapen faces
and those colors, touches his cheeks, which feel hollow.

Whenever he eats, Masino returns to his search,
since it means he's finished a job. He walks down the street
no longer looking at anyone's face. At night he returns
and lies for a while in the field with that girl.
When alone, he likes to rest in the fields
between the sparse houses and faint noises,
and sometimes he naps. No shortage of women,
like back in his days as a mechanic, but now it's Masino
who wants only one, and one who'll be faithful.
Once, when making his rounds, he knocked down a rival—
some guys he had worked with found them both in a ditch
and had to bandage his hand up. Some of those guys,
out of work also, and hungry, had started a band,
a clarinet and guitars, and they wanted Masino
to sing, they wanted to play in the streets for change.
Masino replied that he sang when he wanted,
for nothing; but wandering streets and waking up servant girls
was something they did down South. On days when he eats,

porta ancora con sé pochi amici a metà la collina:
là si chiudono in qualche osteria e ne cantano un pezzo
loro soli, da uomini. Andavano un tempo anche in barca,
ma dal fiume si vede la fabbrica, e fa brutto sangue.

Dopo un giorno a strisciare le suole davanti agli affissi,
alla sera Masino finisce al cinema
dove ha già lavorato, una volta. Fa bene quel buio
alla vista spossata dai troppi lampioni.
Tener dietro alla storia non è una fatica:
vi si vede una bella ragazza e talvolta c'è uomini
che si picchiano secco. Vi sono paesi
che varrebbe la pena di viverci, al posto
degli stupidi attori. Masino contempla,
su un paese di nude colline, di prati e di fabbriche,
la sua testa ingrandita in primissimi piani.
Quelli almeno non dànno la rabbia che dànno i cartelli
colorati, sugli angoli, e i musi di donna dipinti.

he gathers some friends and they go up the hill
to a tavern, they sing for a while, just for themselves,
among men. They used to go out in a boat,
but the factory faces the river—it ruined their mood.

After a day of shuffling his feet beneath posters,
in the evening Masino ends up at the cinema,
where he worked once. That dark does you good
when your eyes are worn out from too many streetlamps.
And it isn't hard work to follow the story:
you see a beautiful girl, and sometimes some men
punching each other. You see, too, a country
where it might be worth it to live, in place
of those idiot actors. Masino reflects,
in his country of bare hills, of fields and of factories,
and that head like his own, giant in close-ups.
But that doesn't make him as mad as the colorful placards
on the corners, or the painted faces of women.

Proprietari

Il mio prete che è nato in campagna, è vissuto vegliando
giorno e notte in città i moribondi e ha riunito in tanti anni
qualche soldo di lasciti per l'ospedale.
Risparmiava soltanto le donne perdute e i bambini
e nel nuovo ospedale — lettucci di ferro imbiancato —
c'è un'intera sezione per donne e bambini perduti.
Ma i morenti che sono scampati, lo vengono ancora a trovare
e gli chiedon consigli di affari. Lo zelo l'ha reso ben magro
tra il sentore dei letti e i discorsi con gente che rantola
e seguire, ogni volta che ha tempo, i suoi morti alla fossa
e pregare per loro, spruzzandoli e benedicendoli.

Una sera di marzo già calda, il mio prete ha sepolto
una vecchia coperta di piaghe: era stata sua madre.
La donnetta era morta al paese, perché l'ospedale
le faceva paura e voleva morir nel suo letto.
Il mio prete quel giorno portava la stola
dei suoi altri defunti, ma sopra la bara
spruzzò a lungo acqua santa e pregò anche piú a lungo.
Nella sera già calda, la terra rimossa odorava
sulla bara dov'era un marciume: la vecchia era morta
per il sangue cattivo a vedersi sfumare le terre
che — rimasta lei sola — spettava a lei sola salvare.
Sotto terra, un rosario era avvolto alle mani piagate
che, da vive, con tre o quattro croci su pezzi di carta
s'eran messe in miseria. E il mio prete pregava
che potesse venir perdonata la temerità
della vedova che, mentre il figlio studiava coi preti,
s'era — senza cercare consiglio — presunta da tanto.

L'ospedale ha un giardino che odora di terra,
messo insieme a fatica, per dare ai malati aria buona.
Il mio prete conosce le piante e i cespugli

Landholders

My priest, born in the country, watched over the dying
day and night in the city, and over the years scraped together
some money in bequests for the hospital.
He exempted only fallen women and children,
and in the new hospital, full of whited iron cots,
a whole ward's set aside just for them.
The dying who managed to live still come to him
to ask his advice. Zeal renders him thin,
what with the odor of beds and the talks with ranting patients
and the trips, when he has time, with the dead to their graves
to pray for them, blessing and sprinkling them.

One late afternoon—it was March and already warm—my priest
buried an old woman covered with sores: it was his mother.
The small woman died in her village, because hospitals
scared her and she wanted to die in her own bed.
That day my priest wore the same stole he wore
to his other funerals, but over the coffin
he sprinkled more holy water, and he prayed longer, too.
In the warm afternoon, earth scented the air as it fell
over the coffin and its corruption: the old lady died
from heartache after watching her land come to nothing
while she, the only one left, was expected to save it.
Under that earth, a rosary twined her sore-covered hands
which, when alive, couldn't scrawl crosses on paper
without crippling pain. And my priest prayed
that the old widow's temerity might be forgiven,
the old widow whose son studied with priests
while she—never seeking advice—shouldered so much.

The hospital has a garden that smells of earth mixed
with hard work—it's good air for the sick.
My priest knows the plants and the bushes

anche piú dei suoi morti, ché quelli rinnovano,
ma le piante e i cespugli son sempre gli stessi.
Tra quel verde borbotta — a quel modo che fa sulle tombe —
negli istanti che ruba ai malati, e dimentica sempre
di fermarsi davanti alla grotta, che han fatto le suore,
della Natività, in fondo al viale. Si lagna talvolta
che le cure gli han sempre impedito di dare un'occhiata
ai bisogni degli alberi secchi e che mai, da trent'anni,
ha potuto pensare alla requiem eterna.

better than even his dead, whose faces change,
while the plants and the bushes are always the same.
Amid that green, in his moments away from the sick,
he mumbles as he does over graves, and always forgets
to pause by the grotto the nuns put together,
a nativity scene, at the end of the walk. He sometimes laments
that his cures have kept him from keeping an eye
on the needs of the dry trees and that, in thirty years,
he's never had time to reflect on eternal rest.

Paesaggio (II)

La collina biancheggia alle stelle, di terra scoperta;
si vedrebbero i ladri, lassú. Tra le ripe del fondo
i filari son tutti nell'ombra. Lassú che ce n'è
e che è terra di chi non patisce, non sale nessuno:
qui nell'umidità, con la scusa di andare a tartufi,
entran dentro alla vigna e saccheggiano le uve.

Il mio vecchio ha trovato due graspi buttati
tra le piante e stanotte borbotta. La vigna è già scarsa:
giorno e notte nell'umidità, non ci viene che foglie.
Tra le piante si vedono al cielo le terre scoperte
che di giorno gli rubano il sole. Lassú brucia il sole
tutto il giorno e la terra è calcina: si vede anche al buio.
Là non vengono foglie, la forza va tutta nell'uva.

Il mio vecchio appoggiato a un bastone nell'erba bagnata,
ha la mano convulsa: se vengono i ladri stanotte,
salta in mezzo ai filari e gli fiacca la schiena.
Sono gente da farle un servizio da bestie,
ché non vanno a contarla. Ogni tanto alza il capo
annusando nell'aria: gli pare che arrivi nel buio
una punta d'odore terroso, tartufi scavati.

Sulle coste lassú, che si stendono al cielo,
non c'è l'uggia degli alberi: l'uva strascina per terra,
tanto pesa. Nessuno può starci nascosto:
si distinguono in cima le macchie degli alberi
neri e radi. Se avesse la vigna lassú,
il mio vecchio farebbe la guardia da casa, nel letto,
col fucile puntato. Qui, al fondo, nemmeno il fucile
non gli serve, perché dentro il buio non c'è che fogliami.

Landscape (II)

The hill is whitened by starlight, the land revealed;
up there, a thief would be seen. Below in the valley,
the vineyards are dark. The one on the hill
does well for its owner, but thieves stay away.
Down here where it's damp, they pretend to be truffling,
then sneak down the rows, filling their sacks.

The old man found two clusters of stems, picked clean
and tossed to the ground, and he's mad. The crop's poor enough
as it is: damp day and night, nothing coming in but leaves.
Beyond them, the hill rises up against the sky
with its vineyards that steal his sun. It blazes all day
up there, and the soil is all lime: you can see in the dark.
Those vines are less leafy; the strength all goes to the grapes.

The old man leans on his cane in the wet grass,
his hand shaking. If the thieves dare to return tonight,
he'll jump them and thrash them good with the cane.
These people deserve to be treated like animals,
and it's not like they'll tell. Now and then, the old man
lifts his head: he thinks he detects in the dark
a trace of an earthy odor, someone digging for truffles.

Up there, on the slopes that stretch to the sky,
no trees block the light: the vines sag with their load
toward earth. No one could hide in that vineyard:
the few patches of trees stand out, black and sparse,
on the peak. If only he had his vineyard up there —
he'd be guarding his harvest from home, from his bed,
his rifle at the ready. But down here, even the gun
is no good, since all you can see in this dark are these leaves.

Paesaggio (III)

Tra la barba e il gran sole la faccia va ancora,
ma è la pelle del corpo, che biancheggia tremante
fra le toppe. Non basta lo sporco a confonderla
nella pioggia e nel sole. Villani anneriti
l'han guardato una volta, ma l'occhiata perdura
su quel corpo, cammini o si accasci al riposo.

Nella notte le grandi campagne si fondono
in un'ombra pesante, che sprofonda i filari
e le piante: soltanto le mani conoscono i frutti.
L'uomo lacero pare un villano, nell'ombra,
ma rapisce ogni cosa e i cagnacci non sentono.
Nella notte la terra non ha piú padroni,
se non voci inumane. Il sudore non conta.
Ogni pianta ha un suo freddo sudore nell'ombra
e non c'è piú che un campo, per nessuno e per tutti.

Al mattino questo'uomo stracciato e tremante
sogna, steso ad un muro non suo, che i villani
lo rincorrono e vogliono morderlo, sotto un gran sole.
Ha una barba stillante, di fredda rugiada
e tra i buchi la pelle. Compare un villano
con la zappa sul collo, e s'asciuga la bocca.
Non si scosta nemmeno, ma scavalca quell'altro:
un suo campo quest'oggi ha bisogno di forza.

Landscape (III)

With the beard and the bright sun, the face can pass.
But the rest of his skin—it's a whiteness shimmering
through torn clothes. Even the dirt doesn't mask it,
no matter the weather. The dark-skinned peasants
took one look at this man, and that look stuck
to his body, whether he's walking or lying around.

At night the fields and the countryside melt
into heavy shadow; vineyards and trees
are swallowed—only a hand can know fruit.
In this dark, the rag man could pass for a peasant,
except that he steals and even the dogs don't hear him.
At night the land no longer has owners,
except for inhuman voices. Sweat doesn't count.
In this dark, the plants have their own cold sweat,
and the fields are one field, and each man's, and none's.

Come morning, this man, ragged and shivering
near a wall that's not his, dreams of peasants
who chase him through sunlight, wanting to bite him.
His beard glistens with cold dew, his skin shines
through holes in his clothes. A peasant appears
with a hoe on his shoulder. Wiping his mouth,
he steps over the man and walks on without pausing:
today one of his fields will need all of his strength.

Una stagione

Questa donna una volta era fatta di carne
fresca e solida: quando portava un bambino,
si teneva nascosta e intristiva da sola.
Non amava mostrarsi sformata per strada.
Le altre volte (era giovane e senza volerlo
fece molti bambini) passava per strada
con un passo sicuro e sapeva godersi gli istanti.
I vestiti diventano vento le sere di marzo
e si stringono e tremano intorno alle donne che passano.
Il suo corpo di donna muoveva sicuro nel vento
che svaniva lasciandolo saldo. Non ebbe altro bene
che quel corpo, che adesso è consunto dai troppi figliuoli.

Nelle sere di vento si spande un sentore di linfe,
il sentore che aveva da giovane il corpo
tra le vesti superflue. Un sapore di terra bagnata,
che ogni marzo ritorna. Anche dove in città non c'è viali
e non giunge col sole il respiro del vento,
il suo corpo viveva, esalando di succhi
in fermento, tra i muri di pietra. Col tempo, anche lei,
che ha nutrito altri corpi, si è rotta e piegata.
Non è bello guardarla, ha perduto ogni forza;
ma, dei molti, una figlia ritorna a passare
per le strade, la sera, e ostentare nel vento
sotto gli alberi, solido e fresco, il suo corpo che vive.

E c'è un figlio che gira e sa stare da solo
e si sa divertire da solo. Ma guarda nei vetri,
compiaciuto del modo che tiene a braccetto
la compagna. Gli piace, d'un gioco di muscoli,
accostarsela mentre rilutta e baciarla sul collo.
Sopratutto gli piace, poi che ha generato
su quel corpo, lasciarlo intristire e tornare a se stesso.

A Season

This woman was once made of firm, young flesh:
when she grew heavy with her first child, she grew sad,
she kept herself hidden, she wilted alone.
She hated to be seen, misshapen, in public.
After the first (she was young and the children
kept coming, unplanned) she'd walk down the street
with a confident air, she learned to enjoy each moment.
Some March evenings, dresses are one with the wind,
clinging and rippling around the bodies of women.
Her own body moved with a sureness through wind
as it weakened, leaving her standing. She'd been given
no gifts but that body, consumed now by too many children.

In the evenings, wind carries an odor like sap,
like the smell of her body when it was still young
under too many clothes. The smell of wet earth
that comes back each March. Even far from the avenues,
in parts of the city where the sun and the wind's breath
don't reach, her body lived, trailing the scent
of its fermenting juices, behind stone walls. But in time,
she, who had fed other bodies, became broken and bent.
It's not pleasant to look at her, she's lost all her powers;
but a daughter (one of the many) still comes around
and walks down the street, beneath trees, in the evening,
flaunting the wind, her young body firm and alive.

And a son's roaming around who knows how to live
on his own and enjoy it. He looks in shop windows,
he likes how he looks with a girl on his arm.
He shows off his strength by pulling her close
as she tries to push him away, and kissing her neck.
He likes, above all, after he's planted his seed
in a body, to leave it to wilt, to return to himself.

Un amplesso lo fa solamente sorridere e un figlio
lo farebbe indignare. Lo sa la ragazza, che attende,
e prepara se stessa a nascondere il ventre sformato
e si gode con lui, compiacente, e gli ammira la forza
di quel corpo che serve per compiere tante altre cose.

An embrace will just make him smile, but a child
would offend him. The girl, who's expecting, knows this
and plans to hide her misshapen belly. Right now
she's enjoying his company, she's willing, she's admiring
the strength of his body and all the things it can do.

Pensieri di Dina

Dentro l'acqua che scorre ormai limpida e fresca di sole,
è un piacere gettarsi: a quest'ora non viene nessuno.
Fanno rabbrividire, le scorze dei pioppi, a toccarle col corpo,
piú che l'acqua scrosciante di un tuffo. Sott'acqua è ancor buio
e fa un gelo che accoppa, ma basta saltare nel sole
e si torna a guardare le cose con occhi lavati.

È un piacere distendersi nuda sull'erba già calda
e cercare con gli occhi socchiusi le grandi colline
che sormontano i pioppi e mi vedono nuda
e nessuno di là se ne accorge. Quel vecchio in mutande
e cappello, che andava a pescare, mi ha vista tuffarmi,
ma ha creduto che fossi un ragazzo e nemmeno ha parlato.

Questa sera ritorno una donna nell'abito rosso
—non lo sanno che sono ora stesa qui nuda quegli uomini
che mi fanno i sorrisi per strada—ritorno vestita
a pigliare i sorrisi. Non sanno quegli uomini
che stasera avrò fianchi piú forti, nell'abito rosso,
e sarò un'altra donna. Nessuno mi vede quaggiú:
e di là dalle piante ci son sabbiatori piú forti
di quegli altri che fanno i sorrisi: nessuno mi vede.
Sono sciocchi gli uomini—stasera ballando con tutti
io sarò come nuda, come ora, e nessuno saprà
che poteva trovarmi qui sola. Sarò come loro.
Solamente, gli sciocchi, vorranno abbracciarmi ben stretta,
bisbigliarmi proposte da furbi. Ma cosa m'importa
delle loro carezze? So farmi carezze da me.
Questa sera dovremmo poter stare nudi e vederci
senza fare sorrisi da furbi. Io sola sorrido
a distendermi qui dentro l'erba e nessuno lo sa.

Dina Thinking

It's a joy to jump in this water, now flowing so clear
and fresh in the sun: nobody's here at this hour.
The husks of the poplars startle me more, when they touch me,
than the slap of the water as I plunge in. It's still dark under there,
and the cold is killing, but as soon as you jump back out
into the sunlight, you see the world with washed eyes.

It's a joy to lie naked in grass that's already warm
and to gaze up with half-closed eyes at the high hills
that rise over the poplars and look down on me naked
and nobody up there can tell. That old man in his hat
and his underwear, fishing one day, saw me dive in,
but thought I was a boy and never uttered a word.

This evening I'll return as a woman in a red dress—
those men who smile at me out on the street don't know
I'm lying here naked right now—I'll go back dressed
to gather their smiles. Those men don't know it
but tonight in my red dress my hips will be stronger
and I'll be a new woman. Nobody sees me down here:
and beyond these bushes are sand-diggers stronger
than those men who smile: but nobody sees me.
Men are so silly—tonight as I dance with them all
it'll be as if I was naked, like now, and no one will know
they could've found me right here. I'll be just like them.
Except that those fools will want to pull me too close
and whisper proposals like con men. But what do I care
for the caresses of men? I can touch me all by myself.
But I wish we could be naked in front of each other tonight
without smiling like con men. I smile to myself now,
and stretch out in the tall grass, and nobody knows.

Tradimento

Stamattina non sono piú solo. Una donna recente
sta distesa sul fondo e mi grava la prua
della barca, che avanza a fatica nell'acqua tranquilla
ancor gelida e torba del sonno notturno.
Sono uscito dal Po tumultuante e echeggiante nel sole
di onde rapide e di sabbiatori, e vincendo la svolta
dopo molti sussulti mi sono cacciato
nel Sangone. «Che sogno», ha osservato colei
senza muovere il corpo supino, guardando nel cielo.
Non c'è un'anima in giro e le rive son alte
e a monte piú anguste, serrate di pioppi.

Quant'è goffa la barca in quest'acqua tranquilla.
Dritto a poppa a levare e abbassare la punta,
vedo il legno che avanza impacciato: è la prua che sprofonda
per quel peso di un corpo di donna, ravvolto di bianco.
La compagna mi ha detto che è pigra e non s'è ancora mossa.
Sta distesa a fissare da sola le vette degli alberi
ed è come in un letto e m'ingombra la barca.
Ora ha messo una mano nell'acqua e la lascia schiumare
e m'ingombra anche il fiume. Non posso guardarla
—sulla prua dove stende il suo corpo—che piega la testa
e mi fissa curiosa dal basso, muovendo la schiena.
Quando ho detto che venga piú in centro, lasciando la prua,
mi ha risposto un sorriso vigliacco: «Mi vuole vicina?»

Altre volte, gocciante di un tuffo fra i tronchi e le pietre,
continuavo a puntare nel sole, finch'ero ubriaco,
e approdando a quest'angolo, mi gettavo riverso,
accecato dall'acqua e dai raggi, buttato via il palo,
a calmare il sudore e l'affanno al respiro
delle piante e alla stretta dell'erba. Ora l'ombra è estuosa
al sudore che pesa nel sangue e alle membra infiacchite,

Betrayal

This morning I'm no longer alone. A new woman
is lying before me and weighs down the prow
of my boat, which labors slowly through placid water,
still murky and cold from last night's sleep.
I left the boisterous Po, its bright sun, its echoes
of quick waves and sand-diggers, rounded the bend
after much heaving, and I've finally made it
into the Sangone. "So enchanting," she said
without moving her body or taking her eyes off the sky.
Not a soul in sight, and moving upstream the banks
grow narrow and steep, crowded with poplars.

How clumsy the boat is in this placid water.
I stand in the stern as the prow rises and falls,
and we make our awkward way: the nose dips
with the weight of her body, wrapped up in white.
My companion told me she's lazy; she hasn't yet moved.
Stretched on her back, she stares at the treetops
as if from her bed—she slows down my boat.
Now she's draped a hand in the water and drags it,
slowing my river too. I can't look at her—
stretched out there on the prow, tilting her head
and looking up at me curiously, shifting her back.
When I told her to come to the center, away from the prow,
she answered, with a cowardly smile: "So we can be closer?"

Other times, soaked from a swim among tree trunks and stones,
I'd keep on toward the sun, until I felt drunk,
until I hit land and threw myself down on my back,
blinded by water and light, my pole tossed aside—
sweating and breathless, I was calmed by the breath
of the plants, the grip of the grass. Now the shade warms
my tired limbs and the sweat that thickens my blood,

e la volta degli alberi filtra la luce
di un'alcova. Seduto sull'erba, non so cosa dire
e m'abbraccio i ginocchi. La compagna è sparita
dentro il bosco dei pioppi, ridendo, e io debbo inseguirla.
La mia pelle è annerita di sole e scoperta.
La compagna che è bionda, poggiando le mani
alle mie per saltare sul greto, mi ha fatto sentire,
con la fragilità delle dita, il profumo
del suo corpo nascosto. Altre volte il profumo
era l'acqua seccata sul legno e il sudore nel sole.
La compagna mi chiama impaziente. Nell'abito bianco
sta girando fra i tronchi e io debbo inseguirla.

and the vault of the trees filters the light
of an alcove. I sit in the grass, at a loss for words,
clasping my knees. My companion has vanished
into the poplars, laughing, and I'm meant
to follow. My bare skin is dark from the sun.
When my companion, a blonde, took hold of my hand
and jumped to the gravel bank, I couldn't help notice
as I held her thin fingers in mine the scent
of her hidden body. Other times the scent
was dried water on boat-wood or sweat in the sun.
My companion calls me impatiently. In her white frock
she wanders among trunks and I'm meant to follow.

Mania di solitudine

Mangio un poco di cena seduto alla chiara finestra.
Nella stanza è già buio e si guarda nel cielo.
A uscir fuori, le vie tranquille conducono
dopo un poco, in aperta campagna.
Mangio e guardo nel cielo—chi sa quante donne
stan mangiando a quest'ora—il mio corpo è tranquillo;
il lavoro stordisce il mio corpo e ogni donna.

Fuori, dopo la cena, verranno le stelle a toccare
sulla larga pianura la terra. Le stelle son vive,
ma non valgono queste ciliege, che mangio da solo.
Vedo il cielo, ma so che fra i tetti di ruggine
qualche lume già brilla e che, sotto, si fanno rumori.
Un gran sorso e il mio corpo assapora la vita
delle piante e dei fiumi e si sente staccato da tutto.
Basta un po' di silenzio e ogni cosa si ferma
nel suo luogo reale, cosí com'è fermo il mio corpo.

Ogni cosa è isolata davanti ai miei sensi,
che l'accettano senza scomporsi: un brusío di silenzio.
Ogni cosa, nel buio, la posso sapere
come so che il mio sangue trascorre le vene.
La pianura è un gran scorrere d'acque tra l'erbe,
una cena di tutte le cose. Ogni pianta e ogni sasso
vive immobile. Ascolto i miei cibi nutrirmi le vene
di ogni cosa che vive su questa pianura.

Non importa la notte. Il quadrato di cielo
mi susurra di tutti i fragori, e una stella minuta
si dibatte nel vuoto, lontano dai cibi,
dalle case, diversa. Non basta a se stessa,
e ha bisogno di troppe compagne. Qui al buio, da solo,
il mio corpo è tranquillo e si sente padrone.

Passion for Solitude

I'm eating a little supper by the bright window.
The room's already dark, the sky's starting to turn.
Outside my door, the quiet roads lead,
after a short walk, to open fields.
I'm eating, watching the sky—who knows
how many women are eating now. My body is calm:
labor dulls all the senses, and dulls women too.

Outside, after supper, the stars will come out to touch
the wide plain of the earth. The stars are alive,
but not worth these cherries, which I'm eating alone.
I look at the sky, know that lights already are shining
among rust-red roofs, noises of people beneath them.
A gulp of my drink, and my body can taste the life
of plants and of rivers. It feels detached from things.
A small dose of silence suffices, and everything's still,
in its true place, just like my body is still.

All things become islands before my senses,
which accept them as a matter of course: a murmur of silence.
All things in this darkness—I can know all of them,
just as I know that blood flows in my veins.
The plain is a great flowing of water through plants,
a supper of all things. Each plant, and each stone,
lives motionlessly. I hear my food feeding my veins
with each living thing that this plain provides.

The night doesn't matter. The square patch of sky
whispers all the loud noises to me, and a small star
struggles in emptiness, far from all foods,
from all houses, alien. It isn't enough for itself,
it needs too many companions. Here in the dark, alone,
my body is calm, it feels it's in charge.

Il dio-caprone

La campagna è un paese di verdi misteri
al ragazzo, che viene d'estate. La capra, che morde
certi fiori, le gonfia la pancia e bisogna che corra.
Quando l'uomo ha goduto con qualche ragazza
—hanno peli là sotto—il bambino le gonfia la pancia.
Pascolando le capre, si fanno bravate e sogghigni,
ma al crepuscolo ognuno comincia a guardarsi alle spalle.
I ragazzi conoscono quando è passata la biscia
dalla striscia sinuosa che resta per terra.
Ma nessuno conosce se passa la biscia
dentro l'erba. Ci sono le capre che vanno a fermarsi
sulla biscia, nell'erba, e che godono a farsi succhiare.
Le ragazze anche godono, a farsi toccare.

Al levar della luna le capre non stanno piú chete,
ma bisogna raccoglierle a spingerle a casa,
altrimenti si drizza il caprone. Saltando nel prato
sventra tutte le capre e scompare. Ragazze in calore
dentro i boschi ci vengono sole, di notte,
e il caprone, se belano stese nell'erba, le corre a trovare.
Ma, che spunti la luna: si drizza e le sventra.
E le cagne, che abbaiano sotto la luna,
è perché hanno sentito il caprone che salta
sulle cime dei colli e annusato l'odore del sangue.
E le bestie si scuotono dentro le stalle.
Solamente i cagnacci piú forti dan morsi alla corda
e qualcuno si libera e corre a seguire il caprone,
che li spruzza e ubriaca di un sangue piú rosso del fuoco,
e poi ballano tutti, tenendosi ritti e ululando alla luna.

Quando, a giorno, il cagnaccio ritorna spelato e ringhioso,
i villani gli dànno la cagna a pedate di dietro.
E alla figlia, che gira di sera, e ai ragazzi, che tornano

The Billy-Goat God

To the boy who comes here in summer, the country
is a land of green mysteries. Certain flowers
make the goat's belly swell; then she must run.
When a man has had a good time with a girl—
they're furry down there—her belly swells with a baby.
The boys who herd the goats sneer and they brag,
but at sundown they all start watching their step.
They can tell by the sinuous stripes in the dust
when a grass snake has crawled through the dirt.
But none of them know when the grass snake is moving
through grass. There are goats who like to lie down
on the snakes, in the grass, they like to be suckled.
And there are girls, too, who like to be touched.

Come moonrise the goats can no longer keep still,
they have to be gathered together and prodded back home,
or else the billy starts bucking. Jumping around,
he gores the she-goats and runs off. Girls in heat
go alone, at night, to the woods, and lie bleating
on the ground, and the billy comes running to find them.
But when the moon rises, he goes wild and gores them.
And the bitches bay in the moonlight, because
they've heard the billy goat jumping way up
in the hills, they've caught a whiff of the blood.
And the animals tremble inside their stalls.
But the strong hounds keep gnawing away at their leashes,
until several break loose and give chase, and the billy
sprays them with blood redder than fire, gets them drunk on it,
and they all dance on their hind legs and howl at the moon.

The next day, each hound will return, scabby and snarling,
and the peasants will give him a bitch, kicking her to him.
And the girl who goes roaming at night, and the boys

quand'è buio, smarrita una capra, gli fiaccano il collo.
Riempion donne, i villani, e faticano senza rispetto.
Vanno in giro di giorno e di notte e non hanno paura
di zappare anche sotto la luna o di accendere un fuoco
di gramigne nel buio. Per questo, la terra
è cosí bella verde e, zappata, ha il colore,
sotto l'alba, dei volti bruciati. Si va alla vendemmia
e si mangia e si canta; si va a spannocchiare
e si balla e si beve. Si sente ragazze che ridono,
ché qualcuno ricorda il caprone. Su, in cima, nei boschi,
tra le ripe sassose, i villani l'han visto
che cercava la capra e picchiava zuccate nei tronchi.
Perché, quando una bestia non sa lavorare
e si tiene soltanto da monta, gli piace distruggere.

who come home after dark, a she-goat missing, are beaten.
They get women with child, these peasants, they work
and get no respect. They wander day or night, unafraid
to hoe fields by the light of the moon, or burn brush
in the dark. They are the reason the land
is so beautifully green and the furrows, at dawn,
are like sunburned faces. They harvest the grapes,
they eat and they sing; they husk the corn,
they dance and they drink. You can hear their girls laugh
when one of them mentions the billy goat—up there
in the woods, in the stony ravines, the peasants
see him looking for she-goats and butting the trees.
Because animals that don't know how to work,
that are kept only for stud—they like to destroy things.

Il tempo passa

Quel vecchione, una volta, seduto sull'erba,
aspettava che il figlio tornasse col pollo
mal strozzato, e gli dava due schiaffi. Per strada
— camminavano all'alba su quelle colline —
gli spiegava che il pollo si strozza con l'unghia
— tra le dita — del pollice, senza rumore.
Nel crepuscolo fresco marciavano sotto le piante
imbottiti di frutta e il ragazzo portava
sulle spalle una zucca giallastra. Il vecchione diceva
che la roba nei campi è di chi ne ha bisogno
tant'è vero che al chiuso non viene. Guardarsi d'attorno
bene prima, e poi scegliere calmi la vite più nera
e sedersele all'ombra e non muovere fin che si è pieni.

C'è chi mangia dei polli in città. Per le vie
non si trovano i polli. Si trova il vecchiotto
— tutto ciò ch'è rimasto dell'altro vecchione —
che, seduto su un angolo, guarda i passanti
e, chi vuole, gli getta due soldi. Non apre la bocca
il vecchiotto: a dir sempre una cosa, vien sete,
e in città non si trova le botti che versano,
né in ottobre né mai. C'è la griglia dell'oste
che sa puzzo di mosto, specialmente la notte.
Nell'autunno, di notte, il vecchiotto cammina,
ma non ha più la zucca, e le porte fumose
delle tampe dan fuori ubriachi che cianciano soli.
È una gente che beve soltanto di notte
(dal mattino ci pensa) e cosí si ubriaca.
Il vecchiotto, ragazzo, beveva tranquillo;
ora, solo annusando, gli balla la barba:
fin che ficca il bastone tra i piedi a uno sbronzo
che va in terra. Lo aiuta a rialzarsi, gli vuota le tasche
(qualche volta allo sbronzo è avanzato qualcosa),

Time Passes

That old guy, in the old days, would sit in the grass
waiting for his son to come back with a chicken
badly strangled, then slap him a couple of times.
Later, walking the hills at dawn, he'd explain
that when wringing their necks you press your thumbnail
between your two fingers: that way they die quiet.
In the cool half-light, they'd walk beneath vines
bursting with fruit, the boy with a yellowish gourd
strapped to his back, the old guy saying that whatever
grows in a field belongs to whoever needs it—
that's why it won't grow indoors. Make sure
to take a good look around, then pick the ripe fruit,
sit down in the shade, don't move till you're full.

In the city, some people eat chicken. But chickens
don't live on the streets. The little old man—
all that's left of that guy from the old days—
now sits on a corner, just watching the people.
Some toss him a couple of coins. The old man
says nothing: all he could say is, I'm thirsty,
can't find an unguarded barrel of wine in these parts,
not in October, not ever. The grate at the tavern,
though, reeks of new wine, especially at night.
In autumn, at night, the old man goes walking,
but he doesn't have any gourd, and the taverns
turn mumbling drunks out of their smoky doors.
They drink only at night (they think of it first thing
in the morning) and that's how they get drunk.
The old man, as a boy, could drink calmly;
now just the smell will make his beard twitch:
he'll end up tripping some other drunk with his cane,
then empty his pockets while helping him back to his feet
(sometimes even a drunk has a little left over),

e alle due lo buttano fuori anche lui
dalla tampa fumosa, che canta, che sgrida
e che vuole la zucca e distendersi sotto la vite.

and at two, they kick him out of the smoky tavern
with all the rest, and he sings, and he shouts,
and he wants to stretch out with his gourd beneath vines.

Grappa a settembre

I mattini trascorrono chiari e deserti
sulle rive del fiume, che all'alba s'annebbia
e incupisce il suo verde, in attesa del sole.
Il tabacco, che vendono nell'ultima casa
ancor umida, all'orlo dei prati, ha un colore
quasi nero e un sapore sugoso: vapora azzurrino.
Tengon anche la grappa, colore dell'acqua.

È venuto un momento che tutto si ferma
e matura. Le piante lontano stan chete:
sono fatte più scure. Nascondono frutti
che a una scossa cadrebbero. Le nuvole sparse
hanno polpe mature. Lontano, sui corsi,
ogni casa matura al tepore del cielo.

Non si vede a quest'ora che donne. Le donne non fumano
e non bevono, sanno soltanto fermarsi nel sole
e riceverlo tiepido addosso, come fossero frutta.
L'aria, cruda di nebbia, si beve a sorsate
come grappa, ogni cosa vi esala un sapore.
Anche l'acqua del fiume ha bevuto le rive
e le macera al fondo, nel cielo. Le strade
sono come le donne, maturano ferme.

A quest'ora ciascuno dovrebbe fermarsi
per la strada e guardare come tutto maturi.
C'è persino una brezza, che non smuove le nubi,
ma che basta a dirigere il fumo azzurrino
senza romperlo: è un nuovo sapore che passa.
E il tabacco va intinto di grappa. È così che le donne
non saranno le sole a godere il mattino.

Grappa in September

The mornings pass clear and deserted
on the river's banks, fogged over by dawn,
their green darkened, awaiting the sun.
In that last house, still damp, at the edge
of the field, they're selling tobacco, blackish,
juicy in flavor: its smoke is pale blue.
They also sell grappa, the color of water.

The moment has come when everything stops
to ripen. The trees in the distance are quiet,
growing darker and darker, concealing fruit
that would fall at a touch. The scattered clouds
are pulpy and ripe. On the distant boulevards,
houses are ripening beneath the mild sky.

This early you see only women. Women don't smoke
and don't drink, they know only to stop in the sun
to let their bodies grow warm, as if they were fruit.
The air's raw with this fog, you drink it in sips
like grappa, everything here has a flavor.
Even the river water has swallowed the banks
and steeps them below, in the sky. The streets
are like women, they grow ripe without moving.

This is the time when each person should pause
in the street to see how everything ripens.
There's even a breeze, it won't move the clouds,
but it's enough to carry the blue smoke
without breaking it: a new flavor passing. And tobacco
is best when steeped in some grappa. That's why the women
won't be the only ones enjoying the morning.

Atlantic Oil

Il meccanico sbronzo è felice buttato in un fosso.
Dalla piola, di notte, con cinque minuti di prato,
uno è a casa: ma prima c'è il fresco dell'erba
da godere, e il meccanico dorme che viene già l'alba.
A due passi, nel prato, è rizzato il cartello
rosso e nero: chi troppo s'accosti, non riesce piú a leggerlo,
tanto è largo. A quest'ora è ancor umido
di rugiada. La strada, di giorno, lo copre di polvere,
come copre i cespugli. Il meccanico, sotto, si stira nel sonno.

È l'estremo silenzio. Tra poco, al tepore del sole,
passeranno le macchine senza riposo, svegliando la polvere.
Improvvise alla cima del colle, rallentano un poco,
poi si buttano giú dalla curva. Qualcuno si ferma
nella polvere, avanti al garage, che la imbeve di litri.
I meccanici, un poco intontiti, saranno al mattino
sui bidoni, seduti, aspettando un lavoro.
Fa piacere passare il mattino seduto nell'ombra.
Qui la puzza degli olii si mesce all'odore di verde,
di tabacco e di vino, e il lavoro li viene a trovare
sulla porta di casa. Ogni tanto, c'è fino da ridere:
contadine che passano e dànno la colpa, di bestie e di spose
spaventate, al garage che mantiene il passaggio;
contadini che guardano bieco. Ciascuno, ogni tanto,
fa una svelta discesa a Torino e ritorna piú sgombro.
Poi, tra il ridere e il vendere litri, qualcuno si ferma:
questi campi, a guardarli soltanto, son pieni di polvere
della strada e, a sedersi sull'erba, si viene scacciati.
Tra le coste, c'è sempre una vigna che piace sulle altre:
finirà che il meccanico sposa la vigna che piace
con la cara ragazza, e uscirà dentro il sole,
ma a zappare, e verrà tutto nero sul collo
e berrà del suo vino, torchiato le sere d'autunno in cantina.

Atlantic Oil

The drunk mechanic is happy to be in the ditch.
From the tavern, five minutes through the dark field
and you're home. But first, there's the cool grass
to enjoy, and the mechanic will sleep here till dawn.
A few feet away, the red and black sign that rises
from the field: if you're too close, you can't read it,
it's that big. At this hour, it's still wet with dew.
Later, the street will cover it with dust, as it covers
the bushes. The mechanic, beneath it, stretches in sleep.

Silence is total. Shortly, in the warmth of the sun,
one car after another will pass, waking the dust.
At the top of the hill they slow down for the curve,
then plunge down the slope. A few of the cars
stop at the garage, in the dust, to drink a few liters.
At this time of morning, the mechanics, still dazed,
will be sitting on oil drums, waiting for work.
It's a pleasure to spend the morning sitting in shade,
where the stink of oil's cut with the smell of green,
of tobacco, of wine, and where work comes to them,
right to their door. Sometimes it's even amusing:
peasants' wives come to scold them, blaming the garage
for the traffic—it frightens animals and women—
and for making their husbands look sullen: quick trips
down the hill into Turin that lighten their wallets.
Between laughing and selling gas, one of them will pause:
these fields, it's plain to see, are covered with road dust,
if you try to sit on the grass, it'll drive you away.
On the hillside, there's a vineyard he prefers to all others,
and in the end he'll marry that vineyard and the sweet girl
who comes with it, and he'll go out in the sun to work,
but now with a hoe, and his neck will turn brown,
and he'll drink wine pressed on fall evenings from his own grapes.

Anche a notte ci passano macchine, ma silenziose,
tantoché l'ubriaco, nel fosso, non l'hanno svegliato.
Nella notte non levano polvere e il fascio dei fari
svela in pieno il cartello sul prato, alla curva.
Sotto l'alba trascorrono caute e non s'ode rumore,
se non brezza che passa, e toccata la cima
si dileguano nella pianura, affondando nell'ombra.

Cars pass during the night, too, but more quietly,
so quiet the drunk in the ditch hasn't woken. At night
they don't raise much dust, and the beams of their headlights,
as they round the curve, reveal in full the sign in the field.
Near dawn, they glide cautiously along, you can't hear a thing
except maybe the breeze, and from the top of the hill
they disappear into the plain, sinking in shadow.

Città in campagna

Papà beve al tavolo avvolto da pergole verdi
e il ragazzo s'annoia seduto. Il cavallo s'annoia
posseduto da mosche: il ragazzo vorrebbe acchiapparne,
ma Papà l'ha sott'occhio. Le pergole dànno nel vuoto
sulla valle. Il ragazzo non guarda piú al fondo,
perché ha voglia di fare un gran salto. Alza gli occhi:
non c'è piú belle nuvole; gli ammassi splendenti
si son chiusi a nascondere il fresco del cielo.

Si lamenta, Papà, che ci sia da patire piú caldo
nella gita per vendere l'uva, che a mietere il grano.
Chi ha mai visto in settembre quel sole rovente
e doversi fermare al ritorno dall'oste,
altrimenti gli crepa il cavallo. Ma l'uva è venduta;
qualcun altro ci pensa, di qui all vendemmia:
se anche grandina, il prezzo è già fatto. Il ragazzo s'annoia,
il suo sorso Papà gliel'ha già fatto bere.
Non c'è piú che guardare quel bianco maligno,
sotto il nero dell'afa, e sperare nell'acqua.

Le vie fresche di mezza mattina eran piene di portici
e di gente. Gridavano in piazza. Girava il gelato
bianco e rosa: pareva le nuvole sode nel cielo.
Se faceva 'sto caldo in città, si fermavano a pranzo
nell'albergo. La polvere e il caldo non sporcano i muri
in città: lungo i viali le case son bianche
e ogni tanto qualcuno si siede nei viali a far niente.
In città stanno al fresco a far niente, ma comprano l'uva,
la lavorano in grandi cantine e diventano ricchi.
Se restavano ancora, vedevano in mezzo alle piante,
nella sera, ogni viale una fila di luci.

City in the Country

Father drinks at the table, wrapped in the green of the arbor;
the boy beside him is bored. The horse is bored too
and covered with flies: the boy wants to swat them,
but Father is watching. The arbor looks over a steep drop
toward the valley. The boy no longer looks over that ledge,
because he'd like to take a great leap. He raises his eyes:
the fine clouds are gone: their masses, once splendid,
have clotted together to block out the blue of the sky.

Father complains that the heat has been harder to bear
on this grape-selling trip than it was for the wheat harvest.
Unheard-of, the sun blazing like this in September,
having to stop at the inn on your way home
to keep from killing your horse. But now they've been sold.
From now till the harvest, let someone else worry:
so what if it hails—the price has been set. The boy is still bored,
the small drink his father gave him is already gone.
Nothing to do now but stare at the malevolent whiteness
beneath the black haze of heat, hoping for rain.

The cool streets of midmorning were lined with arcades
and people. Shouts in the square. Vendors of ice cream,
white and pink: like firm clouds piled in the sky.
If the heat were this bad in the city, they'd have eaten
in the hotel. The dust and the heat don't stick to the walls
in the city: along the avenues, the houses are white.
The boy raises his eyes to the terrible clouds.
City folks sit in the shade doing nothing, but they're the ones
who buy all the grapes and make all the wine and get rich.
If they'd stayed the night in the city, they'd have seen,
through the leaves at evening, the avenues strung with lights.

Tra le pergole nasce un gran vento. Il cavallo si scuote
e Papà guarda in aria. Laggiú nella valle
c'è la casa nel prato e la vigna matura.
Tutt'a un tratto fa freddo e le foglie si staccano
e la polvere vola. Papà beve sempre.
Il ragazzo alza gli occhi alle nuvole orribili.
Sulla valle c'è ancora una chiazza di sole.
Se si fermano qui, mangeranno dall'oste.

A gust of wind rattles the arbor. The horse shudders,
and Father looks to the sky. Down in the valley,
their house sits in their field among ripening grapes.
All of a sudden it's cold, leaves let go of their branches,
and dust starts to fly. Father's still drinking.
The boy raises his eyes to the terrible clouds.
Patches of sun still shine on the valley below.
If they stay here tonight, they'll eat at the inn.

Gente che non capisce

Sotto gli alberi della stazione si accendono i lumi.
Gella sa che a quest'ora sua madre ritorna dai prati
col grembiale rigonfio. In attesa del treno,
Gella guarda tra il verde e sorride al pensiero
di fermarsi anche lei, tra i fanali, a raccogliere l'erba.

Gella sa che sua madre da giovane è stata in città
una volta: lei tutte le sere col buio ne parte
e sul treno ricorda vetrine specchianti
e persone che passano e non guardano in faccia.
La città di sua madre è un cortile rinchiuso
tra muraglie, e la gente s'affaccia ai balconi.
Gella torna ogni sera con gli occhi distratti
di colori e di voglie, e, spaziando dal treno,
pensa, al ritmo monotono, netti profili di vie
tra le luci, e colline percorse di viali e di vita
e gaiezze di giovani, schietti nel passo e nel riso padrone.

Gella è stufa di andare e venire, e tornare la sera
e non vivere né tra le case né in mezzo alle vigne.
La città la vorrebbe su quelle colline,
luminosa, segreta, e non muoversi piú.
Cosí, è troppo diversa. Alla sera ritrova
i fratelli, che tornano scalzi da qualche fatica,
e la madre abbronzata, e si parla di terre
e lei siede in silenzio. Ma ancora ricorda
che, bambina, tornava anche lei col suo fascio dell'erba:
solamente, quelli erano giochi. E la madre che suda
a raccogliere l'erba, perché da trent'anni
l'ha raccolta ogni sera, potrebbe una volta
ben restarsene in casa. Nessuno la cerca.

People Who Don't Understand

Beneath the trees by the station, streetlamps come on.
Gella knows it's the time her mother comes in from the fields,
her apron bulged out. As she waits for the train,
Gella looks toward some bushes and smiles at the thought
of herself stopping, there by the signal-lights, to pick greens.

Gella knows that her mother went once, as a girl,
to the city: she herself leaves it each evening at dark,
and recalls, as she rides, the mirrorlike windows
and the people who pass and won't look at your face.
To her mother, the city's a courtyard closed off
with high walls, its residents posing on balconies.
Gella leaves each evening, her eyes distracted
by colors and longings, and imagines, as she's lulled
by the train's dull rhythm, the crisp outlines of streets
lined with lamps, and hills overrun by avenues and life,
and the joy of the young, their pure walk, their loud laughter.

Gella's fed up with going and coming, traveling at night,
living neither among buildings nor out in the vineyards.
She wishes the city were up on those hills,
luminous, secret: never again would she leave it.
Now, it's all split. She's back in the evening to see
her brothers returning barefoot from some chore
and her sun-bronzed mother: they talk of the fields,
and she sits in silence. Still, she remembers
herself as a girl, returning with her own bundle of greens—
but that, of course, was a game. It was her mother
who sweated to gather them, for thirty-odd years
she's done it each evening, though she could, for once,
relax and stay home: nobody needs them.

Anche Gella vorrebbe restarsene, sola, nei prati,
ma raggiungere i piú solitari, e magari nei boschi.
E aspettare la sera e sporcarsi nell'erba
e magari nel fango e mai piú ritornare in città.
Non far nulla, perché non c'è nulla che serva a nessuno.
Come fanno le capre strappare soltanto le foglie piú verdi
e impregnarsi i capelli, sudati e bruciati,
di rugiada notturna. Indurirsi le carni
e annerirle e strapparsi le vesti, cosí che in città
non la vogliano piú. Gella è stufa di andare e venire
e sorride al pensiero di entrare in città
sfigurata e scomposta. Finché le colline e le vigne
non saranno scomparse, e potrà passeggiare
per i viali, dov'erano i prati, le sere, ridendo,
Gella avrà queste voglie, guardando dal treno.

Gella, too, would like to relax, alone, in the fields,
the farthest, loneliest field, or maybe the woods.
And to wait for evening, and to get grass on her clothes,
perhaps even mud, and to never go back to the city.
Not to do anything, because nothing does anyone good.
To pluck, like the goats, only the greenest of leaves,
to steep her hair, sweaty and sun-bleached, in the dew
that falls in the night. To harden and darken
her flesh, and to throw off her clothes—so the city
would no longer want her. Gella's fed up with going and coming,
and she smiles at the thought of arriving in Turin
disheveled and monstrous. But until the hills and vineyards
have vanished, until she can stroll, laughing,
down avenues, where fields were, in the evening,
Gella will gaze, with these longings, through train windows.

Casa in costruzione

Coi canneti è scomparsa anche l'ombra. Già il sole, di sghembo,
attraversa le arcate e si sfoga per vuoti
che saranno finestre. Lavorano un po' i muratori,
fin che dura il mattino. Ogni tanto rimpiangono
quando qui ci frusciavano ancora le canne,
e un passante accaldato poteva gettarsi sull'erba.

I ragazzi cominciano a giungere a sole piú alto.
Non lo temono il caldo. I pilastri isolati nel cielo
sono un campo di gioco migliore che gli alberi
o la solita strada. I mattoni scoperti
si riempion d'azzurro, per quando le volte
saran chiuse, e ai ragazzi è una gioia vedersi dal fondo
sopra il capo i riquadri del cielo. Peccato il sereno,
ché un rovescio di pioggia lassú da quei vuoti
piacerebbe ai ragazzi. Sarebbe un lavare la casa.

Certamente stanotte — poterci venire — era meglio:
la rugiada bagnava i mattoni e, distesi tra i muri,
si vedevan le stelle. Magari potevano accendere
un bel fuoco e qualcuno assalirli e pigliarsi a sassate.
Una pietra di notte può uccidere senza rumore.
Poi ci sono le bisce che scendono i muri
e che cadono come una pietra, soltanto piú molli.
Cosa accada di notte là dentro, lo sa solo il vecchio
che al mattino si vede discendere per le colline.
Lascia braci di fuoco là dentro e ha la barba strinata
dalla vampa e ha già preso tant'acqua, che, come il terreno,
non potrebbe cambiare colore. Fa ridere tutti
perché dice che gli altri si fanno la casa
col sudore e lui senza sudare ci dorme. Ma un vecchio
non dovrebbe durare alla notte scoperta.
Si capisce una coppia in un prato: c'è l'uomo e la donna

House under Construction

The shade disappeared with the canebrake. Early sun
angles through passageways, spills through the spaces
where windows will be. The masons will work
most of the morning, recalling occasionally
the days when this place still rustled with cane leaves,
and a person could lie in the grass to cool off.

The kids will arrive when the sun is higher,
not afraid of the heat. The piers that cut into the sky
make better playgrounds, they think, than the trees
or the usual street. The bare bricks gather in
as much of the sky as they can before the roof
will close over them, and the kids love to look up
at the rectangles of sky. The nice weather's a shame:
these kids would love to see a good rain, pouring down
through those open spaces — a housecleaning.

Last night, could they have come, would've surely been better:
on bricks bathed in dew, you could have stretched out
and stared at the stars. Perhaps they'd have lit a nice fire
and gotten attacked and fought back, the stones flying.
A stone in the night can kill without making a noise.
And then there are grass snakes who crawl up the walls
and fall down like stones, only softer.
Only the old man knows what really goes on at night,
the man you see in the morning coming down from the hill.
He leaves ashes in there, and his beard has been singed,
and he's soaked up so much water that he, like the earth,
will never change color. He makes everyone laugh
by saying that others are building that house
with their sweat, while he gets to sleep there. But old men
shouldn't have to endure nights out in the open.
A couple out in a field is one thing: a man and a woman

che si tengono stretti, e poi tornano a casa.
Ma quel vecchio non ha piú una casa e si muove a fatica.
Certamente qualcosa gli accade là dentro,
perché ancora al mattino borbotta tra sé.

Dopo un po' i muratori si buttano all'ombra.
È il momento che il sole ha investito ogni cosa
e un mattone a toccarlo ci scotta le mani.
S'è già visto una biscia piombare fuggendo
in un pozzo di calce: è il momento che il caldo
fa impazzire persino le bestie. Si beve una volta
e si vedono le altre colline ogn'intorno, bruciate,
tremolare nel sole. Soltanto uno scemo
resterebbe al lavoro e difatti quel vecchio
a quest'ora attraversa le vigne, rubando le zucche.
Poi ci sono i ragazzi sui ponti, che salgono e scendono.
Una volta una pietra è finita sul cranio
del padrone e hanno tutti interrotto il lavoro
per portarlo al torrente e lavargli la faccia.

holding each other, then going back home.
But the old man no longer has any home, he moves slow.
Surely something must happen at night in that house,
because he's still mumbling to himself in the morning.

After a while, the masons go look for some shade.
It's that time when sun has soaked into everything,
and touching a brick with a bare hand will burn.
They saw a grass snake that was fleeing from something
fall into the lime-pit: the heat's gotten so bad
it drives even the animals crazy. You take a drink
and you look at the hills around you, scorched
and wavering in sunlight. In this heat, only a fool
would keep working, that's why the old man
is raiding the vineyards now, filling his gourds.
And the boys are climbing all over the scaffolding.
Once, a stone fell from up there, hitting the owner
in the head, and everyone took a break from his work
to carry him down to the stream and wash off his face.

Civiltà antica

Il ragazzo respira piú fresco, nascosto
dalle imposte, fissando la strada. Si vedono i ciottoli
per la chiara fessura, nel sole. Nessuno cammina
per la strada. Il ragazzo vorrebbe uscir fuori
cosí nudo — la strada è di tutti — e affogare nel sole.

In città, non si può. Si potrebbe in campagna,
se non fosse, sul capo, il profondo del cielo
che atterrisce e avvilisce. C'è l'erba che fredda
fa il solletico ai piedi, ma le piante che guardano
ferme, e i tronchi e i cespugli son occhi severi
per un debole corpo slavato, che trema.
Fino l'erba è diversa e ripugna al contatto.

Ma la strada è deserta. Passasse qualcuno
il ragazzo dal buio oserebbe fissarlo
e pensare che tutti nascondono un corpo.
Passa invece un cavallo dai muscoli grossi
e rintronano i ciottoli. Da tempo il cavallo
se ne va, nudo e senza ritegno, nel sole:
tantoché marcia in mezzo alla strada. Il ragazzo
che vorrebbe esser forte a quel modo e annerito
e magari tirare a quel carro, oserebbe mostrarsi
anche sotto le strisce del cielo. Le case, che guardano,
avviliscono meno che il prato deserto.

Se si ha un corpo, bisogna vederlo. Il ragazzo non sa
se ciascuno abbia un corpo. Il vecchiotto rugoso
che passava al mattino, non può avere un corpo
cosí pallido e triste, non può avere nulla
che atterrisca a quel modo. E nemmeno gli adulti
o le spose che danno la poppa al bambino
sono nudi. Hanno un corpo soltanto i ragazzi.

Ancient Civilization

The boy breathes in the cool air, hidden
behind shutters, watching the street. He watches
the cobbles gleam through the slats. The street
is deserted. He wants to go out, naked like this —
the street is for everyone — to drown in the sun.

You can't in the city. You could in the country,
if the sky wasn't so huge overhead —
it's daunting and scary. Then there's the cold grass
that tickles your feet, and the plants that just stare,
while the trees and the bushes look harshly
on a body so thin and weak that it trembles.
Even the grass there is strange and unpleasant.

But the street is deserted. If anyone passed,
the boy would stare out from the darkness
and think to himself: everyone's hiding a body.
Instead, a muscled brown horse clomps into view,
rattling the cobbles. It passes by slowly,
naked in broad daylight, and so lacking in shame
that it walks in the middle of the street. The boy
would like such strength and such color, would even
consider pulling that cart — he'd dare show himself
even under those strips of sky. The houses that watch you
are less daunting than wide-open fields.

People with bodies should let them be seen. The boy
isn't sure that everyone has one. The craggy old man
who passed this morning can't have a body
as pale and as sad as his face, couldn't have anything
as frightening as that. No adults, not even
a young wife giving her breast to her baby,
are really naked. Only children have bodies.

Il ragazzo non osa guardarsi nel buio,
ma sa bene che deve affogarsi nel sole
e abituarsi agli sguardi del cielo, per crescere un uomo.

The boy's afraid to look at himself in the dark,
but he knows he'll have to drown in the sun
and get used to the gaze of the sky, to grow into a man.

Cattive compagnie

Questo è un uomo che fuma la pipa. Laggiú nello specchio,
ce n'è un altro che fuma la pipa. Si guardano in faccia.
Quello vero è tranquillo perché vede l'altro sorridere.

Prima ha visto altre cose. Su un fondo di fumo
una faccia di donna protesa a sorridere
e un idiota leccarla con gli occhi parlando.
Poi l'idiota, parlando, afferrare anche lui
e strappargli un sogghigno. Un sogghigno da idiota.
E la donna piegarsi e serrare le labbra
come avesse veduto qualcosa di nudo.

Ora, corpi di uomini nudi la donna ne vede
dal mattino alla sera, ma spoglia anche sé
e là sopra lavora, ridendo. E sogghigni ne vede
e ne fa, sul lavoro: anzi, è mezzo lavoro
un sogghigno ben fatto. Ma quando una è lí per scherzare
a parole, ferisce vedere anche l'altro,
che in silenzio ascoltava parlare l'idiota,
lampeggiare lo stesso pensiero brutale.

Donna e idiota son già ritornati a alitarsi sul volto
—si somigliano un poco le donne e gli idioti—
e la pipa vapora una faccia contratta.
Dentro il fumo è possibile fare una smorfia
e socchiudere gli occhi. La donna ridendo
schiva quello che parla pendendole addosso.

Bad Company

This is a man smoking a pipe. There in the mirror
sits another who smokes. They look at each other.
The real one's relieved to see the other one smile.

He's seen other things: against a backdrop of smoke
a woman lying prone with a smile on her face,
an idiot licking her with his eyes as he talks.
And later the idiot looking at him too,
wringing a sneer from him. The sneer of an idiot.
And the woman turning and closing her mouth
as if she had seen something naked.

These days she sees the naked bodies of men
from morning till evening, and she too undresses
and laughs as she works. She sees plenty of sneers
and gives back her share: a good sneer, in fact,
and half the job's done. But when a woman's there only to play
word games, it's wounding to see the other man,
who had listened in silence as the idiot spoke,
brighten with the identical animal thought.

Woman and idiot are breathing in each other's faces
again. They're similar, women and idiots,
and a drawn face dissolves in the pipesmoke.
Surrounded by smoke it's easy to grimace
and half-close your eyes. The woman who laughs
eludes the talking man leaning against her.

Piaceri notturni

Anche noi ci fermiamo a sentire la notte
nell'istante che il vento è piú nudo: le vie
sono fredde di vento, ogni odore è caduto;
le narici si levano verso le luci oscillanti.

Abbiam tutti una casa che attende nel buio
che torniamo: una donna ci attende nel buio
stesa al sonno: la camera è calda di odori.
Non sa nulla del vento la donna che dorme
e respira; il tepore del corpo di lei
è lo stesso del sangue che mormora in noi.

Questo vento ci lava, che giunge dal fondo
delle vie spalancate nel buio; le luci
oscillanti e le nostre narici contratte
si dibattono nude. Ogni odore è un ricordo.
Da lontano nel buio sbucò questo vento
che s'abbatte in città: giú per prati e colline,
dove pure c'è un'erba che il sole ha scaldato
e una terra annerita di umori. Il ricordo
nostro è un aspro sentore, la poca dolcezza
della terra sventrata che esala all'inverno
il respiro del fondo. Si è spento ogni odore
lungo il buio, e in città non ci giunge che il vento.

Torneremo stanotte alla donna che dorme,
con le dita gelate a cercare il suo corpo,
e un calore ci scuoterà il sangue, un calore di terra
annerita di umori: un respiro di vita.
Anche lei si è scaldata nel sole e ora scopre
nella sua nudità la sua vita piú dolce,
che nel giorno scompare, e ha sapore di terra.

Nocturnal Pleasures

And we too stop to smell the night air
just when the wind is most naked: the streets
are chilled by this wind, each odor drops down,
and nostrils rise toward the shimmering lights.

We all have a house that waits in the dark
for us to return: a woman waits for us too,
asleep in the dark, in a room warm with odors.
The woman sleeping and breathing knows nothing
at all about wind; the warmth of her body
matches the blood that murmurs in us.

It washes us clean, this wind, it reaches the ends
of streets that open on darkness; the lights
that shimmer and the nostrils that flare
are struggling, naked. Each odor's a memory.
It came a long way, through darkness, this wind
that dies in the city: down hills and through fields
where the grasses are warmed by the sun
and the earth is blackened by humors. Our memory
is a sour scent, barely a trace of sweetness
in the deep breath exhaled from the gutted earth
in winter. Each odor fades in the darkness;
nothing reaches us here in the city but wind.

Tonight we'll return to the woman who sleeps,
we'll reach for her body with fingers of ice,
heat shaking our blood, the heat of earth
blackened by humors: a breath of life.
She too was warmed by the sun and discovers,
in her nakedness now, her sweetest life —
it leaves with the daylight, it tastes like the earth.

Balletto

È un gigante che passa volgendosi appena,
quando attende una donna, e non sembra che attenda.
Ma non fa mica apposta: lui fuma e la gente lo guarda.

Ogni donna che va con quest'uomo è una bimba
che si addossa a quel corpo ridendo, stupita
della gente che guarda. Il gigante s'avvia
e la donna è una parte di tutto il suo corpo,
solamente piú viva. La donna non conta,
ogni sera è diversa, ma sempre una piccola
che ridendo contiene il culetto che danza.

Il gigante non vuole un culetto che danzi
per la strada, e pacato lo porta a sedersi
ogni sera alla sfida e la donna è contenta.
Alla sfida, la donna è stordita dagli urli
e, guardando il gigante, ritorna bambina.
Dai due pugilatori si sentono i tonfi
del saltelli e dei pugni, ma pare che danzino
cosí nudi allacciati, e la donna li fissa
con gli occhietti e si morde le labbra contenta.
Si abbandona al gigante e ritorna bambina:
è un piacere appoggiarsi a una rupe che accoglie.

Se la donna e il gigante si spogliano insieme
—lo faranno piú tardi—, il gigante somiglia
alla placidità di una rupe, una rupe bruciante,
e la bimba, a scaldarsi, si stringe a quel masso.

Ballet

He's a giant who turns only barely when passing,
who waits for a woman without seeming to wait.
But it isn't on purpose: he smokes and people just stare.

Every woman who goes with this man is a child
who attaches herself to his body, laughing, amazed
by the people who watch. The giant moves on,
the woman having become part of his body,
more alive than the rest. The women don't matter—
each night there's a new one, they're always petite
with cute little asses that dance when they laugh.

The giant doesn't want the cute little ass to dance
in the street, so he quietly guides it each evening
to a seat at the fights, and the woman is happy.
At the fight, the woman is deafened by shouts,
and watching her giant, becomes childlike again.
You can hear the thudding of fists and the scraping
of feet, but it looks like they're dancing together,
naked and close, and the woman is staring
with wide little eyes, biting her lips—she's happy.
She abandons herself to the giant, childlike again:
it's a pleasure to lie back against cliffs that support you.

If the woman and the giant take off their clothes—
and later they will—the giant will resemble
the serenity of cliffs grown hot in the sun,
the girl-child pressing against them for warmth.

Paternità (1)

Fantasia della donna che balla, e del vecchio
che è suo padre e una volta l'aveva nel sangue
e l'ha fatta una notte, godendo in un letto, bel nudo.
Lei s'affretta per giungere in tempo a svestirsi,
e ci sono altri vecchi che attendono. Tutti
le divorano, quando lei salta a ballare, la forza
delle gambe con gli occhi, ma i vecchi ci tremano.
Quasi nuda è la giovane. E i giovani guardano
con sorrisi, e qualcuno vorrebbe esser nudo.

Sembran tutti suo padre i vecchiotti entusiasti
e son tutti, malfermi, un avanzo di corpo
che ha goduto altri corpi. Anche i giovani un giorno
saran padri, e la donna è per tutti una sola.
È accaduto in silenzio. Una gioia profonda
prende il buio davanti alla giovane viva.
Tutti i corpi non sono che un corpo, uno solo
che si muove inchiodando gli sguardi di tutti.

Questo sangue, che scorre le membra diritte
della giovane, è il sangue che gela nei vecchi;
e suo padre che fuma in silenzio, a scaldarsi,
lui non salta, ma ha fatto la figlia che balla.
C'è un sentore e uno scatto nel corpo di lei
che è lo stesso nel vecchio, e nei vecchi. In silenzio
fuma il padre e l'attende che ritorni, vestita.
Tutti attendono, giovani e vecchi, e la fissano;
e ciascuno, bevendo da solo, ripenserà a lei.

Fatherhood (1)

Fond notion of the dancer, and of the old man,
her father, who had her once in his blood
and made her one night, romping in bed, stark naked.
She hurries to get there in time to undress,
knowing other old men are there waiting. They all
devour, when she jumps in the air, the strength
of her legs with their eyes, and the old men tremble.
She's young, almost naked. The young men
smile as they watch—some wish they were naked.

All these admiring old men resemble her father,
and all of them, feeble, are what's left of bodies
that enjoyed other bodies. Someday the young men too
will be fathers—for them, this woman's just one
among many. And then this, in silence: a deep joy
takes hold of the darkness in front of the woman.
All bodies are suddenly one body, one only,
and each gaze is riveted to it as it moves.

This blood that flows through the dancer's strong limbs
is the blood that freezes the veins of old men;
her father smokes in the silence to keep warm,
he doesn't dance, but he made a daughter who does.
The same feeling that pulses through her body,
pulses in his, and in the rest of the old men. Her father
smokes quietly, waiting—she's gone to get dressed.
They all wait, young men and old, fixing her image.
Each one, when drinking alone, will call her to mind.

Disciplina antica

Gli ubriachi non sanno parlare alle donne
e si sono sbandati; nessuno li vuole.
Vanno adagio per strada, la strada e i lampioni
non han fine. Qualcuno fa i giri piú larghi:
ma non c'è da temere, domani ritornano a casa.

L'ubriaco che sbanda, si crede con donne
—i lampioni son sempre gli stessi e le donne, di notte,
sono sempre le stesse—: nessuna lo ascolta.
L'ubriaco ragiona e le donne non vogliono.
Queste donne che ridono sono il discorso che fa:
perché ridono tanto le donne o, se piangono, gridano?
L'ubriaco vorrebbe una donna ubriaca
che ascoltasse sommessa. Ma quelle lo assordano
«Per avere 'sto figlio, bisogna passare da noi».

L'ubriaco si stringe a un compagno ubriaco,
che stasera è suo figlio, non nato da quelle.
Come può una donnetta che piange e che sgrida
fargli un figliolo compagno? Se quello è ubriaco,
non ricorda le donne nel passo malfermo,
e i due avanzano in pace. Il figliolo che conta
non è nato di donna—sarebbe una donna
anche lui—. Lui cammina col padre e ragiona:
i lampioni gli durano tutta la notte.

Ancient Discipline

Drunkards don't know how to speak to a woman,
they straggle and drift; nobody wants them.
They move slow down the street; the street and its lamps
are endless. Some make longer journeys:
but nothing to fear, they'll come home tomorrow.

The drunkard who drifts, he thinks he's with women —
the streetlamps are always the same and the women, at night,
are always the same. He talks but none listen.
The drunkard expounds and the women don't want to.
These women, who laugh, they are his subject:
why do they laugh so, and why, when they cry, do they shout?
The drunkard would like a woman who's drunk
to listen submissively. Instead they are deafening:
"You want a kid, you gotta go through us."

The drunkard holds on to a fellow drunk,
who tonight is his son, not born of those women.
How could a little woman who scolds him and cries
give him such a companionable son? If he's drunk,
he won't remember the women as he totters along,
and they can move on in peace. The son that counts
wasn't born of a woman — or he'd be a woman
himself. He walks with his father and expounds:
the streetlamps will last them the whole night.

Indisciplina

L'ubriaco si lascia alle spalle le case stupite.
Mica tutti alla luce del sole si azzardano
a passare ubriachi. Traversa tranquillo la strada,
e potrebbe infilarsi nei muri, ché i muri ci stanno.
Solo un cane trascorre a quel modo, ma un cane si ferma
ogni volta che sente la cagna e la fiuta con cura.
L'ubriaco non guarda nessuno, nemmeno le donne.

Per la strada la gente, stravolta a guardarlo, non ride
e non vuole che sia l'ubriaco, ma i molti che inciampano
per seguirlo con gli occhi, riguardano innanzi
bestemmiando. Passato che c'è l'ubriaco,
tutta quanta la strada si muove piú lenta
nella luce del sole. Qualcuno che corre
come prima, è qualcuno che non sarà mai l'ubriaco.
Gli altri fissano, senza distinguere, il cielo e le case
che continuano a esserci, se anche nessuno li vede.

L'ubriaco non vede né case né cielo,
ma li sa, perché a passo malfermo percorre uno spazio
netto come le strisce di cielo. La gente impacciata
non comprende piú a cosa ci stiano le case,
e le donne non guardano gli uomini. Tutti
hanno come paura che a un tratto la voce
rauca scoppi a cantare e li segua nell'aria.
Ogni casa ha una porta, ma è inutile entrarci.
L'ubriaco non canta, ma tiene una strada
dove l'unico ostacolo è l'aria. Fortuna
che di là non c'è il mare, perché l'ubriaco
camminando tranquillo entrerebbe anche in mare
e, scomparso, terrebbe sul fondo lo stesso cammino.
Fuori, sempre, la luce sarebbe la stessa.

Indiscipline

The drunk leaves a wake of stunned houses behind him.
Not everyone dares, even in daylight, to walk
past a drunk. He casually crosses the street—
he could slip right into the wall, since it's there.
Only dogs travel like this, but a dog will stop
when it catches the scent of a bitch, to sniff her.
The drunk doesn't see anyone, not even women.

In the street, people cringe at the sight, not laughing,
not wanting to be him, and sometimes they stumble,
because their eyes are on him, then look straight ahead
and curse. When the drunk's finally gone,
the whole street moves a bit slower
in the sunlight. Whoever still rushes along
the same as before won't be the drunk, ever.
The rest stare, without focusing, at houses or sky,
which continue existing, even if nobody sees them.

The drunk sees neither the sky nor the houses,
but he knows them, since he sways through a space
as sharply defined as the strips of sky. The people,
uneasy, are no longer sure what houses are for,
and the women won't look at the men. They all
feel somehow afraid that a sudden hoarse voice
will start singing and follow them home through the air.
Every house has a door, but it's useless to use it.
The drunk doesn't sing, just sticks to his road
where the only obstacle's air. Lucky for him
this road doesn't lead to the sea—if it did
the drunk, walking calmly, would enter the water,
vanish beneath it, and continue along the seafloor.
Outside, the light would remain, forever, unchanged.

Paesaggio (v)

Le colline insensibili che riempiono il cielo
sono vive nell'alba, poi restano immobili
come fossero secoli, e il sole le guarda.
Ricoprirle di verde sarebbe una gioia
e nel verde, disperse, le frutta e le case.
Ogni pianta nell'alba sarebbe una vita
prodigiosa e le nuvole avrebbero un senso.

Non ci manca che un mare a risplendere forte
e inondare la spiaggia in un ritmo monotono.
Su dal mare non sporgono piante, non muovono foglie;
quando piove sul mare, ogni goccia è perduta,
come il vento su queste colline, che cerca le foglie
e non trova che pietre. Nell'alba, è un istante:
si disegnano in terra le sagome nere
e le chiazze vermiglie. Poi torna il silenzio.

Hanno un senso le coste buttate nel cielo
come case di grande città? Sono nude.
Passa a volte un villano stagliato nel vuoto,
cosí assurdo che pare passeggi su un tetto
di città. Viene in mente la sterile mole
delle case ammucchiate, che prende la pioggia
e si asciuga nel sole e non dà un filo d'erba.

Per coprire le case e le pietre di verde
—sí che il cielo abbia un senso—bisogna affondare
dentro il buio radici ben nere. Al tornare dell'alba
scorrerebbe la luce fin dentro la terra
come un urto. Ogni sangue sarebbe piú vivo:
anche i corpi son fatti di vene nerastre.
E i villani che passano avrebbero un senso.

Landscape (v)

The unfeeling hills that fill up the sky
come alive at dawn, then hold still, it seems,
for centuries, as the sun watches them.
Such a joy it would be to wrap them in green again,
and to scatter the green with houses and fruit.
Each plant would be a miraculous life
at dawn, and the clouds would make sense.

The only thing missing's a dazzling sea
flooding the shore with monotonous rhythm.
Nothing grows by the sea, no leaf moves;
when it rains on the sea, each drop is lost,
like the wind on these hills, which seeks leaves
and finds only rock. There's a moment at dawn
when black silhouettes appear on the ground,
and blotches of red. Then silence again.

Do these slopes, slapped up in front of the sky
like city buildings, make sense? They're naked.
A peasant up there, stark against the sky's void,
is absurd, as if he were taking a walk on a rooftop
in the city. It brings to mind a sterile colossus
of clustered houses: they get rained on, they dry
in the sun, and not one blade of grass grows.

To cover the houses and the rocks with green—
so the sky would make sense—you'd need
black roots to sink deep in the darkness. At dawn
the light would gush into the earth, with force.
Everything's blood would be more alive: bodies,
too, are made of veins so dark they look black.
Then the peasants who walk past would make sense.

Disciplina

I lavori cominciano all'alba. Ma noi cominciamo
un po' prima dell'alba a incontrare noi stessi
nella gente che va per la strada. Ciascuno ricorda
di esser solo e aver sonno, scoprendo i passanti
radi—ognuno trasogna fra sé,
tanto sa che nell'alba spalancherà gli occhi.
Quando viene il mattino ci trova stupiti
a fissare il lavoro che adesso comincia.
Ma non siamo piú soli e nessuno piú ha sonno
e pensiamo con calma i pensieri del giorno
fino a dare in sorrisi. Nel sole che torna
siamo tutti convinti. Ma a volte un pensiero
meno chiaro—un sogghigno—ci coglie improvviso
e torniamo a guardare come prima del sole.
La città chiara assiste ai lavori e ai sogghigni.
Nulla può disturbare il mattino. Ogni cosa
può accadere e ci basta di alzare la testa
dal lavoro e guardare. Ragazzi scappati
che non fanno ancor nulla, camminano in strada
e qualcuno anche corre. Le foglie dei viali
gettan ombre per strada e non manca che l'erba,
tra le case che assistono immobili. Tanti
sulla riva del fiume si spogliano al sole.
La città ci permette di alzare la testa
a pensarci, e sa bene che poi la chiniamo.

Discipline

The jobs start at dawn. But even before,
we begin to encounter ourselves in the faces
we occasionally pass on the street. Seeing them
reminds us that we're alone and we're tired —
each of us walks through a waking dream,
knowing that dawn will force our eyes open.
When morning does come, it finds us dazed
in the face of work that now has begun.
But no one's alone anymore, no one's tired,
and we think the day's thoughts with such calm
that we smile. Beneath the returning sun,
we all are convinced. But darker thoughts,
sneering thoughts, sometimes surprise us,
and we look again as we did before dawn.
The bright city watches the work, the sneers.
Nothing can bother the morning. Anything
can happen, you just have to lift your eyes
from your work and watch. Boys on the loose,
not doing anything yet, walk back and forth,
some of them run. Leaves throw their shadows
on avenues, the only thing missing is grass
between the still, watching houses. And down
on the banks of the river they undress in the sun.
The city allows us to lift up our heads
to reflect, knowing we'll lower them later.

Legna verde

L'uomo fermo ha davanti colline nel buio.
Fin che queste colline saranno di terra,
i villani dovranno zapparle. Le fissa e non vede,
come chi serri gli occhi in prigione ben sveglio.
L'uomo fermo—che è stato in prigione—domani riprende
il lavoro coi pochi compagni. Stanotte è lui solo.

Le colline gli sanno di pioggia: è l'odore remoto
che talvolta giungeva in prigione nel vento.
Qualche volta pioveva in città: spalancarsi
del respiro e del sangue alla libera strada.
La prigione pigliava la pioggia, in prigione la vita
non finiva, ogni giorno filtrava anche il sole:
i compagni attendevano e il futuro attendeva.

Ora è solo. L'odore inaudito di terra
gli par sorto dal suo stesso corpo, e ricordi remoti
—lui conosce la terra—costringerlo al suolo,
a quel suolo reale. Non serve pensare
che la zappa i villani la picchiano in terra
come sopra un nemico e che si odiano a morte
come tanti nemici. Hanno pure una gioia
i villani: quel pezzo di terra divelto.
Cosa importano gli altri? Domani nel sole
le colline saranno distese, ciascuno la sua.

I compagni non vivono nelle colline,
sono nati in città dove invece dell'erba
c'è rotaie. Talvolta lo scorda anche lui.
Ma l'odore di terra che giunge in città
non sa piú di villani. È una lunga carezza
che fa chiudere gli occhi e pensare ai compagni
in prigione, alla lunga prigione che attende.

Green Wood

The still man stands facing the hills in the dark.
As long as these hills are made out of earth,
peasants must work them. He stares at the hills, not seeing,
like a prisoner who closes his eyes but stays wide awake.
The still man, who knows prison, starts work again
in the morning, with his comrades. Tonight he's alone.

He thinks the hills smell like rain: that distant scent
that sometimes came on the wind into prison.
When it rained in the city, one's breath and blood
would open like doors onto wide public streets.
But prison deprived him of rain; in prison his life
became endless, and each day leeched even the sun:
his comrades were waiting, his future was waiting.

Now he's alone. The astonishing smell of the earth
(this man knows the earth) seems to rise up from his body,
and he's bound by old memories to that ground,
to that actual ground. It's pointless to think
that the peasants hack up the earth with their hoes
as if hacking an enemy, or hate one another
with murderous hatred. They even have joy,
these peasants: that piece of cleared land. Why worry
about anyone else? Tomorrow the hills
will spread out in the sun, each man to his own.

His comrades, his friends, don't live in these hills,
they were born in the city: no grass on that ground,
just tram-tracks. Even he sometimes forgets that.
And the earth-smell that reaches the city has nothing
of the peasants left in it. It's one long caress,
and you close your eyes and you think of your comrades
in prison, and of the long prison that's waiting.

Rivolta

Quello morto è stravolto e non guarda le stelle:
ha i capelli incollati al selciato. La notte è piú fredda.
Quelli vivi ritornano a casa, tremandoci sopra.
È difficile andare con loro; si sbandano tutti
e chi sale una scala, chi scende in cantina.
C'è qualcuno che va fino all'alba e si butta in un prato
sotto il sole. Domani qualcuno sogghigna
disperato, al lavoro. Poi, passa anche questa.

Quando dormono, sembrano il morto: se c'è anche una donna,
è piú greve il sentore, ma paiono morti.
Ogni corpo si stringe stravolto al suo letto
come al rosso selciato: la lunga fatica
fin dall'alba, val bene una breve agonia.
Su ogni corpo coagula un sudicio buio.
Solamente, quel morto è disteso alle stelle.

Pare morto anche il mucchio di cenci, che il sole
scalda forte, appoggiato al muretto. Dormire
per la strada dimostra fiducia nel mondo.
C'è una barba tra i cenci e vi corrono mosche
che han da fare; i passanti si muovono in strada
come mosche; il pezzente è una parte di strada.
La miseria ricopre di barba i sogghigni
come un'erba, e dà un'aria pacata. 'Sto vecchio
che poteva morire stravolto, nel sangue,
pare invece una cosa ed è vivo. Cosí,
tranne il sangue, ogni cosa è una parte di strada.
Pure, in strada le stelle hanno visto del sangue.

Revolt

That dead man, facedown, isn't gazing at stars:
his hair's glued to the pavement. The night's getting colder.
The living return to their homes, shivering still.
It's hard to follow them all as they scatter:
some climb stairs, others go down into basements.
One will walk until dawn, then lie down in a field
in the sun. And tomorrow, another will grimace
at work, despairing. Then this too will pass.

Asleep, they look like the dead man: if a woman's there too,
the smell might be thicker, but both will look dead.
Each body, facedown, clings to its bed,
as to red pavement: their long labor since dawn
has earned them the quick death of sleep.
On each body, a dark filth coagulates.
But the dead man's laid out under starlight.

That rag heap also looks dead, propped there
in the blistering sun, against that low wall. To sleep
on the street, you have to have faith in the world.
There's a beard in those rags, and the gathering flies
have plenty to do. People move down the street
like flies—the beggar's just part of the street.
His miserable grimaces are hidden by beard;
like grass, it imparts an air of serenity. He's old
and could die anytime, facedown in blood,
yet he looks like an inanimate thing, and he lives.
Except for the blood, everything's part of the street.
And stars have seen blood in the street before.

Esterno

Quel ragazzo scomparso al mattino, non torna.
Ha lasciato la pala, ancor fredda, all'uncino
—era l'alba—nessuno ha voluto seguirlo:
si è buttato su certe colline. Un ragazzo
dell'età che comincia a staccare bestemmie,
non sa fare discorsi. Nessuno
ha voluto seguirlo. Era un'alba bruciata
di febbraio, ogni tronco colore del sangue
aggrumato. Nessuno sentiva nell'aria
il tepore futuro.
                    Il mattino è trascorso
e la fabbrica libera donne e operai.
Nel bel sole, qualcuno—il lavoro riprende
tra mezz'ora—si stende a mangiare affamato.
Ma c'è un umido dolce che morde nel sangue
e alla terra dà brividi verdi. Si fuma
e si vede che il cielo è sereno, e lontano
le colline son viola. Varrebbe la pena
di restarsene lunghi per terra nel sole.
Ma a buon conto si mangia. Chi sa se ha mangiato
quel ragazzo testardo? Dice un secco operaio,
che, va bene, la schiena si rompe al lavoro,
ma mangiare si mangia. Si fuma persino.
L'uomo è come una bestia, che vorrebbe far niente.

Son le bestie che sentono il tempo, e il ragazzo
l'ha sentito dall'alba. E ci sono dei cani
che finiscono marci in un fosso: la terra
prende tutto. Chi sa se il ragazzo finisce
lungo un fosso, affamato? È scappato nell'alba
senza fare discorsi, con quattro bestemmie,
alto il naso nell'aria.
                    Ci pensano tutti
aspettando il lavoro, come un gregge svogliato.

Outside

That boy who vanished this morning's not back.
He left his shovel, still cold, on its hook—
it was dawn, nobody wanted to follow him:
he took off for those hills. He's that age
when boys start stringing curses together
and can't have real conversations.
No one went after him. A biting-cold dawn
in February, each tree trunk the color
of blood clots. No one could smell in that air
the warm weather coming.
                              Morning is over,
the factory sets free women and workers.
A few stretch out in the beautiful sun
to wolf down their lunch—they've got a half hour.
The air's humid and sweet, it gnaws at the blood
and sends green shivers into the earth.
You smoke, you look at the calm sky, the hills
in the distance purple. It would be a fine thing
to lie on this ground, in this sun, for hours.
But regardless you eat. That hardheaded boy—
who knows if he ate? And the skinniest worker
says, Sure, they break your back with this work,
but at least you can eat. You can smoke too.
A man's like a beast: he'd rather do nothing.

It's beasts that can smell the weather—the boy
smelled it at dawn. And there are dogs
that end up rotting in ditches: the earth
takes it all. Who knows if that boy will wind up
starving in some ditch? He ran off at dawn
without explanation, cursing four times,
his nose high in the air.
                              That's what they're thinking
as they wait, like a flock with no will, to go work.

Lavorare stanca (II)

Traversare una strada per scappare di casa
lo fa solo un ragazzo, ma quest'uomo che gira
tutto il giorno le strade, non è piú un ragazzo
e non scappa di casa.
                    Ci sono d'estate
pomeriggi che fino le piazze son vuote, distese
sotto il sole che sta per calare, e quest'uomo, che giunge
per un viale di inutili piante, si ferma.
Val la pena esser solo, per essere sempre piú solo?
Solamente girarle, le piazze e le strade
sono vuote. Bisogna fermare una donna
e parlarle e deciderla a vivere insieme.
Altrimenti, uno parla da solo. È per questo che a volte
c'è lo sbronzo notturno che attacca discorsi,
e racconta i progetti di tutta la vita.

Non è certo attendendo nella piazza deserta
che s'incontra qualcuno, ma chi gira le strade
si sofferma ogni tanto. Se fossero in due,
anche andando per strada, la casa sarebbe
dove c'è quella donna e varrebbe la pena.
Nella notte la piazza ritorna deserta
e quest'uomo, che passa, non vede le case
tra le inutili luci, non leva piú gli occhi:
sente solo il selciato, che han fatto altri uomini
dalle mani indurite, come sono le sue.
Non è giusto restare sulla piazza deserta.
Ci sarà certamente quella donna per strada
che, pregata, vorrebbe dar mano alla casa.

Work's Tiring (II)

Crossing a street to run away from your home,
only a child would do that. But this man, who all day
wanders these streets, is no longer a child,
and he isn't running from home.
                              Some late afternoons
in summer, even the piazzas are empty, sprawling
under the sun that will soon set. And this man,
as he comes to an avenue of useless trees, stops.
Is it worth it to be alone, and always more alone?
If you're just wandering, the streets and piazzas
will always be empty. You get a woman to stop
and talk with you, you convince her to live with you.
The rest is just talking to yourself. And that's why
you might hear the drunkard talking during the night,
discussing the plans he's made for his life.

You can't, of course, just wait in an empty piazza
hoping to meet someone, but if you wander the streets
people stop now and then. If he had a companion,
they could walk through the streets together, and home
would be where she was, and it would be worth it.
At night, the piazza will empty again,
and this man, as he passes, won't see the houses
among the useless lights, he won't raise his eyes:
he feels only the pavement, which other men made
with their hardened hands, as hard as his hands.
It's not right to remain in the empty piazza.
Somewhere, on some street, that woman is waiting
and would, if he asked, lead him home by the hand.

Ritratto d'autore

a Leone

La finestra che guarda il selciato sprofonda
sempre vuota. L'azzurro d'estate, sul capo,
pare invece piú fermo e vi spunta una nuvola.
Qui non spunta nessuno. E noi siamo seduti per terra.

Il collega — che puzza — seduto con me
sulla pubblica strada, senza muovere il corpo
s'è levato i calzoni. Io mi levo la maglia.
Sulla pietra fa un gelo e il collega lo gode
piú di me che lo guardo, ma non passa nessuno.
La finestra di botto contiene una donna
color chiaro. Magari ha sentito quel puzzo
e ci guarda. Il collega è già in piedi che fissa.
Ha una barba, il collega, dalle gambe alla faccia,
che gli scusa i calzoni e germoglia tra i buchi
della maglia. È una barba che puzza da sola.
Il collega è saltato per quella finestra,
dentro il buio, e la donna è scomparsa. Mi scappano gli occhi
alla striscia di cielo bel solido, nudo anche lui.

Io non puzzo perché non ho barba. Mi gela, la pietra,
questa mia schiena nuda, che piace alle donne
perché è liscia: che cosa non piace alle donne?
Ma non passano donne. Passa invece la cagna
inseguita da un cane che ha preso la pioggia
tanto puzza. La nuvola liscia, nel cielo,
guarda immobile: pare un ammasso di foglie.
Il collega ha trovato la cena stavolta.
Trattan bene, le donne, chi è nudo. Compare
finalmente alla svolta un gorbetta che fuma.
Ha le gambe d'anguilla anche lui, testa riccia,
pelle dura: le donne vorranno spogliarlo

Portrait of the Author

to Leone

The window that faces this street is always
an empty abyss. The summer blue overhead
seems firmer somehow, with its passing cloud.
Here, nobody passes. It's just us sitting here.

My colleague—who stinks—is sitting beside me
on the public street, and without moving his body
he strips off his pants. I take off my sweater.
The stones beneath us are cold, and my colleague
likes this, and I look at him, and nobody passes.
And suddenly, framed in the window, a woman,
brightly colored. Maybe she noticed the stink
and wanted to see. My colleague stands and looks back.
He has a sort of continuous beard from his face
to his ankles, it covers what pants do and pokes out
through his sweater. That beard stinks all by itself.
When he jumped through the window, into the dark,
the woman vanished. My eyes wander up
toward the nice solid strip of sky—it's naked too.

I don't stink, since I don't have a beard. The stones
are cold on the skin of my back, which women like
because it's so smooth: what don't women like?
But no women pass by. Some bitch passes by
followed by a male whose fur is rain-drenched
and stinks bad. The smooth cloud in the sky
looks down, unmoving: it resembles a leaf pile.
My colleague has found himself supper tonight.
Women treat you well when you're naked. At last
a kid appears from around a corner. He's smoking,
he's got curly hair, tough skin, and legs like an eel,
like me. Some fine day, the women will want

un bel giorno e annusare se puzza di buono.
Quando è qui, stendo un piede. Va subito in terra
e gli chiedo una cicca. Fumiamo in silenzio.

to take off his clothes and sniff for the good stink.
I stick out a foot as he passes. He falls to the ground,
and I ask for a cig. We smoke there in silence.

Mediterranea

Parla poco l'amico, e quel poco è diverso.
Val la pena incontrarlo un mattino di vento?
Di noi due uno, all'alba, ha lasciato una donna.
Si potrebbe discorrere del vento umidiccio,
della calma o di qualche passante, guardando la strada;
ma nessuno comincia. L'amico è lontano
e a fumare non pensa. Non guarda.

       Fumava
anche il negro, un mattino, che insieme vedemmo
fisso, in piedi, nell'angolo a bere quel vino
—fuori il mare aspettava. Ma il rosso del vino
e la nuvola vaga non erano suoi:
non pensava ai sapori. Neanche il mattino
non pareva un mattino di quelli dell'alba;
era un giorno monotono fuori dei giorni
per il negro. L'idea di una terra lontana
gli faceva da sfondo. Ma lui non quadrava.

C'era donne per strada e una luce piú fresca,
e il sentore del mare correva le vie.
Noi, nemmeno le donne o girare: bastava
star seduti e ascoltare la vita e pensare che il mare
era là, sotto il sole ancor fresco di sonno.
Donne bianche passavano, nostre, sul negro
che nemmeno abbassava lo sguardo alle mani
troppo fosche, e nemmeno muoveva il respiro.
Avevamo lasciato una donna, e ogni cosa
sotto l'alba sapeva di nostro possesso:
calma, strade, e quel vino.

      Stavolta i passanti
mi distraggono e piú non ricordo l'amico
che nel vento bagnato si è messo a fumare,

Mediterraneans

My friend says little, and that little is strange.
Should I bother to meet him on mornings like this?
Only one of us left a woman at dawn.
We could chat idly about this damp wind,
the stillness, some passerby, while watching the street;
but neither begins. My friend is far off,
he smokes without thinking. Or watching.

                                    The black guy
was smoking too, when we saw him one morning,
standing still in a corner, drinking that wine —
the sea waited outside. But the red of the wine
and the wandering cloud didn't belong to him:
he wasn't thinking of flavors. Nor did the morning
seem like a morning that had come from a dawn;
it was, for the black guy, a monotonous day
outside of days. The idea of a distant country
provided his backdrop. But he didn't fit in.

In the street, there were women, and light
that was cool and fresh, and the smell of the sea.
For us, neither women nor walking: enough
to sit there and listen to life and know that the sea
was there, beneath a sun still fresh from its sleep.
White women, ours, passed right in front of the black guy,
who didn't even lower his gaze to his somber hands,
his too-dark hands, didn't even catch his breath.
We had left a woman behind, and everything
beneath the dawn sky tasted of our possessing:
stillness, streets, and that wine.

                                    The passersby now
have distracted me, I've forgotten my friend
who's just lit a cigarette in the damp wind

ma non pare che goda.

                    Tra poco mi chiede:
Lo ricordi quel negro che fumava e beveva?

but doesn't seem to enjoy it.
                    He says before long:
Remember that black guy who was smoking and drinking?

La cena triste

Proprio sotto la pergola, mangiata la cena.
C'è lí sotto dell'acqua che scorre sommessa.
Stiamo zitti, ascoltando e guardando il rumore
che fa l'acqua a passare nel solco di luna.
Quest'indugio è il piú dolce.
                                    La compagna, che indugia,
pare ancora che morda nel grappolo d'uva
tanto ha viva la bocca; e il sapore perdura,
come il giallo lunare, nell'aria. Le occhiate, nell'ombra,
hanno il dolce dell'uva, ma le solide spalle
e le guance abbrunite rinserrano tutta l'estate.

Son rimasti uva e pane sul tavolo bianco.
Le due sedie si guardano in faccia deserte.
Chissà il solco di luna che cosa schiarisce,
con quel suo lume dolce, nei boschi remoti.
Può accadere anzi l'alba che un soffio piú freddo
spenga luna e vapori, e qualcuno compaia.
Una debole luce ne mostri la gola
sussultante e le mani febbrili serrarsi
vanamente sui cibi. Continua il sussulto dell'acqua,
ma nel buio. Né l'uva né il pane son mossi.
I sapori tormentano l'ombra affamata,
che non riesce nemmeno a leccare sul grappolo
la rugiada che già si condensa. E, ogni cosa stillando
sotto l'alba, le sedie si guardano, sole.

Qualche volta alla riva dell'acqua un sentore,
come d'uva, di donna ristagna sull'erba,
e la luna fluisce in silenzio. Compare qualcuno,
ma traversa le piante incorporeo, e si lagna
con quel gemito rauco di chi non ha voce,
e si stende sull'erba e non trova la terra:

Sad Supper

We're under the arbor. Supper is finished.
Below us, some water that flows softly by.
We're silent, hearing and watching the noise
the water makes as it passes in the moon's wake.
The sweetest lingering.
                              My companion is lingering, too,
and her mouth is so vivid she might have just eaten
a handful of grapes. Their scent still hangs in the air,
like the moon's yellow light. In these shadows, her glances
are sweet as the grapes, but her strong shoulders
and tan cheeks contain the whole of the summer.

Some bread and some grapes are left on the table.
The two empty chairs are facing each other.
Who knows what the moon's wake illuminates,
with its sweet glow, in the distant forests?
It could happen, even at dawn, that a cold gust
blows moon and mist away, and someone appears.
A weak light reveals his throat rippling
and his feverish hands grasping in vain
for the food. The water continues to ripple,
in darkness now. Neither the bread nor the grapes
have moved. The smells torment this famished shade,
unable even to lick the dew already condensed
on the cluster of grapes. All things are distilled
by the dawn; the chairs face one another, alone.

Sometimes on the banks of the river a scent,
as of grapes or a woman, pools in the grass,
and the moon flows silently by. Someone appears,
passing over the plants, incorporeal, grieving
in the hoarse tones of the voiceless: he lies
down on the grass and can't feel the ground—

solamente, gli treman le nari. Fa freddo, nell'alba,
e la stretta di un corpo sarebbe la vita.
Piú diffusa del giallo lunare, che ha orrore
di filtrare nei boschi, è quest'ansia inesausta
di contatti e sapori che macera i morti.
Altre volte, nel suolo li tormenta la pioggia.

yet his nostrils are quivering. It's cold here at dawn,
and a body's embrace would restore him to life.
More pervasive than the moon's yellow light, with its fear
of deep forests, is this inexhaustible ache
for flavor and touch that gnaws at the dead.
When they're in the ground, their torment is rain.

Paesaggio (IV)

I due uomini fumano a riva. La donna che nuota
senza rompere l'acqua, non vede che il verde
del suo breve orizzonte. Tra il cielo e le piante
si distende quest'acqua e la donna vi scorre
senza corpo. Nel cielo si posano nuvole
come immobili. Il fumo si ferma a mezz'aria.

Sotto il gelo dell'acqua c'è l'erba. La donna
vi trascorre sospesa; ma noi la schiacciamo,
l'erba verde, col corpo. Non c'è lungo le acque
altro peso. Noi soli sentiamo la terra.
Forse il corpo allungato di lei, che è sommerso,
sente l'avido gelo assorbirle il torpore
delle membra assolate e discioglierla viva
nell'immobile verde. Il suo capo non muove.

Era stesa anche lei, dove l'erba è piegata.
Il suo volto socchiuso posava sul braccio
e guardava nell'erba. Nessuno fiatava.
Stagna ancora nell'aria quel primo sciacquío
che l'ha accolta nell'acqua. Su noi stagna il fumo.
Ora è giunta alla riva e ci parla, stillante
nel suo corpo annerito che sorge fra i tronchi.
La sua voce è ben l'unico suono che si ode sull'acqua
—rauca e fresca, è la voce di prima.
                            Pensiamo, distesi
sulla riva, a quel verde piú cupo e piú fresco
che ha sommerso il suo corpo. Poi, uno di noi
piomba in acqua e traversa, scoprendo le spalle
in bracciate schiumose, l'immobile verde.

Landscape (IV)

The two men smoke on the bank. A woman swims
without breaking the water, seeing only the green
of her narrow horizon. Between trees and the sky,
this water stretches away, and the woman
glides bodiless over it. Clouds perch in the sky,
unmoving. The men's smoke hangs in midair.

Beneath the cold water are grasses. She floats,
suspended, above them. But the grass beneath us
is crushed by our bodies. Along these banks,
there's no weight but ours. We alone feel the earth.
Maybe her body, stretched out in that water,
can feel the greed of the cold as it soaks
her sun-dulled limbs, as it melts her alive
in the motionless green. Her head doesn't move.

She too was lying there where the grass is bent down.
Her face was resting, half-hidden, on her arm
as she stared into grass. None of us breathed.
The first splash of the water, rinsing around her,
still hangs in this air. Our smoke, too, hangs in the air.
Now she's back on the shore, she's speaking to us
as she rises up, dripping and dark, among trees.
Her voice is the only thing audible over the water —
husky and fresh, the same as before.
                              We think,
as we lie on the bank, of the darker, cooler green
that swallowed her body. Then one of us dives
into the water, moving, with churning strokes
of the shoulders, into that motionless green.

Maternità

Questo è un uomo che ha fatto tre figli: un gran corpo
poderoso, che basta a sé stesso; a vederlo passare
uno pensa che i figli han la stessa statura.
Dalle membra del padre (la donna non conta)
debbon esser usciti, già fatti, tre giovani
come lui. Ma comunque sia il corpo dei tre,
alle membra del padre non manca una briciola
o uno scatto: si sono staccati da lui
camminandogli accanto.
                          La donna c'è stata,
una donna di solido corpo, che ha sparso
su ogni figlio del sangue e sul terzo c'è morta.
Pare strano ai tre giovani vivere senza la donna
che nessuno conosce e li ha fatti, ciascuno, a fatica
annientandosi in loro. La donna era giovane
e rideva e parlava, ma è un gioco rischioso
prender parte alla vita. È cosí che la donna
c'è restata in silenzio, fissando stravolta il suo uomo.

I tre figli hanno un modo di alzare le spalle
che quell'uomo conosce. Nessuno di loro
sa di avere negli occhi e nel corpo una vita
che a suo tempo era piena e saziava quell'uomo.
Ma, a vedere piegarsi un suo giovane all'orlo del fiume
e tuffarsi, quell'uomo non ritrova piú il guizzo
delle membra di lei dentro l'acqua, e la gioia
dei due corpi sommersi. Non ritrova piú i figli,
se li guarda per strada e confronta con sé.
Quanto tempo è che ha fatto dei figli? I tre giovani
vanno invece spavaldi e qualcuno per sbaglio
s'è già fatto un figliolo, senza farsi la donna.

Motherhood

Here is a man who has made three sons: a large body,
strong, enough for itself. Seeing him pass,
you can tell that his sons are built the same way.
They must have emerged from their father's limbs
(forget the woman) already formed, all three
like him. But no matter how they were made,
their father never lost an ounce or a step:
as he walked, their bodies split off from his
and kept walking beside him.
                                        There was a woman,
a strong-bodied woman, who spilled her own blood
on each boy; with the birth of the third she died.
It's strange for the boys, living without this woman,
who none of them knew, who labored to make them,
erased herself in them. The woman was young,
she laughed and she talked, but to take part in life
is a dangerous game. In the end, that's how
she wound up: staring in silence, undone, at her man.

His sons have a way of shrugging their shoulders
their father knows well. The sons, without knowing it,
carry a life, in their eyes and their bodies,
that once was a full one, that met a man's needs.
And now, watching one of them lean from the riverbank
and dive in, the man can no longer recall the flash
of her limbs in the water, or the joy of two bodies
swimming together. And watching his boys
walk down the street, he no longer sees himself.
How long has it been since he had them? The boys,
though, are fearless and vain, and one, by mistake,
has already made a son of his own, without making a woman.

Una generazione

Un ragazzo veniva a giocare nei prati
dove adesso s'allungano i corsi. Trovava nei prati
ragazzotti anche scalzi e saltava di gioia.
Era bello scalzarsi nell'erba con loro.
Una sera di luci lontane echeggiavano spari,
in città, e sopra il vento giungeva pauroso
un clamore interrotto. Tacevano tutti.
Le colline sgranavano punti di luce
sulle coste, avvivati dal vento. La notte
che oscurava, finiva per spegnere tutto
e nel sonno duravano solo freschezze di vento.

(Domattina i ragazzi ritornano in giro
e nessuno ricorda il clamore. In prigione
c'è operai silenziosi e qualcuno è già morto.
Nelle strade han coperto le macchie di sangue.
La città di lontano si sveglia nel sole
e la gente esce fuori. Si guardano in faccia.)
I ragazzi a quel tempo giravano in strada
e guardavano in faccia le donne. Persino le donne
non dicevano nulla e lasciavano fare.
I ragazzi pensavano al buio dei prati
dove qualche bambina veniva. Era bello far piangere
le bambine nel buio. Eravamo i ragazzi.
La città ci piaceva di giorno: la sera, tacere
e guardare le luci in distanza e ascoltare i clamori.

Vanno ancora ragazzi a giocare nei prati
dove giungono i corsi. E la notte è la stessa.
A passarci si sente l'odore dell'erba.
In prigione ci sono gli stessi. E ci sono le donne
come allora, che fanno bambini e non dicono nulla.

A Generation

A boy used to come here to play in the fields,
now covered by boulevards. He met other boys,
barefoot like him, and he jumped and was happy.
A fine thing to kick off your shoes in that grass.
One evening gunshots rang out in the distance,
from the lit city, and the wind carried scraps
of frightening noises. The boys all fell silent.
Over their slopes, the hills, like sowers,
scattered points of light that flared in the wind,
till night, as it fell, extinguished each one.
In sleep, only the freshness of wind remained.

(In the morning, the boys will come back
and none will remember the noises. In prison,
the workers are silent. And people are dead.
They've covered the stains of blood on the street.
In the distance, the city wakes up to the sun,
and people go out. They look at each other.)
The boys in those days would wander the streets
and look women right in the face. The women
even allowed this, they didn't say anything.
The boys were thinking of the darkness of fields
and the girls who would come there. A fine thing to make
a girl cry in the dark. And we were those boys.
We stuck to the city by day; at night we fell silent
and looked at the lights in the distance, and listened to noises.

And still there are boys who play in the fields
at the end of these boulevards. The night's still the same,
and passing those fields, you smell grass on the air.
The same men are in prison. And still there are women,
just as then, who make babies and don't say a word.

Ulisse

Questo è un vecchio deluso, perché ha fatto suo figlio
troppo tardi. Si guardano in faccia ogni tanto,
ma una volta bastava uno schiaffo. (Esce il vecchio
e ritorna col figlio che si stringe una spalla
e non leva piú gli occhi). Ora il vecchio è seduto
fino a notte, davanti a una grande finestra,
ma non viene nessuno e la strada è deserta.

Stamattina, è scappato il ragazzo, e ritorna
questa notte. Starà sogghignando. A nessuno
vorrà dire se a pranzo ha mangiato. Magari
avrà gli occhi pesanti e andrà a letto in silenzio:
due scarponi infangati. Il mattino era azzurro
sulle piogge di un mese.
                                    Per la fresca finestra
scorre amaro un sentore di foglie. Ma il vecchio
non si muove dal buio, non ha sonno la notte,
e vorrebbe aver sonno e scordare ogni cosa
come un tempo al ritorno dopo un lungo cammino.
Per scaldarsi, una volta gridava e picchiava.

Il ragazzo che torna fra poco, non prende piú schiaffi.
Il ragazzo comincia a esser giovane e scopre
ogni giorno qualcosa e non parla a nessuno.
Non c'è nulla per strada che non possa sapersi
stando a questa finestra. Ma il ragazzo cammina
tutto il giorno per strada. Non cerca ancor donne
e non gioca piú in terra. Ogni volta ritorna.
Il ragazzo ha un suo modo di uscire di casa
che, chi resta, s'accorge di non farci piú nulla.

Ulysses

The old man's disappointed: his one son was born
too late. These days their eyes meet occasionally,
but once a slap was enough. (The man goes out,
comes back with the boy clutching a shoulder,
eyes lowered.) Now the old man will sit here,
waiting for dark, before a large window,
but no one's coming and the road is deserted.

This morning the boy escaped, won't return
till tonight. He'll come in with a sneer. No one
will know whether he's eaten today. Perhaps
his eyes will be dull and he'll go quiet to bed,
boots caked with mud. After weeks of rain,
the morning was blue.
                              The leaves' bitter scent
comes in through the window. But the old man
stays there in the dark, he can't sleep at night,
though he wishes he could, so he could forget things
as he once could coming back from a long walk.
To keep himself warm, he'd shout and throw punches.

The boy will be back soon, but can no longer be slapped.
The boy's becoming a man, and each day
he learns something new, not speaking to anyone.
Nothing goes on in this street that can't be seen
from this window. But the boy spends his day
roaming the street, not looking yet for a woman
and no longer playing in dirt. He always returns.
The boy has a way of leaving the house
that tells the old man there's no way to stop him.

Atavismo

Certo il giorno non trema, a guardarlo. E le case
sono ferme, piantate ai selciati. Il martello
di quell'uomo seduto scalpiccia su un ciottolo
dentro il molle terriccio. Il ragazzo che scappa
al mattino, non sa che quell'uomo lavora,
e si ferma a guardarlo. Nessuno lavora per strada.

L'uomo siede nell'ombra, che cade dall'alto
di una casa, piú fresca che un'ombra di nube,
e non guarda, ma tocca i suoi ciottoli assorto.
Il rumore dei ciottoli echeggia lontano
sul selciato velato dal sole. Ragazzi
non ce n'è per le strade. Il ragazzo è ben solo
e s'accorge che tutti sono uomini o donne
che non vedono quel che lui vede e trascorrono svelti.

Ma quell'uomo lavora. Il ragazzo lo guarda,
esitante al pensiero che un uomo lavori
sulla strada, seduto come fanno i pezzenti.
E anche gli altri che passano, paiono assorti
a finire qualcosa e nessuno si guarda
alle spalle o dinanzi, lungo tutta la strada.
Se la strada è di tutti, bisogna goderla
senza fare nient'altro, guardandosi intorno,
ora all'ombra ora al sole, nel fresco leggero.

Ogni via si spalanca che pare una porta,
ma nessuno l'infila. Quell'uomo seduto
non s'accorge nemmeno, come fosse un pezzente,
della gente che viene e che va, nel mattino.

Atavism

Of course the day doesn't tremble, not visibly. And houses
hold still, planted in pavement. The hammer
in the hand of that man is striking a cobblestone
into the soft dirt below. The boy, who's running away
this morning, can't tell the man's working,
and pauses to watch him. No one works in the street.

The man's sitting in shade that slants down
from a house, cooler than the shade of a cloud,
he's tapping the cobbles, absorbed, but not looking.
The hammering echoes into the distance
over the pavement with its sheen of sun. No kids
in the street but this boy — he's completely alone,
and notices the rest are either women or men:
they don't see what he sees, they just hurry along.

But that man is working. The boy, as he watches,
struggles with the thought that a man might work
in the street, sitting right there like a beggar.
And the people rushing by are absorbed
in accomplishing something, and no one at all,
in the whole street, is looking ahead or behind.
If the streets belong to us all, we should enjoy them
without distraction, looking around as we walk —
now in shade, now in sunlight — through the fresh air.

And every street opens wide like a door
that nobody enters. That man sitting there
seems not to notice, as if he were a beggar,
the people as they come and they go, all morning.

Avventure

Sulla nera collina è l'alba e sui tetti
s'assopiscono i gatti. Un ragazzo è piombato
giú dal tetto stanotte, spezzandosi il dorso.
Vibra un vento tra gli alberi freschi: le nubi
rosse, in alto, so tiepide e viaggiano lente.
Giú nel vicolo spunta un cagnaccio, che fiuta
il ragazzo sui ciottoli, ma un rauco gnaulio
sale su tra i comignoli: qualcuno è scontento.

Nella notte cantavano i grilli, e le stelle
si spegnevano al vento. Al chiarore dell'alba
si son spenti anche gli occhi del gatti in amore
che il ragazzo spiava. La gatta, che piange,
è perché non ha gatto. Non c'è nulla che valga
—né le vette degli alberi né le nuvole rosse—
piange al cielo scoperto, come fosse ancor notte.

Il ragazzo spiava gli amori dei gatti.
Il cagnaccio, che fiuta 'sto corpo ringhiando,
è arrivato e non era ancor l'alba: fuggiva
il chiarore dell'altro versante. Nuotando
dentro il fiume che infradicia come nei prati
la rugiada, l'ha colto la luce. Le cagne
ululavano ancora.
                    Scorre il fiume tranquillo
e lo schiumano uccelli. Tra le nuvole rosse
piomban giú dalla gioia di trovarlo deserto.

Affairs

Dawn on the black hill, and up on the roof
cats drowsing. Last night, there was a boy
who fell off this roof, breaking his back.
The wind riffles the cool leaves of the trees.
The red clouds above are warm and move slowly.
A stray dog appears in the alley below, sniffing
the boy on the cobblestones, and a raw wail
rises up among chimneys: someone's unhappy.

The crickets were singing all night, and the stars
were blown out by the wind. In dawn's glow,
even the eyes of cats in love were extinguished,
the cats the boy watched. The female is crying,
no toms are around and nothing can soothe her:
not the tops of the trees, not the red clouds.
She cries to the wide sky, as if it were still night.

The boy was spying on cats making love.
The stray dog sniffs the boy's body and growls;
he got here at dawn, fleeing the glow
that crept down the far hill. Swimming the river
that drenched him as dew drenches fields,
he was finally caught by the light. The bitches
were still howling.
                    The river runs smoothly,
skimmed by birds that drop from red clouds,
elated to find their river deserted.

Donne appassionate

Le ragazze al crepuscolo scendono in acqua,
quando il mare svanisce, disteso. Nel bosco
ogni foglia trasale, mentre emergono caute
sulla sabbia e si siedono a riva. La schiuma
fa i suoi giochi inquieti, lungo l'acqua remota.

Le ragazze han paura delle alghe sepolte
sotto le onde, che afferrano le gambe e le spalle:
quant'è nudo, del corpo. Rimontano rapide a riva
e si chiamano a nome, guardandosi intorno.
Anche le ombre sul fondo del mare, nel buio.
sono enormi e si vedono muovere incerte,
come attratte dai corpi che passano. Il bosco
è un rifugio tranquillo, nel sole calante,
piú che il greto, ma piace alle scure ragazze
star sedute all'aperto, nel lenzuolo raccolto.

Stanno tutte accosciate, serrando il lenzuolo
alle gambe, e contemplano il mare disteso
come un prato al crepuscolo. Oserebbe qualcuna
ora stendersi nuda in un prato? Dal mare
balzerebbero le alghe, che sfiorano i piedi,
a ghermire e ravvolgere il corpo tremante.
Ci son occhi nel mare, che traspaiono a volte.

Quell'ignota straniera, che nuotava di notte
sola e nuda, nel buio quando muta la luna,
è scomparsa una notte e non torna mai piú.
Era grande e doveva esser bianca abbagliante
perché gli occhi, dal fondo del mare, giungessero a lei.

Passionate Women

The girls go down to the water at dusk,
as the sea fades and lies calm. Each leaf
trembles as they emerge from the woods, cautious,
onto the sand, to sit by the water. The froth
plays its restless games, the shore stretching away.

The girls are afraid of the seaweed buried
beneath waves: it clings to legs and shoulders,
any bare skin. They scramble back to the beach,
calling friends' names, peering behind them.
Even the shadows on the seabed, in this light,
grow huge, they seem to be shifting uneasily,
as if drawn to the bodies above them. The woods,
at sunset, can be a haven more peaceful
than the rock beach, but the dark girls enjoy
sitting out in the open on a pale sheet.

They huddle together, wrapping the sheet
around their legs, regarding the calm sea
like a meadow at twilight. Would any girl dare
lie naked now in a meadow? The seaweed,
brushing her feet, would suddenly rise
to seize and surround her shuddering body.
There are eyes in the sea; sometimes they gleam.

That foreign woman, who would swim at night
alone and naked, even in the moonless dark,
disappeared one night and never came back.
She was big, and must have been dazzling white
for those eyes at the bottom of the sea to have seen her.

Luna d'agosto

Al di là delle gialle colline c'è il mare,
al di là delle nubi. Ma giornate tremende
di colline ondeggianti e crepitanti nel cielo
si frammettono prima del mare. Quassú c'è l'ulivo
con la pozza dell'acqua che non basta a specchiarsi,
e le stoppie, le stoppie, che non cessano mai.

E si leva la luna. Il marito è disteso
in un campo, col cranio spaccato dal sole
— una sposa non può trascinare un cadavere
come un sacco—. Si leva la luna, che getta un po' d'ombra
sotto i rami contorti. La donna nell'ombra
leva un ghigno atterrito al faccione di sangue
che coagula e inonda ogni piega dei colli.
Non si muove il cadavere disteso nei campi
né la donna nell'ombra. Pure l'occhio di sangue
pare ammicchi a qualcuno e gli segni una strada.

Vengon brividi lunghi per le nude colline
di lontano, e la donna se li sente alle spalle,
come quando correvano il mare del grano.
Anche invadono i rami dell'ulivo sperduto
in quel mare di luna, e già l'ombra dell'albero
pare stia per contrarsi e inghiottire anche lei.

Si precipita fuori, nell'orrore lunare,
e la segue il fruscio della brezza sui sassi
e una sagoma tenue che le morde le piante,
e la doglia nel grembo. Rientra curva nell'ombra
e si butta sui sassi e si morde la bocca.
Sotto, scura la terra si bagna di sangue.

August Moon

There, beyond the yellowing hills, is the sea,
beyond the clouds. But between the sea and here,
terrible days full of hills that waver and crackle
in the sky. Up here there's an olive tree
and a puddle too small to give any reflection,
and stubble: stubble as far as the eye can see.

And the moon rises. The husband is stretched out
in a field, his skull split wide by the sun—
a wife can't drag a dead body around
like some sack. The moon rises, casting thin shadows
under gnarled branches. The woman in the shadows
is gaping in horror at the huge face of blood,
clotting now, that drenches each crease in these hills.
The body stretched out in the field doesn't move,
nor does the woman in shadows. The bleeding eye
seems to be winking at someone, pointing the way.

Long shudders come over the naked hills
from afar, and the woman can hear them behind her,
like when they'd run through that sea of wheat.
The branches of the olive, lost in that sea of moon,
begin to advance, and now the tree's shadow
seems ready to turn on itself, to swallow her too.

The woman runs forward, beneath the moon's horror,
chased by the rustle of wind on the stones,
by a shadowy form that gnaws at the soles of her feet,
by pain in her belly. She returns, bent double, to the shadows,
collapsing onto the stones and biting her lip.
Beneath her, the dark earth darkens with blood.

Terre bruciate

Parla il giovane smilzo che è stato a Torino.
Il gran mare si stende, nascosto da rocce,
e dà in cielo un azzurro slavato. Rilucono gli occhi
di ciascuno che ascolta.

                   A Torino si arriva di sera
e si vedono subito per la strada le donne
maliziose, vestite per gli occhi, che camminano sole.
Là, ciascuna lavora per le veste che indossa,
ma l'adatta a ogni luce. Ci sono colori
da mattino, colori per uscire nei viali,
per piacere di notte. Le donne, che aspettano
e si sentono sole, conoscono a fondo la vita.
Sono libere. A loro non rifiutano nulla.

Sento il mare che batte e ribatte spossato alla riva.
Vedo gli occhi profondi di questi ragazzi
lampeggiare. A due passi il filare di fichi
disperato s'annoia sulla roccia rossastra.

Ce ne sono di libere che fumano sole.
Ci si trova la sera e abbandona il mattino
al caffè, come amici. Sono giovani sempre.
Voglion occhi e prontezza nell'uomo e che scherzi
e che sia sempre fine. Basta uscire in collina
e che piova: si piegano come bambine,
ma si sanno godere l'amore. Più esperte di un uomo.
Sono vive e slanciate e, anche nude, discorrono
con quel brio che hanno sempre.

                   Lo ascolto.
Ho fissato le occhiaie del giovane smilzo
tutte intente. Han veduto anche loro una volta quel verde.
Fumerò a notte buia, ignorando anche il mare.

Burnt Lands

The thin young man back from Turin is speaking.
The great sea stretches away, hidden by rocks,
lending its tenuous blue to the sky, lighting the eyes
of everyone listening:

            Go to Turin some evening
and first thing you see on the street is these women —
dangerous, dressed for the eyes, walking alone.
Each one of them works for the dress on her back,
and she's got one for every occasion. One color
for morning, others for strolling the avenues
or the pleasures of night. These women, they wait,
they feel lonely, they know life to its depths.
They're loose. And nothing is ever refused them.

I hear the sea beating and again beating the shore.
I see, deep in the eyes of each boy, a light
gleaming. Nearby, the long row of fig trees
looks hopelessly bored on the reddish rocks.

These are loose women who smoke by themselves.
You meet up at night and leave after coffee, like friends,
in the morning. They're all young, they all want
your eyes, your attention. They like you to laugh
and act so refined. If you go for a walk in the hills,
watch out for the rain: they fold up like little girls.
But they know how to make love. Know more than a man.
They're alive and so sleek, and even when naked
they'll talk with their usual spirit.

            I listen.
I stare at the thin young man, at his sunken eyes
that are so absorbed. They've seen that green before, too.
I'll smoke into the night, not noticing even the sea.

Poggio Reale

Una breve finestra nel cielo tranquillo
calma il cuore; qualcuno c'è morto contento.
Fuori, sono le piante e le nubi, la terra
e anche il cielo. Ne giunge quassú il mormorio:
i clamori di tutta la vita.
                              La vuota finestra
non rivela che, sotto le piante, ci sono colline
e che un fiume serpeggia lontano, scoperto.
L'acqua è limpida come il respiro del vento,
ma nessuno ci bada.
                        Compare una nube
soda e bianca, che indugia, nel quadrato del cielo.
Scorge case stupite e colline, ogni cosa
che traspare nell'aria, vede uccelli smarriti
scivolare nell'aria. Viandanti tranquilli
vanno lungo quel fiume e nessuno s'accorge
della piccola nube.
                        Ora è vuoto l'azzurro
nella breve finestra: vi piomba lo strido
di un uccello, che spezza il brusio. Quella nube
forse tocca le piante o discende nel fiume.

L'uomo steso nel prato potrebbe sentirla
nel respiro dell'erba. Ma non muove lo sguardo,
l'erba sola si muove. Dev'essere morto.

Poggio Reale

Small windows on clear skies can soothe hearts:
some of the prisoners must have died happy.
Outside: the trees and the clouds and the earth,
and sky, of course. A murmur reaches us here:
the clamor of life.
                    The empty window
doesn't reveal that, beneath the trees, there are hills,
and winding into the distance, a river, uncovered.
The water's as clear as the breath of the wind,
but nobody notices.
                    A cloud appears
and lingers, solid and white, in the square of sky.
It looks down on hills and stunned houses,
on things that shine in the air, on lost birds
that slip through the air. People walk leisurely
along the banks of that river, unaware
of the little cloud.
                    Now, the small window
holds nothing but blue: the cry of a bird
comes through it, piercing the murmur. The cloud
might be touching the trees or approaching the river.

The man lying out in the field ought to sense it
in the breath of the grass. But his gaze remains fixed,
and only the grass moves. Surely he's dead.

Paesaggio (VI)

Quest'è il giorno che salgono le nebbie dal fiume
nella bella città, in mezzo a prati e colline,
e la sfumano come un ricordo. I vapori confondono
ogni verde, ma ancora le donne dai vivi colori
vi camminano. Vanno nella bianca penombra
sorridenti: per strada può accadere ogni cosa.
Può accadere che l'aria ubriachi.

                      Il mattino
si sarà spalancato in un largo silenzio
attutendo ogni voce. Persino il pezzente,
che non ha una città né una casa, l'avrà respirato,
come aspira il bicchiere di grappa a digiuno.
Val la pena aver fame o esser stato tradito
dalla bocca piú dolce, pur di uscire a quel cielo
ritrovando al respiro i ricordi piú lievi.

Ogni via, ogni spigolo schietto di casa
nella nebbia, conserva un antico tremore:
chi lo sente non può abbandonarsi. Non può abbandonare
la sua ebrezza tranquilla, composta di cose
dalla vita pregnante, scoperte a riscontro
d'una casa o d'un albero, d'un pensiero improvviso.
Anche i grossi cavalli, che saranno passati
tra la nebbia nell'alba, parleranno d'allora.

O magari un ragazzo scappato di casa
torna proprio quest'oggi, che sale la nebbia
sopra il fiume, e dimentica tutta la vita,
le miserie, la fame e le fedi tradite,
per fermarsi su un angolo, bevendo il mattino.
Val la pena tornare, magari diverso.

Landscape (VI)

This is the day the fog rises up from the river
into the beautiful city, surrounded by fields and hills,
and blurs it like memory. In this haze, all green
melts together, but still the bright-colored women
go walking. They walk through the white penumbra
smiling: anything's possible here on the street.
You might get drunk on the air.

                      The morning
will burst suddenly open into a wide silence,
muffling each voice. And even the beggar,
with no home and no city, will inhale it,
like a glass of grappa on an empty stomach.
It's worth being hungry, worth being betrayed
by the sweetest mouth, if it gets you out into that sky,
where breath can bring back the slightest of memories.

The streets, the pure lines of the houses,
retain, in this fog, an ancient tremor:
you can't, once you feel it, give up on yourself. You can't
give up the gentle intoxication that comes
from the things of a pregnant life, things discovered
as you meet a house, or a tree, or a startling thought.
Even the big horses, who will have passed,
at dawn, through the fog, will speak of it.

Or maybe a runaway boy will return
this very day to his home, as the fog rises
to cover the river. Maybe he'll forget his whole life,
the hard times, the hunger, the betrayals of trust,
as he stops on a corner, to drink in the morning.
It's worth going home—maybe everything's different.

Part Two

Work's Tiring

1943

Il figlio della vedova

Può accadere ogni cosa nella bruna osteria,
può accadere che fuori sia un cielo di stelle,
al di là della nebbia autunnale e del mosto.
Può accadere che cantino dalla collina
le arrochite canzoni sulle aie deserte
e che torni improvvisa sotto il cielo d'allora
la donnetta seduta in attesa del giorno.

Tornerebbero intorno alla donna i villani
dalle scarne parole, in attesa del sole
e del pallido cenno di lei, rimboccati
fino al gomito, chini a fissare la terra.
Alla voce del grillo si unirebbe il frastuono
della cote sul ferro e un più rauco sospiro.
Tacerebbero il vento e i brusii della notte.
La donnetta seduta parlerebbe con ira.

Lavorando i villani ricurvi lontano,
la donnetta è rimasta sull'aia e li segue
con lo sguardo, poggiata allo stipite, affranta
dal gran ventre maturo. Sul volto consunto
ha un amaro sorriso impaziente, e una voce
che non giunge ai villani le solleva la gola.
Batte il sole sull'aia e sugli occhi arrossati
ammiccanti. Una nube purpurea vela la stoppia
seminata di gialli covoni. La donna
vacillando, la mano sul grembo, entra in casa.

Donne corrono con impazienza le stanze deserte
comandate dal cenno e dall'occhio che, soli,
di sul letto le seguono. La grande finestra
che contiene colline e filari e il gran cielo,
manda un fioco ronzio che è il lavoro di tutti.

The Widow's Son

All things seem possible in the gloom of the tavern.
The sky outside could be brilliant with stars,
beyond autumn's fog and the scent of pressed grapes.
Even now, the ragged songs of the harvesters
could be rising from the emptied fields on the hill;
even now, the dark sky of a lost time could return,
a small woman seated beneath it, waiting for day.

Her peasants too would return, milling around her
with their thin words, waiting for first light
and the slightest nod of her head, their sleeves
rolled to their elbows, their faces tilted toward earth.
And the cricket's voice would merge with the scraping
of iron on the whetstone and a hoarse, rasping sigh.
The wind and the low hums of night would die down.
The small woman would speak, from her chair, in anger.

In the distance the peasants bend to their labors.
The small woman leans on a wall by the threshing yard,
following the men with her gaze, exhausted
by her belly, huge now, and ripe. On her worn face,
her smile is impatient and bitter, her voice
heaves in her throat; it won't reach the peasants.
The sun beats on the threshing yard, her eyes
redden and blink. A purplish mist shrouds the stubble,
yellow sheaves scattered across it. The small woman
staggers, hand on her belly, and goes back in the house.

Women run hurriedly through empty rooms,
spurred by her nod and the look in her eyes;
she follows their movements from bed. The big window
that frames the hills and the vineyards and the wide sky
lets in the soft drone that is everyone working.

La donnetta dal pallido viso ha serrate le labbra
alle fitte del ventre e si tende in ascolto
impaziente. Le donne la servono, pronte.

The small woman with the pale face tightens her lips against the fits of her belly, listening to footsteps, impatient. And the women return, and they're ready.

Gente che c'è stata

Luna tenera e brina sui campi nell'alba
assassinano il grano.

       Sul piano deserto,
qua e là putrefatto (ci vuole del tempo
perché il sole e la pioggia sotterrino i morti),
era ancora un piacere svegliarsi e guardare
se la brina copriva anche quelli. La luna
inondava, e qualcuno pensava al mattino
quando l'erba sarebbe spuntata piú verde.

Ai villani che guardano piangono gli occhi.
Per quest'anno al ritorno del sole, se torna,
foglioline bruciate saran tutto il grano.
Trista luna—non sa che mangiare le nebbie,
e le brine al sereno hanno un morso di serpe,
che del verde fa tanto letame. Ne han dato letame
alla terra; ora torna in letame anche il grano,
e non serve guardare, e sarà tutto arso,
putrefatto. È un mattino che toglie ogni forza
solamente svegliarsi e girare da vivi
lungo i campi.

       Vedranno piú tardi spuntare
qualche timido verde sul piano deserto,
sulla tomba del grano, e dovranno lottare
a ridurre anche quello in letame, bruciando.
Perché il sole e la pioggia proteggono solo le erbacce
e la brina, toccato che ha il grano, non torna.

People Who've Been There

Tender moon and frost in the fields at dawn
murder the wheat.

          On the empty expanse,
spotted with putrefaction (it takes a while
for the sun and the rain to bury the dead),
it was still a pleasure to wake up and see
whether frost had covered that too. In the flood
of the moon, some of us thought of the morning
when new stalks would sprout, even greener.

The peasants' eyes fill with tears as they look.
This year, when the sun comes back, if it does,
burnt-looking leaves will be the sole harvest.
Malevolent moon — it just eats the mist,
and frost, on clear nights, bites like a snake,
reducing the green to manure. That's what the land
was fed, and that's what the grain has become.
No point in looking, all of it's blackened
and rotted. Such mornings it's all you can do
to wake up and walk, like one of the living,
into the fields.

          Later, on that empty expanse,
they'll see a new crop sprouting, timid and green
on the grave of that wheat, and they'll have to toil
to turn that to manure as well, burning it off.
Because the sun and the rain protect only the weeds,
and the frost, having finished the wheat, won't return.

La notte

Ma la notte ventosa, la limpida notte
che il ricordo sfiorava soltanto, è remota,
è un ricordo. Perdura una calma stupita
fatta anch'essa di foglie e di nulla. Non resta,
di quel tempo di là dai ricordi, che un vago
ricordare.

       Talvolta ritorna nel giorno
nell'immobile luce del giorno d'estate,
quel remoto stupore.

         Per la vuota finestra
il bambino guardava la notte sui colli
freschi e neri, e stupiva di trovarli ammassati:
vaga e limpida immobilità. Fra le foglie
che stormivano al buio, apparivano i colli
dove tutte le cose del giorno, le coste
e le piante e le vigne, eran nitide e morte
e la vita era un'altra, di vento, di cielo,
e di foglie e di nulla.

       Talvolta ritorna
nell'immobile calma del giorno il ricordo
di quel vivere assorto, nella luce stupita.

The Night

But the windy night, the transparent night,
which memory touched only briefly, has faded,
is memory. An astonished calm remains,
it too made of leaves and of nothing. All gone,
from that time beyond memories, but a blurred
remembering.

        Sometimes it returns,
in the motionless light of a summer day,
that fading astonishment.

            Through the empty window
the small boy watched the night on the hills,
the cool, dark hills, astonished to find them
massing together: a blurred and transparent stillness.
Through leaves that fluttered in darkness rose hills
where the things of the day—the slopes, the trees,
the vineyards—stood clearly defined and dead,
and life was another thing, made of wind, of sky,
of leaves, and of nothing.

           Sometimes it returns,
in the motionless calm of daylight, that memory
of immersion in life, in astonished light.

Incontro

Queste dure colline che han fatto il mio corpo
e lo scuotono a tanti ricordi, mi han schiuso il prodigio
di costei, che non sa che la vivo e non riesco a comprenderla.

L'ho incontrata, una sera: una macchia più chiara
sotto le stelle ambigue, nella foschía d'estate.
Era intorno il sentore di queste colline
più profondo dell'ombra, e d'un tratto suonò
come uscisse da queste colline, una voce più netta
e aspra insieme, una voce di tempi perduti.

Qualche volta la vedo, e mi vive dinanzi
definita, immutabile, come un ricordo.
Io non ho mai potuto afferrarla: la sua realtà
ogni volta mi sfugge e mi porta lontano.
Se sia bella, non so. Tra le donne è ben giovane:
mi sorprende, a pensarla, un ricordo remoto
dell'infanzia vissuta tra queste colline,
tanto è giovane. È come il mattino. Mi accenna negli occhi
tutti i cieli lontani di quei mattini remoti.
E ha negli occhi un proposito fermo: la luce più netta
che abbia avuto mai l'alba su queste colline.

L'ho creata dal fondo di tutte le cose
che mi sono più care, e non riesco a comprenderla.

Meeting

These hard hills, which built my body and rock it
with such memories, have disclosed to me the miracle
of she who doesn't know I live her while failing to grasp her.

I met her one evening, a bright, clear spot
beneath ambiguous stars and a summer haze.
We were surrounded by the scent of these hills,
a smell deeper than darkness, and a sudden sound
rose up as if from these hills, a voice
both clean and strident, a voice of lost times.

Sometimes I still see her—she lives in my gaze
distinct and unchanging, like a memory.
I've never been able to hold her: her reality
eludes me each time, removes me to a distance.
I don't know if she's beautiful. For a woman, she's young:
so young I'm surprised, when I think of her,
by an old memory of childhood spent
among these hills. She's like morning, her eyes hinting
at all the remote skies of those old mornings.
And she has in those eyes a firm purpose: the cleanest light
that sunrise ever cast upon these hills.

I've created her from the essence of all things
dearest to me, and I've never been able to grasp her.

Rivelazione

L'uomo solo rivede il ragazzo dal magro
cuore assorto a scrutare la donna ridente.
Il ragazzo levava lo sguardo a quegli occhi,
dove i rapidi sguardi trasalivano nudi
e diversi. Il ragazzo raccoglieva un segreto
in quegli occhi, un segreto come il grembo nascosto.

L'uomo solo si preme nel cuore il ricordo.
Gli occhi ignoti bruciavano come brucia la carne,
vivi d'umida vita. La dolcezza del grembo
palpitante di calda ansietà traspariva
in quegli occhi. Sbocciava angoscioso il segreto
come un sangue. Ogni cosa era fatta tremenda
nella luce tranquilla delle piante e del cielo.

Il ragazzo piangeva nella sera sommessa
rade lacrime mute, come fosse già uomo.
L'uomo solo ritrova sotto il cielo remoto
quello sguardo raccolto che la donna depone
sul ragazzo. E rivede quegli occhi e quel volto
ricomporsi sommessi al sorriso consueto.

Revelation

The man alone sees again the thin-hearted boy
watching, absorbed, as the woman laughs.
The boy used to lift his gaze to those eyes,
where sudden glances darted naked
and strange. The boy gathered a secret
from those eyes, a secret as veiled as the womb.

The man alone presses into his heart that memory.
The unknowable eyes burned like flesh burns,
alive with damp life. All the womb's sweetness,
pulsing with nervous heat, shone
from those eyes. The secret bloomed in anguish,
like blood. All things were made terrible
in the calm light of the trees and the sky.

The boy sometimes cried a few silent tears
in the softness of evening, as if already a man.
The man alone rediscovers, beneath the old sky,
that self-contained gaze that the woman let fall
on the boy. He sees those eyes again, and that face
gently shaping itself toward its usual smile.

Mattino

La finestra socchiusa contiene un volto
sopra il campo del mare. I capelli vaghi
accompagnano il tenero ritmo del mare.

Non ci sono ricordi su questo viso.
Solo un'ombra fuggevole, come di nube.
L'ombra è umida e dolce come la sabbia
di una cavità intatta, sotto il crepuscolo.
Non ci sono ricordi. Solo un susurro
che è la voce del mare fatta ricordo.

Nel crepuscolo l'acqua molle dell'alba
che s'imbeve di luce, rischiara il viso.
Ogni giorno è un miracolo senza tempo,
sotto il sole: una luce salsa l'impregna
e un sapore di frutto marino vivo.

Non esiste ricordo su questo viso.
Non esiste parola che lo contenga
o accomuni alle cose passate. Ieri,
dalla breve finestra è svanito come
svanirà tra un istante, senza tristezza
né parole umane, sul campo del mare.

Morning

The half-open window frames a face
over the field of sea. The loose hair
accompanies the sea's tender rhythm.

No memories at all pass over this face.
Only a fugitive shadow, as if from a cloud.
The shadow's damp and sweet like the sand
of an undisturbed pool at twilight.
No memories at all. Only a whisper
that is the sea's voice made into memory.

In the twilight, the soft water of dawn
drinks in the glow, brightens the face.
Each day is a miracle outside of time,
beneath the hot sun: a salt light and the taste
of what lives in the sea suffuse the day.

No memories exist on this face.
No words exist that could contain it
or connect it to past things. Yesterday,
it vanished from the brief window
as it will again soon, without sadness
or human words, over the field of sea.

Estate (1)

C'è un giardino chiaro, fra mura basse,
di erba secca e di luce, che cuoce adagio
la sua terra. È una luce che sa di mare.
Tu respiri quell'erba. Tocchi i capelli
e ne scuoti il ricordo.

            Ho veduto cadere
molti frutti, dolci, su un'erba che so,
con un tonfo. Cosí trasalisci tu pure
al sussulto del sangue. Tu muovi il capo
come intorno accadesse un prodigio d'aria
e il prodigio sei tu. C'è un sapore uguale
nei tuoi occhi e nel caldo ricordo.

                Ascolti.
Le parole che ascolti ti toccano appena.
Hai nel viso calmo un pensiero chiaro
che ti finge alle spalle la luce del mare.
Hai nel viso un silenzio che preme il cuore
con un tonfo, e ne stilla una pena antica
come il succo dei frutti caduti allora.

Summer (1)

There's a bright garden, low walls around it,
made of dry grass and of light that's slowly
cooking the soil. A light that smells of the sea.
You breathe the grass in. You touch your hair
and shake the memory out.

                                I've often seen
fruit falling, ripe, landing on grass I know
with a thud. Even you are startled at times
by quickening blood. You move your head
as if miracles of air were swirling around you,
but the miracle's you. Your eyes and the heat
of memory: they taste just the same.

                                    You listen.
The words reaching your ears barely touch you.
On your calm face, a bright thought bathes you,
as if from behind, in something like sea light.
On your face, a silence that lands on my heart
with a thud, and draws from it pain as ancient
as the juice from fruit that fell in those days.

Notturno

La collina è notturna, nel cielo chiaro.
Vi s'inquadra il tuo capo, che muove appena
e accompagna quel cielo. Sei come una nube
intravista fra i rami. Ti ride negli occhi
la stranezza di un cielo che non è il tuo.

La collina di terra e di foglie chiude
con la massa nera il tuo vivo guardare,
la tua bocca ha la piega di un dolce incavo
tra le coste lontane. Sembri giocare
alla grande collina e al chiarore del cielo:
per piacermi ripeti lo sfondo antico
e lo rendi piú puro.

           Ma vivi altrove.
Il tuo tenero sangue si è fatto altrove.
Le parole che dici non hanno riscontro
con la scabra tristezza di questo cielo.
Tu non sei che una nube dolcissima, bianca
impigliata una notte fra i rami antichi.

Nocturne

The hill is night-dark against the bright sky.
The scene frames your head, which moves slightly
as the sky moves. You're like a cloud
glimpsed between branches. In your eyes gleams
the strangeness of a sky that isn't yours.

The hill, made of earth and leaves, surrounds
your living gaze with its darkening mass.
Your mouth gently curves, like the dip
between distant ridges. You seem to double
both the great hill and the sky's glow,
repeating, to please me, the ancient scene,
and making it purer.

               But you live elsewhere.
Your tender blood has its origins elsewhere.
The words you utter don't resonate here
with the harsh desolation of this sky.
You're nothing but the softest white cloud
that snagged one night in some ancient branches.

Agonia

Girerò per le strade finché non sarò stanca morta
saprò vivere sola e fissare negli occhi
ogni volto che passa e restare la stessa.
Questo fresco che sale a cercarmi le vene
è un risveglio che mai nel mattino ho provato
cosí vero: soltanto, mi sento piú forte
che il mio corpo, e un tremore piú freddo accompagna il mattino.

Son lontani i mattini che avevo vent'anni.
E domani, ventuno: domani uscirò per le strade,
ne ricordo ogni sasso e le striscie di cielo.
Da domani la gente riprende a vedermi
e sarò ritta in piedi e potrò soffermarmi
e specchiarmi in vetrine. I mattini di un tempo,
ero giovane e non lo sapevo, e nemmeno sapevo
di esser io che passavo — una donna, padrona
di se stessa. La magra bambina che fui
si è svegliata da un pianto durato per anni:
ora è come quel pianto non fosse mai stato.

E desidero solo colori. I colori non piangono,
sono come un risveglio: domani i colori
torneranno. Ciascuna uscirà per la strada,
ogni corpo un colore — perfino i bambini.
Questo corpo vestito di rosso leggero
dopo tanto pallore riavrà la sua vita.
Sentirò intorno a me scivolare gli sguardi
e saprò d'esser io: gettando un'occhiata,
mi vedrò tra la gente. Ogni nuovo mattino,
uscirò per le strade cercando i colori.

Agony

I'll wander these streets until I'm dead tired,
I'll learn how to live by myself, how to meet the eyes
of each passing face and remain the same woman.
This coolness that rises, reaching into my veins,
is a truer awakening than any I've felt
at morning: the only thing is, I feel stronger
than my body, and the morning's edge is colder than ever.

The mornings when I was twenty are gone.
Tomorrow, twenty-one: tomorrow I'll walk down the street;
I remember each stone, each wide strip of sky.
Tomorrow people will start to see me again,
and my head will be higher and I might even pause
to glance at myself in the windows. Other mornings,
I was young without knowing it, not even aware
that it was me walking by, that I was a woman,
my own woman. The skinny child that I was
awoke from a wail that had lasted for years:
now it's as if that wail never happened.

And all I want now are colors. Colors don't cry,
they're like waking up: tomorrow the colors
come back. Each woman will walk down the street,
each body a color—even the children.
And my body, dressed in a frivolous red
after so much pallor, will get its life back.
I'll feel the gazes of others gliding around me,
and I'll know that I'm me. And glancing around,
I'll see myself among people. Every new morning
I'll walk down the street, looking for colors.

Paesaggio (VII)

Basta un poco di giorno negli occhi chiari
come il fondo di un'acqua, e la invade l'ira,
la scabrezza del fondo che il sole riga.
Il mattino che torna e la trova viva,
non è dolce né buono: la guarda immoto
tra le case di pietra, che chiude il cielo.

Esce il piccolo corpo tra l'ombra e il sole
come un lento animale, guardandosi intorno,
non vedendo null'altro se non colori.
Le ombre vaghe che vestono la strada e il corpo
le incupiscono gli occhi, socchiusi appena
come un'acqua, e nell'acqua traspare un'ombra.

I colori riflettono il cielo calmo.
Anche il passo che calca i ciottoli lento
sembra calchi le cose, pari al sorriso
che le ignora e le scorre come acqua chiara.
Dentro l'acqua trascorrono minacce vaghe.
Ogni cosa nel giorno s'increspa al pensiero
che la strada sia vuota, se non per lei.

Landscape (VII)

A little light in the clear pools of her eyes
is all it takes, and anger invades them—
the way sun shows the edges of sunken rocks.
The morning, returning to find her living,
isn't gentle or kind: it sits still amid
stone houses, surrounded by sky, and watches.

Her small body emerges into sun and shadow
like a slow animal taking a look around,
not seeing anything except maybe colors.
Vague shadows drape the street, her body,
the slits of her eyes, barely open, like pools
with shadows that show through their surfaces.

The colors mirror the tranquil sky.
And the steps that tread slowly over cobbles
seem to tread on all things, oblivious to them
like her smile, passing over them like water.
Beneath the surface move threatening shapes.
Every thing here ripples at the thought
that except for her, this street is empty.

Tolleranza

Piove senza rumore sul prato del mare.
Per le luride strade non passa nessuno.
È discesa dal treno una femmina sola:
tra il cappotto si è vista la chiara sottana
e le gambe sparire nella porta annerita.

Si direbbe un paese sommerso. La sera
stilla fredda su tutte le soglie, e le case
spandon fumo azzurrino nell'ombra. Rossastre
le finestre s'accendono. S'accende una luce
tra le imposte accostate nella casa annerita.

L'indomani fa freddo e c'è il sole sul mare.
Una donna in sottana si strofina la bocca
alla fonte, e la schiuma è rosata. Ha capelli
biondo-ruvido, simili alle bucce d'arancia
sparse in terra. Protesa alla fonte, sogguarda
un monello nerastro che la fissa incantato.
Donne fosche spalancano imposte alla piazza
—i mariti sonnecchiano ancora, nel buio.

Quando torna la sera, riprende la pioggia
scoppiettante sui molti bracieri. Le spose,
ventilando i carboni, dànno occhiate alla casa
annerita e alla fonte deserta. La casa
ha le imposte accecate, ma dentro c'è un letto,
e sul letto una bionda si guadagna la vita.
Tutto quanto il paese riposa la notte,
tutto, tranne la bionda, che si lava al mattino.

Tolerance

It's raining quietly on the field of sea.
The filthy streets and sidewalks are empty.
A female steps down from the train alone:
a bright skirt and legs flash through her coat
then vanish through the darkened doorway.

You'd think the town was buried in water.
The evening chills each doorway, the houses
spread a blue haze in the darkness. Red
windows are lit. Behind the closed shutters
of a darkened house, a light is turned on.

The next day it's cold, the sun's on the sea.
A woman in a skirt is scrubbing her mouth
at the fountain, spitting pink foam. Her hair
is a kind of blond, like the orange peels
that litter the ground. She bends to the fountain,
half-watching an urchin who's staring at her,
enchanted. Women fling open their shutters,
somber, their husbands still sleeping inside.

When evening returns, the rain starts again,
spattering on all the braziers. The wives
stand fanning the coals, eyeing the dark house,
the deserted fountain. The house's windows
are shuttered tight, but inside there's a bed,
and in bed is a blonde who's earning her living.
Everyone sleeps at night here, the town sleeps,
all but the blonde, who'll wash in the morning.

La puttana contadina

La muraglia di fronte che accieca il cortile
ha sovente un riflesso di sole bambino
che ricorda la stalla. E la camera sfatta
e deserta al mattino quando il corpo si sveglia,
sa l'odore del primo profumo inesperto.
Fino il corpo, intrecciato al lenzuolo, è lo stesso
dei primi anni, che il cuore balzava scoprendo.

Ci si sveglia deserte al richiamo inoltrato
del mattino e riemerge nella greve penombra
l'abbandono di un altro risveglio: la stalla
dell'infanzia e la greve stanchezza del sole
caloroso sugli usci indolenti. Un profumo
impregnava leggero il sudore consueto
dei capelli, e le bestie annusavano. Il corpo
si godeva furtivo la carezza del sole
insinuante e pacata come fosse un contatto.

L'abbandono del letto attutisce le membra
stese giovani e tozze, come ancora bambine.
La bambina inesperta annusava il sentore
del tabacco e del fieno e tremava al contatto
fuggitivo dell'uomo: le piaceva giocare.
Qualche volta giocava distesa con l'uomo
dentro il fieno, ma l'uomo non fiutava i capelli:
le cercava nel fieno le membra contratte,
le fiaccava, schiacciandole come fosse suo padre.
Il profumo eran fiori pestati sui sassi.

Molte volte ritorna nel lento risveglio
quel disfatto sapore di fiori lontani
e di stalla e di sole. Non c'è uomo che sappia

The Country Whore

The big front wall that blocks off the courtyard
often catches the newborn light of the sun
like the side of a barn. The body awakes
in the morning to a room, messy and empty,
that smells of the first, clumsy perfume.
Even that body, wrapped now in sheets,
is the same as it was when it thrilled in discovery.

Her body wakes alone to the extended call
of morning, the languor of another morning
returning in the heavy shadows: the barn
of childhood and the heavy tiredness of sun
hot in the indolent doorways. A perfume
worked itself into the usual sweat
of her hair, a smell the animals knew.
Her body took secret pleasure in the sun's
suggestive, serene caress—like a real touch.

The languor of bed saps the sprawled limbs,
still youthful and plump, like a child's.
The clumsy child used to smell the mixed scent
of tobacco and hay, used to tremble when touched
by the man's quick hands: she liked playing games.
Sometimes she played lying down with the man
in the hay, but he wasn't smelling her hair:
he'd find her closed legs in the hay and pry
them open, then crush her like he was her father.
The perfume was flowers ground upon stones.

It often returns, in the slow rise from sleep,
that undone aroma of far-off flowers,
of barns and of sun. No man can know

la sottile carezza di quell'acre ricordo.
Non c'è uomo che veda oltre il corpo disteso
quell'infanzia trascorsa nell'ansia inesperta.

the subtle caress of that sour memory.
No man can see, beyond that sprawled body,
that childhood passed in such clumsy anxiety.

Dopo

La collina è distesa e la pioggia l'impregna in silenzio.

Piove sopra le case: la breve finestra
s'è riempita di un verde piú fresco e piú nudo.
La compagna era stesa con me: la finestra
era vuota, nessuno guardava, eravamo ben nudi.
Il suo corpo segreto cammina a quest'ora per strada
col suo passo, ma il ritmo è piú molle; la pioggia
scende come quel passo, leggera e spossata.
La compagna non vede la nuda collina
assopita nell'umidità: passa in strada
e la gente che l'urta non sa.

                    Verso sera
la collina è percorsa da brani di nebbia,
la finestra ne accoglie anche il fiato. La strada
a quest'ora è deserta; la sola collina
ha una vita remota nel corpo piú cupo.
Giacevamo spossati nell'umidità
dei due corpi, ciascuno assopito sull'altro.

Una sera piú dolce, di tiepido sole
e di freschi colori, la strada sarebbe una gioia.
È una gioia passare per strada, godendo
un ricordo del corpo, ma tutto diffuso d'intorno.
Nelle foglie dei viali, nel passo indolente di donne,
nelle voci di tutti, c'è un po' della vita
che i due corpi han scordato ma è pure un miracolo.
E scoprire giú in fondo a una via la collina
tra le case, e guardarla e pensare che insieme
la compagna la guardi, dalla breve finestra.

Afterwards

The hill sprawls and the rain soaks into it silently.

It's raining on houses: the narrow window
fills with a green that's naked and fresh.
My companion was lying with me: the window
was empty, and nobody watching, and us stark naked.
And now, her hidden body is walking the street
with its usual rhythm, but gentler. The rain
falls with that rhythm, soft and exhausted.
My companion won't notice the naked hill
drowsing in the damp air; out in the streets,
she's jostled by people who don't know.

                                    Toward evening,
when thin patches of fog pass over the hill,
the window will gather their breath. The street
at this hour is empty. The lonely hill leads,
in its darker body, a separate, remote life.
We were lying exhausted in the damp air
of two bodies, each drowsing on the other.

If the weather were better, with a warm, fading sun
and fresh colors, the street would be a delight—
delightful to stroll down the street, enjoying
the body's memory as it diffuses around you.
In the avenue's leaves, in the indolent walk of a woman,
in everyone's voice, there's something of life
that both bodies have forgotten, but that still is a miracle.
And to find, down at the end of some street, that hill
among houses, and to stare, and to think that she, too,
is watching that hill through her own narrow window.

Dentro il buio è affondata la nuda collina
e la pioggia bisbiglia. Non c'è la compagna
che ha portato con sé il corpo dolce e il sorriso.
Ma domani nel cielo lavato dall'alba
la compagna uscirà per le strade, leggera
del suo passo. Potremo incontrarci, volendo.

The naked hill has sunk into darkness,
the rain is a whisper. My companion's not here —
she took, when she left, that sweet body, that smile.
But tomorrow, beneath a sky washed clean by dawn,
my companion will walk out into the streets,
her step light. And we can, if we desire, meet again.

Crepuscolo di sabbiatori

I barconi risalgono adagio, sospinti e pesanti:
quasi immobili, fanno schiumare la viva corrente.
È già quasi la notte. Isolati, si fermano:
si dibatte e sussulta la vanga sott'acqua.
Di ora in ora, altre barche son state fin qui.
Tanti corpi di donna han varcato nel sole
su quest'acqua. Son scese nell'acqua o saltate alla riva
a dibattersi in coppia, qualcuna, sull'erba.
Nel crepuscolo, il fiume è deserto. I due o tre sabbiatori
sono scesi con l'acqua alla cintola e scavano il fondo.
Il gran gelo dell'inguine fiacca e intontisce le schiene.
Quelle donne non sono che un bianco ricordo.

I barconi nel buio discendono grevi di sabbia,
senza dare una scossa, radenti: ogni uomo è seduto
a una punta e un granello di fuoco gli brucia alla bocca.
Ogni paio di braccia strascina il suo remo,
un tepore discende alle gambe fiaccate
e lontano s'accendono i lumi. Ogni donna è scomparsa,
che al mattino le barche portavano stesa
e che un giovane, dritto alla punta, spingeva sudando.
Quelle donne eran belle: qualcuna scendeva
seminuda e spariva ridendo con qualche compagno.
Quando un qualche inesperto veniva a cozzare,
sabbiatori levavano il capo e l'ingiuria moriva
sulla donna distesa come fosse già nuda.
Ora tornano tutti i sussulti, intravisti nell'erba,
a occupare il silenzio e ogni cosa s'accentra
sulla punta di fuoco, che vive. Ora l'occhio
si smarrisce nel fumo invisibile ch'esce di bocca
e le membra ritrovano l'urto del sangue.

Sand-Diggers' Twilight

The ponderous barges push their way slowly upriver,
barely moving, the quick current foaming around them.
Already it's near dark. They stop, spaced apart:
under the water, their spades struggle and jerk.
Other boats, in the course of the day, have been here.
The bodies of many women have passed in the sun
over this water. They swam here, perhaps, or hopped
on shore to contend with a boyfriend in the tall grass.
Now twilight, the river's deserted. Two or three diggers
stand in water up to their waists, working the bottom:
it's ice in the groin, tiring and numbing their backs.
Those women are only the palest of memories.

In the dark, the barges float smoothly downstream,
heavy with sand, riding low in the water: each man
sits on the edge of a boat, a grain of fire in his mouth.
Each pair of arms trails its oar over the water,
a warmness suffuses tired legs, and lights gleam
in the distance. The women have all disappeared—
this morning, each was stretched out in a boat,
a young man standing astern, poling and sweating.
Those women were lovely: sometimes they'd get out,
half-naked and laughing, and disappear with their men.
If some clumsy guy bumped one of the barges,
the diggers would look up, and their anger would die
on the woman, who lay there as if naked already.
Now the quick movements, seen through the grass-stalks,
come back, filling the silence, and all things converge
on that point of fire as it flares. Now, eyes blur
in the invisible smoke leaving their mouths,
and limbs discover again the pounding of blood.

In distanza, sul fiume, scintillano i lumi
di Torino. Due o tre sabbiatori hanno acceso
sulla prua il fanale, ma il fiume è deserto.
La fatica del giorno vorrebbe assopirli
e le gambe so quasi spezzate. Qualcuno non pensa
che a attraccare il barcone e cadere sul letto
e mangiare nel sonno, magari sognando.
Ma qualcuno rivede quei corpi nel sole
e avrà ancora la forza di andare in città, sotto i lumi,
a cercare ridendo tra la folla che passa.

Downriver, far in the distance, the bright lights
of Turin. Two or three diggers light lanterns
to hang at the prows, but the river's deserted.
The day's long labor has left them exhausted,
their legs nearly dead. Some can think only
of docking their barges and falling in bed,
of eating, perhaps in a dream, while they sleep.
Others remember the bodies they saw in the sun
and find strength to go to the city, under those lights,
to laugh, and to look through the crowd as it passes.

Il carrettiere

Lo stridore del carro scuote la strada.
Non c'è letto piú solo per chi, sotto l'alba,
dorme ancora disteso, sognando il buio.
Sotto il carro s'è spenta —lo dice il cielo—
la lanterna che dondola notte e giorno.

Va col carro un tepore che sa d'osteria,
di mammelle premute e di notte chiara,
di fatica contenta senza risveglio.
Va col carro nel sonno un ricordo già desto
di parole arrochite, taciute all'alba.
Il calore del vivo camino acceso
si riaccende nel corpo che sente il giorno.

Lo stridore piú roco, del carro che va,
ha dischiuso nel cielo che pesa in alto
una riga lontana di luce fredda.
È laggiú che s'accende il ricordo di ieri.
È laggiú che quest'oggi sarà il calore
l'osteria la veglia le voci roche
la fatica. Sarà sulla piazza aperta.
Ci saranno quegli occhi che scuotono il sangue.

Anche i sacchi, nell'alba che indugia, scuotono
chi è disteso e li preme, con gli occhi al cielo
che si schiude —il ricordo si stringe ai sacchi.
Il ricordo s'affonda nell'ombra di ieri
dove balza il camino e la fiamma viva.

The Wagoner

The squeak of the wagon rattles the street.
For one lying asleep, who dreams beneath dawn
of darkness, there is no lonelier bed.
The lantern that hangs beneath the wagon,
night and day, has blown out—so says the sky.

Moving with the wagon: the warmth of a tavern,
of breasts pressed against him in the clear night,
of happy fatigue and unbroken sleep.
Moving with it: a memory, already awake,
of hoarse words, fading by dawn to silence.
The heat of the high flames in the fireplace
rekindles in the body that feels day coming.

The hoarsest voice, the squeaking voice
of the wagon, discloses beneath the gray
a cold streak of light in the distant sky.
It's there that yesterday's memory shines.
It's there that today will take shape: the heat
the tavern the late night the hoarse voices
the fatigue. All in the open piazza,
and those blood-shaking eyes will be there.

And under the slow dawn, the grain sacks shake
the man lying on top, his eyes toward the sky
as it opens—memory presses into the sacks,
memory sinks down into yesterday's dark,
where the fireplace and the high flames flicker.

Un ricordo

Non c'è uomo che giunga a lasciare una traccia
su costei. Quant'è stato dilegua in un sogno
come via in un mattino, e non resta che lei.
Se non fosse la fronte sfiorata da un attimo,
sembrerebbe stupita. Sorridon le guance
ogni volta.

       Nemmeno s'ammassano i giorni
sul suo viso, a mutare il sorriso leggero
che s'irradia alle cose. Con dura fermezza
fa ogni cosa, ma sembra ogni volta la prima;
pure vive fin l'ultimo istante. Si schiude
il suo solido corpo, il suo sguardo raccolto,
a una voce sommessa e un po' rauca: una voce
d'uomo stanco. E nessuna stanchezza la tocca.

A fissarle la bocca, socchiude lo sguardo
in attesa: nessuno può osare uno scatto.
Molti uomini sanno il suo ambiguo sorriso
o la ruga improvvisa. Se quell'uomo c'è stato
che la sa mugolante, umiliata d'amore,
paga giorno per giorno, ignorando di lei
per chi viva quest'oggi.

       Sorride da sola
il sorriso piú ambiguo camminando per strada.

A Memory

No man yet has left his mark on this one.
Whatever was there dissolves like a dream
in the morning, and nothing is left but her.
But for the moment's light touch on her brow,
she'd seem astonished. She smiles with her cheeks
each time.

      Nor do the days collect
on her face or diminish the easy smile
she shines on the world. All that she does
is done firmly, and every time seems like the first;
she's alive to the end of each moment. Her gaze
is gathered, her body is firm, they unfold
in a voice that's soft, a bit hoarse: the voice
of a tired man. And she is untouched by tiredness.

When shaping her mouth, she narrows her eyes
and she waits: nobody dares to move.
Many men see her ambiguous smile,
her forehead's quick wrinkle. If the man exists
who has seen her moaning, humbled by love,
he pays dearly each day, not knowing who
she's living for now.

      Alone on the street,
she smiles her most ambiguous smile.

La voce

Ogni giorno il silenzio della camera sola
si richiude sul lieve sciacquío d'ogni gesto
come l'aria. Ogni giorno la breve finestra
s'apre immobile all'aria che tace. La voce
rauca e dolce non torna nel fresco silenzio.

S'apre come il respiro di chi sia per parlare
l'aria immobile, e tace. Ogni giorno è la stessa.
E la voce è la stessa, che non rompe il silenzio,
rauca e uguale per sempre nell'immobilità
del ricordo. La chiara finestra accompagna
col suo palpito breve la calma d'allora.

Ogni gesto percuote la calma d'allora.
Se suonasse la voce, tornerebbe il dolore.
Tornerebbero i gesti nell'aria stupita
e parole parole alla voce sommessa.
Se suonasse la voce anche il palpito breve
del silenzio che dura, si farebbe dolore.

Tornerebbero i gesti del vano dolore,
percuotendo le cose nel rombo del tempo.
Ma la voce non torna, e il susurro remoto
non increspa il ricordo. L'immobile luce
dà il suo palpito fresco. Per sempre il silenzio
tace rauco e sommesso nel ricordo d'allora.

The Voice

Each day the silence of the lonely room
closes in on the gentle rustle of gestures
like air. Each day the small window is opened,
motionless, to the hushed air. The voice,
hoarse and sweet, won't break this cool silence.

The motionless air expands like the breath
of one who might speak, then falls silent. Each day
is the same, the same voice not breaking the silence,
hoarse and always the same in the stillness
of memory. The bright window accompanies,
with its brief tremor, the calm of that time.

Each gesture jolts the calm of that time.
At the sound of that voice, the pain would return,
and the gestures, too, in the astonished air,
and words, and words, uttered so softly.
The sound of that voice would be a brief tremor
in lasting silence; even that would cause pain.

The gestures of pointless pain would return,
jolting all things in the rumble of time.
But the voice won't return, and the distant whisper
won't ripple memory's surface. A cool tremor
runs through the still light. In the memory of that time,
the soft, hoarse silence falls silent for good.

La moglie del barcaiolo

Qualche volta nel tiepido sonno dell'alba,
sola in sogno, le accade che ha sposato una donna.

Si distacca dal corpo materno una donna
magra e bianca che abbassa la piccola testa
nella stanza. Nel freddo barlume la donna
non attende il mattino; lavora. Trascorre
silenziosa: fra donne non occorre parola.

Mentre dorme, la moglie sa la barca sul fiume
e la pioggia che fuma sulla schiena dell'uomo.
Ma la piccola moglie chiude svelta la porta
e s'appoggia, e solleva gli sguardi nei suoi.
La finestra tintinna alla pioggia che scroscia
e la donna distesa, che mastica adagio,
tende un piatto. La piccola moglie lo riempie
e si siede sul letto e comincia a mangiare.

Mangia in fretta la piccola moglie furtiva
sotto gli occhi materni, come fosse una bimba
e resiste alla mano che le cerca la nuca.
Corre a un tratto alla porta e la schiude: le barche
sono tutte attraccate alla trave. Ritorna
piedi scalzi nel letto e s'abbracciano svelte.

Sono gelide e magre le labbra accostate,
ma nel corpo si fonde un profondo calore
tormentoso. La piccola moglie ora dorme
stesa accanto al suo corpo materno. È sottile
aspra come un ragazzo, ma dorme da donna.
Non saprebbe portare una barca, alla pioggia.

The Boatman's Wife

Sometimes, alone in the warm sleep of dawn
and dreaming, she finds she has married a woman.

Detaching herself from the motherly body,
a thin pale woman appears in the room,
her little head lowered. The woman's not waiting,
in the cold half-light, for morning; she's working
in silence. Among women, words are not needed.

As she sleeps, the wife knows the boat on the river
and the rain that steams up from the man's back.
But the little wife hurriedly closes the door,
leaning against it, and raises her eyes to the other's.
The rain pours down, pattering against the window,
and the woman in bed is chewing slowly
and holding a plate out. The little wife fills it,
then sits on the bed and starts to eat too.

The little wife eats in a hurry, furtively,
in the gaze of those motherly eyes, like a girl,
and resists the hand that touches her nape.
She runs to the door and looks out: the boats
are tied fast to the pier. She comes back to bed
in her bare feet, and they quickly embrace.

The lips against hers are thin, and cold,
but within her a deep heat melts her away
and troubles her. Now, the little wife sleeps,
lying beside the motherly body. She's lean
and hard, like a boy, but she sleeps like a woman.
She couldn't handle a boat in this rain.

Fuori scroscia la pioggia nella luce sommessa
della porta socchiusa. Entra un poco di vento
nella stanza deserta. Se si aprisse la porta,
entrerebbe anche l'uomo, che ha veduto ogni cosa.
Non direbbe parola: crollerebbe la testa
col suo viso di scherno, alla donna delusa.

Outside the rain pours down in the soft light
of the half-open door. A little wind enters
the empty room. If the door were to open,
the man, too, would enter, having seen everything.
He wouldn't say a word: he'd shake his head
with a sneer of derision at his wife's disappointment.

La vecchia ubriaca

Piace pure alla vecchia distendersi al sole
e allargare le braccia. La vampa pesante
schiaccia il piccolo volto come schiaccia la terra.

Delle cose che bruciano non rimane che il sole.
L'uomo e il vino han tradito e consunto quelle ossa
stese brune nell'abito, ma la terra spaccata
ronza come una fiamma. Non occorre parola
non occorre rimpianto. Torna il giorno vibrante
che anche il corpo era giovane, piú rovente del sole.

Nel ricordo compaiono le grandi colline
vive e giovani come quel corpo, e lo sguardo dell'uomo
e l'asprezza del vino ritornano ansioso
desiderio: una vampa guizzava nel sangue
come il verde nell'erba. Per vigne e sentieri
si fa carne il ricordo. La vecchia, occhi chiusi,
gode immobile il cielo col suo corpo d'allora.

Nella terra spaccata batte un cuore piú sano
come il petto robusto di un padre o di un uomo:
vi si stringe la guancia aggrinzita. Anche il padre,
anche l'uomo, son morti traditi. La carne
si è consunta anche in quelli. Né il calore dei fianchi
né l'asprezza del vino non li sveglia mai piú.

Per le vigne distese la voce del sole
aspra e dolce susurra nel diafano incendio,
come l'aria tremasse. Trema l'erba d'intorno.
L'erba è giovane come la vampa del sole.
Sono giovani i morti nel vivace ricordo.

The Drunk Old Woman

Even the old woman likes to lie in the sun
and stretch out her arms. The heat weighs her down,
pressing her small face as it presses the earth.

Of things that burned, only the sun remains.
Men and wine have betrayed her, have consumed
the dark bones in her dress. But the cracked earth
hums like a flame. No call for words now,
no call for regrets. The shimmering day will return
when her young body burned like the sun.

The great hills reappear in her memory,
young and alive, like her body. The look of a man
or the sharp taste of wine can bring back
desire's tension: a heat hums in her blood
like greenness in grass. Among vineyards and paths
memory becomes flesh. The woman lies still,
eyes closed, enjoying the sky with the body she had.

Beating beneath the cracked earth is a healthier heart,
like a father's strong chest, like the chest of a man:
she presses a wizened cheek to the ground. Even fathers,
even men, are betrayed when they die. Their flesh,
like hers, is consumed. Neither warm thighs
nor the sharp taste of wine will arouse these men now.

In the sprawling vineyards, the sharp, sweet voice
of the sun whispers through the diaphanous blaze,
as if the air trembled. Grass trembles around her.
The grass is young still, like the heat of the sun.
The dead are young too, while memories live.

Paesaggio (VIII)

I ricordi cominciano nella sera
sotto il fiato del vento a levare il volto
e ascoltare la voce del fiume. L'acqua
è la stessa, nel buio, degli anni morti.

Nel silenzio del buio sale uno sciacquo
dove passano voci e risa remote;
s'accompagna al brusío un colore vano
che è di sole, di rive e di sguardi chiari.
Un'estate di voci. Ogni viso contiene
come un frutto maturo un sapore andato.

Ogni occhiata che torna, conserva un gusto
di erba e cose impregnate di sole e sera
sulla spiaggia. Conserva un fiato di mare.
Come un mare notturno è quest'ombra vaga
di ansie e brividi antichi, che il cielo sfiora
e ogni sera ritorna. Le voci morte
assomigliano al frangersi di quel mare.

Landscape (VIII)

Late in the evening, beneath the breath
of wind, memories begin to lift their heads
to listen to the speech of the river. Water
is the same, in this dark, as in the dead years.

From the silence of darkness the sound of water
rises to join the distant laughter and voices;
and along with the murmur, the useless color
coming from sunlight, bright faces, shores.
A summer of voices. Each face contains
a taste of the past, like a ripened fruit.

Each glance that returns preserves the flavor
of grass and of everything soaked with late sun
on the beach. It preserves the breath of the sea.
It's like the night sea, this hazy shadow
of shuddering old anxieties that the sky touches,
and that each evening returns. The dead voices
recall the noise of that sea breaking on itself.

Fumatori di carta

Mi ha condotto a sentir la sua banda. Si siede in un angolo
e imbocca il clarino. Comincia un baccano d'inferno.
Fuori, un vento furioso e gli schiaffi, tra i lampi,
della pioggia fan sí che la luce vien tolta,
ogni cinque minuti. Nel buio, le facce
dànno dentro stravolte, a suonare a memoria
un ballabile. Energico, il povero amico
tiene tutti, dal fondo. E il clarino si torce,
rompe il chiasso sonoro, s'inoltra, si sfoga
come un'anima sola, in un secco silenzio.

Questi poveri ottoni son troppo sovente ammaccati:
contadine le mani che stringono i tasti,
e le fronti, caparbie, che guardano appena da terra.
Miserabile sangue fiaccato, estenuato
dalle troppe fatiche, si sente muggire
nelle note e l'amico li guida a fatica,
lui che ha mani indurite a picchiare una mazza,
a menare una pialla, a strapparsi la vita.

Li ebbe un tempo i compagni e non ha che trent'anni.
Fu di quelli di dopo la guerra, cresciuti alla fame.
Venne anch'egli a Torino, cercando una vita,
e trovò le ingiustizie. Imparò a lavorare
nelle fabbriche senza un sorriso. Imparò a misurare
sulla propria fatica la fame degli altri,
e trovò dappertutto ingiustizie. Tentò darsi pace
camminando, assonnato, le vie interminabili
nella notte, ma vide soltanto a migliaia i lampioni
lucidissimi, su iniquità: donne rauche, ubriachi,
traballanti fantocci sperduti. Era giunto a Torino
un inverno, tra lampi di fabbriche e scorie di fumo;
e sapeva cos'era lavoro. Accettava il lavoro

Smokers of Paper

He's brought me to hear his band. He sits in a corner
mouthing his clarinet. A hellish racket begins.
Outside, through flashes of lightning, wind gusts
and rain whips, knocking the lights out
every five minutes. In the dark, their faces
give it their all, contorted, as they play a dance tune
from memory. Full of energy, my poor friend
anchors them all from behind. His clarinet writhes,
breaks through the din, passes beyond it, releasing
like a lone soul, into a dry, rough silence.

The poor pieces of brass have been dented too often:
the hands working the stops also work in the fields,
and the obstinate brows stay fixed on the ground.
Miserable worn-out blood, weakened
by too many labors—you can hear it groan
in their notes, as my friend struggles to lead them,
his own hands hardened from swinging a hammer,
from pushing a plane, from scraping a living.

He's lost all his old comrades, and he's only thirty.
Part of the postwar group that grew up on hunger.
They all came to Turin, to look for a life,
and discovered injustice. He learned, without smiling,
how to work in a factory. He learned how to measure
the hunger of others with his own fatigue—
injustice was everywhere. He tried to find peace
by walking, at night, down streets without ends,
half-asleep, but found only thousands of streetlamps
blazing down on iniquity: hoarse women and drunks,
staggering puppets, far from their homes. He came,
one winter, to Turin—factory lights, smoke and ash—
and he learned what work is. He accepted that work

come un duro destino dell'uomo. Ma tutti gli uomini
lo accettassero e al mondo ci fosse giustizia.
Ma si fece i compagni. Soffriva le lunghe parole
e dovette ascoltarne, aspettando la fine.
Se li fece i compagni. Ogni casa ne aveva famiglie.
La città ne era tutta accerchiata. E la faccia del mondo
ne era tutta coperta. Sentivano in sé
tanta disperazione da vincere il mondo.

Suona secco stasera, malgrado la banda
che ha istruito a uno a uno. Non bada al frastuono
della pioggia e alla luce. La faccia severa
fissa attenta un dolore, mordendo il clarino.
Gli ho veduto questi occhi una sera, che soli,
col fratello, piú triste di lui di dieci anni,
vegliavamo a una luce mancante. Il fratello studiava
su un inutile tornio costrutto da lui.
E il mio povero amico accusava il destino
che li tiene inchiodati alla pialla e alla mazza
a nutrire due vecchi, non chiesti.

                    D'un tratto gridò
che non era il destino se il mondo soffriva,
se la luce del sole strappava bestemmie:
era l'uomo, colpevole. *Almeno potercene andare,
far la libera fame, rispondere no
a una vita che adopera amore e pietà,
la famiglia, il pezzetto di terra, a legarci le mani.*

was part of a man's hard fate; if all men did that,
there just might be some justice in this world.
And he found new comrades. He suffered their long words,
he listened and waited for them to be over.
He made them his comrades. Families of them
in each house, the city surrounded by them, the face
of the world covered with them. And each of them
felt desperate enough to conquer the world.

They sound harsh tonight, despite all the time
he spent coaching each player. He ignores the loud rain
and the flickering lights. His face is severe,
fixed on some grief, almost biting the mouthpiece.
I've seen this expression before, one evening, just us
and his brother, who's ten years sadder than him.
We were up late in the dim light, the brother studying
a lathe he had built that didn't work right,
and my poor friend cursing the fate that kept him there,
bound to his hammer and plane, feeding a pair
of old people he never had asked for.

                              That's when he yelled
that it wasn't fate that made the world suffer
or made the daylight spark blasphemous outbursts:
man is the guilty one. *If we could just leave,
and be hungry and free, and say no
to a life that uses our love and our piety,
our families, our patches of dirt, to shackle our hands.*

Parole del politico

Si passava sul presto al mercato dei pesci
a lavarci lo sguardo: ce n'era d'argento,
di vermigli, di verdi, colore del mare.
Al confronto col mare tutto scaglie d'argento,
la vincevano i pesci. Si pensava al ritorno.

Belle fino le donne dall'anfora in capo,
ulivigna, foggiata sulla forma dei fianchi
mollemente: ciascuno pensava alle donne,
come parlano, ridono, camminano in strada.
Ridevamo, ciascuno. Pioveva sul mare.

Per le vigne nascoste negli anfratti di terra
l'acqua macera foglie e racimoli. Il cielo
si colora di nuvole scarse, arrossate,
di piacere e di sole. Sulla terra sapori
e colori nel cielo. Nessuno con noi.

Si pensava al ritorno, come dopo una notte
tutta quanta di veglia, si pensa al mattino.
Si godeva il colore dei pesci e l'umore
delle frutta, vivaci nel tanfo del mare.
Ubriachi eravamo, nel ritorno imminente.

Words from Confinement

We would go down to the fish market early
to cleanse our vision: the fish were silver,
and scarlet, and green, and the color of sea.
The fish were lovelier than even the sea
with its silvery scales. We thought of return.

Lovely too the women with jars on their heads,
olive-brown clay, shaped softly like thighs:
we each thought of our women, their voices,
their laughs, the way they walked down the street.
And each of us laughed. And it rained on the sea.

In vineyards that cling to cracks in the earth,
water softens the leaves and the grape-stems. The sky
is colored by occasional clouds that redden
with pleasure and sun. On earth, flavors and smells;
in the sky, color. And we were alone there.

We thought of return the way a man thinks
of morning after an utterly sleepless night.
We took pleasure in the color of fish and the glisten
of fruit, all so alive in the musk of the sea.
We were drunk on the thought of impending return.

Mito

Verrà il giorno che il giovane dio sarà un uomo,
senza pena, col morto sorriso dell'uomo
che ha compreso. Anche il sole trascorre remoto
arrossando le spiagge. Verrà il giorno che il dio
non saprà piú dov'erano le spiagge d'un tempo.

Ci si sveglia un mattino che è morta l'estate,
e negli occhi tumultuano ancora splendori
come ieri, e all'orecchio i fragori del sole
fatto sangue. È mutato il colore del mondo.
La montagna non tocca piú il cielo; le nubi
non s'ammassano piú come frutti; nell'acqua
non traspare piú un ciottolo. Il corpo di un uomo
pensieroso si piega, dove un dio respirava.

Il gran sole è finito, e l'odore di terra,
e la libera strada, colorata di gente
che ignorava la morte. Non si muore d'estate.
Se qualcuno spariva, c'era il giovane dio
che viveva per tutti e ignorava la morte.
Su di lui la tristezza era un'ombra di nube.
Il suo passo stupiva la terra.

                    Ora pesa
la stanchezza su tutte le membra dell'uomo,
senza pena: la calma stanchezza dell'alba
che apre un giorno di pioggia. Le spiagge oscurate
non conoscono il giovane, che un tempo bastava
le guardasse. Né il mare dell'aria rivive
al respiro. Si piegano le labbra dell'uomo
rassegnate, a sorridere davanti alla terra.

Myth

One of these days the young god will become a man,
painlessly, with the dead smile of the man
who now understands. And the faraway sun
will redden the beaches. One of these days the god
will have forgotten the sands he once walked on.

You wake up one morning and the summer's dead,
its splendors fermenting still in your eyes,
as they used to, and in your ears the roar of the sun
turned to blood. The color of the world has changed.
The mountaintop no longer touches the sky;
clouds no longer gather like fruit; small stones
no longer shine through clear water. A man's body
bends forward in thought, where a god used to breathe.

The great sun is gone, and the earth's smell too,
and the wide-open road is colored with people
who know nothing of death. No one dies in the summer.
If anyone vanished, there was always the young god
who lived for us all and knew nothing of death.
He wore sadness lightly, like the shadow of clouds.
His footstep astonished the earth.

                     But now
exhaustion weighs down the limbs of the man,
painlessly: the calm exhaustion of dawn
at the start of a day of rain. The darkening beaches
no longer remember the god, whose mere glance
was enough for them once. Nor is the sea of air
alive with his breath. The man's lips have shut,
resigned, to smile in the presence of earth.

Il paradiso sui tetti

Sarà un giorno tranquillo, di luce fredda
come il sole che nasce o che muore, e il vetro
chiuderà l'aria sudicia fuori del cielo.

Ci si sveglia un mattino, una volta per sempre,
nel tepore dell'ultimo sonno: l'ombra
sarà come il tepore. Empirà la stanza
per la grande finestra un cielo piú grande.
Dalla scala salita un giorno per sempre
non verranno piú voci, né visi morti.

Non sarà necessario lasciare il letto.
Solo l'alba entrerà nella stanza vuota.
Basterà la finestra a vestire ogni cosa
di un chiarore tranquillo, quasi una luce.
Poserà un'ombra scarna sul volto supino.
I ricordi saranno dei grumi d'ombra
appiattati cosí come vecchia brace
nel camino. Il ricordo sarà la vampa
che ancor ieri mordeva negli occhi spenti.

Paradise above the Roofs

The day will be calm, with cold light, as if
from a sun that's newborn or dying; the window
will keep the filthy air out of the sky.

You wake up one morning, once and for all,
in the warmth of your final sleep: the shadow
will resemble that warmth. Through the big window
there comes a bigger sky, filling the room.
From the stairs that were climbed once and for all,
no voices will come, no dead faces.

There'll be no reason to get out of bed.
Only dawn will enter the empty room.
The window will manage to dress each thing
in a calm glow that will be almost a light.
A thin shadow will rest on the face that stares
at the ceiling. Each memory will be a lump
of shadow, crumbled like an old coal
in the fireplace. Memory will be the flame
that burned until yesterday in snuffed eyes.

Semplicità

L'uomo solo — che è stato in prigione — ritorna in prigione
ogni volta che morde in un pezzo di pane.
In prigione sognava le lepri che fuggono
sul terriccio invernale. Nella nebbia d'inverno
l'uomo vive tra muri di strade, bevendo
acqua fredda e mordendo in un pezzo di pane.

Uno crede che dopo rinasca la vita,
che il respiro si calmi, che ritorni l'inverno
con l'odore del vino nella calda osteria,
e il buon fuoco, la stalla, e le cene. Uno crede,
fin che è dentro uno crede. Si esce fuori una sera,
e le lepri le han prese e le mangiano al caldo
gli altri, allegri. Bisogna guardarli dai vetri.

L'uomo solo osa entrare per bere un bicchiere
quando proprio si gela, e contempla il suo vino:
il colore fumoso, il sapore pesante.
Morde il pezzo di pane, che sapeva di lepre
in prigione, ma adesso non sa piú di pane
né di nulla. E anche il vino non sa che di nebbia.

L'uomo solo ripensa a quei campi, contento
di saperli già arati. Nella sala deserta
sottovoce si prova a cantare. Rivede
lungo l'argine il ciuffo di rovi spogliati
che in agosto fu verde. Dà un fischio alla cagna.
E compare la lepre e non hanno piú freddo.

Simplicity

The man alone, who's known prison already, returns
each time he bites down on a piece of bread.
In prison he dreamed of wild hares that flee
across winter's plowed fields. In the wintry fog
the man's life is walled in by streets, he drinks
cold water, he bites down on pieces of bread.

You try to believe that later there'll be a rebirth,
that you can breathe calmly, that winter's come back
with the smell of new wine in a warm tavern—
a good fire, a stable, and your meal. You believe.
While you're there you believe. One evening you go out
and they've caught all the hares, they're eating them hot,
they're happy. And you have to watch through the window.

The man alone dares go inside for a drink
when he's chilled to the bone. He considers his wine,
its smoky color, thick taste. He bites down
on a piece of bread, which tasted in prison
like wild hares, which no longer tastes like bread
or anything. Even the wine tastes like nothing but fog.

The man alone thinks back to those fields,
glad they've already been plowed. In the empty room
he starts singing under his breath. He sees again,
along the embankment, the naked blackberry bushes
that in August were green. He whistles to his dog.
And the hare appears, and they're no longer cold.

L'istinto

L'uomo vecchio, deluso di tutte le cose,
dalla soglia di casa nel tiepido sole
guarda il cane e la cagna sfogare l'istinto.

Sulla bocca sdentata si rincorrono mosche.
La sua donna gli è morta da tempo. Anche lei
come tutte le cagne non voleva saperne,
ma ci aveva l'istinto. L'uomo vecchio annusava
—non ancora sdentato—, la notte veniva,
si mettevano a letto. Era bello l'istinto.

Quel che piace nel cane è la gran libertà.
Dal mattino alla sera gironzola in strada;
e un po' mangia, un po' dorme, un po' monta le cagne:
non aspetta nemmeno la notte. Ragiona,
come fiuta, e gli odori che sente son suoi.

L'uomo vecchio ricorda una volta di giorno
che l'ha fatta da cane in un campo di grano.
Non sa piú con che cagna, ma ricorda il gran sole
e il sudore e la voglia di non smettere mai.
Era come in un letto. Se tornassero gli anni,
lo vorrebbe far sempre in un campo di grano.

Scende in strada una donna e si ferma a guardare;
passa il prete e si volta. Sulla pubblica piazza
si può fare di tutto. Persino la donna,
che ha ritegno a voltarsi per l'uomo, si ferma.
Solamente un ragazzo non tollera il gioco
e fa piovere sassi. L'uomo vecchio si sdegna.

Instinct

The old man, all his hopes disappointed,
watches from the porch as the dog and the bitch
give in to their instincts in the warm sun.

Flies light on his face near his toothless mouth.
His woman's been dead for some time. She too,
like all bitches, wanted nothing to do with it,
but she had the instinct. The man had a nose for it
when he still had his teeth: the night would come,
they'd get in their bed—the instinct was good.

What's great about dogs is their freedom.
From morning till evening they saunter the streets,
now eating, now sleeping, now mounting the bitches—
without even waiting for night. The dog thinks
like he sniffs, and whatever he smells is his.

The old man remembers that once at midday
he did it like a dog in a field of ripe wheat.
He's forgotten the bitch, but not the hot sun
or the sweat or the never wanting to stop.
It was just like a bed. If the years would turn back,
he'd like to do it only in wheat fields.

A woman walks by and stops there to watch.
A priest passes and looks. In the public piazza,
you can do as you please. Even the woman,
reluctant to watch because of the man,
has stopped. Only a boy can't bear this game;
he starts throwing stones. The old man's indignant.

Paternità (II)

Uomo solo dinanzi all'inutile mare,
attendendo la sera, attendendo il mattino.
I bambini vi giocano, ma quest'uomo vorrebbe
lui averlo un bambino e guardarlo giocare.
Grandi nuvole fanno un palazzo sull'acqua
che ogni giorno rovina e risorge, e colora
i bambini nel viso. Ci sarà sempre il mare.

Il mattino ferisce. Su quest'umida spiaggia
striscia il sole, aggrappato alle reti e alle pietre.
Esce l'uomo nel torbido sole e cammina
lungo il mare. Non guarda le madide schiume
che trascorrono a riva e non hanno piú pace.
A quest'ora i bambini sonnecchiano ancora
nel tepore del letto. A quest'ora sonnecchia
dentro il letto una donna, che farebbe l'amore
se non fosse lei sola. Lento, l'uomo si spoglia
nudo come la donna lontana, e discende nel mare.

Poi la notte, che il mare svanisce, si ascolta
il gran vuoto ch'è sotto le stelle. I bambini
nelle case arrossate van cadendo dal sonno
e qualcuno piangendo. L'uomo, stanco di attesa,
leva gli occhi alle stelle, che non odono nulla.
Ci son donne a quest'ora che spogliano un bimbo
e lo fanno dormire. C'è qualcuna in un letto
abbracciata ad un uomo. Dalla nera finestra
entra un ansito rauco, e nessuno l'ascolta
se non l'uomo che sa tutto il tedio del mare.

Fatherhood (II)

A man alone facing the pointless sea,
waiting for evening, waiting for morning.
Children play here, but the man would like
a child of his own to watch. Over the water,
great clouds build a castle that's ruined each day
and rises again, as it colors the faces
of children. The sea will always be there.

The morning is wounding. The sun crawls up
the damp beach, clinging to nets and to stones.
The man goes walking at the sea's edge
in the turbid light, not watching the wet foam
that runs up the sand and is never at peace.
At this hour the children are dozing still
in the warmth of their beds. At this hour a woman
is dozing in bed—she'd like to make love
if she weren't alone. The man undresses and walks,
as naked now as the faraway woman, into the sea.

Then at night, when the sea disappears, you can hear
the great emptiness under the stars. The children
in the reddened houses are falling asleep,
some of them crying. The man, tired of waiting,
looks up at the stars, who don't hear a thing.
It's the hour when women undress their babies
to put them to bed. When some, in their own beds,
are embraced by a man. A hoarse gasping comes in
through darkened windows, and nobody hears it
but the man who knows all the sea's tedium.

Lo steddazzu

L'uomo solo si leva che il mare è ancor buio
e le stelle vacillano. Un tepore di fiato
sale su dalla riva, dov'è il letto del mare,
e addolcisce il respiro. Quest'è l'ora in cui nulla
può accadere. Perfino la pipa tra i denti
pende spenta. Notturno è il sommesso sciacquío.
L'uomo solo ha già acceso un gran fuoco di rami
e lo guarda arrossare il terreno. Anche il mare
tra non molto sarà come il fuoco, avvampante.

Non c'è cosa piú amara che l'alba di un giorno
in cui nulla accadrà. Non c'è cosa piú amara
che l'inutilità. Pende stanca nel cielo
una stella verdognola, sorpresa dall'alba.
Vede il mare ancor buio e la macchia di fuoco
a cui l'uomo, per fare qualcosa, si scalda;
vede, e cade dal sonno tra le fosche montagne
dov'è un letto di neve. La lentezza dell'ora
è spietata, per chi non aspetta piú nulla.

Val la pena che il sole si levi dal mare
e la lunga giornata cominci? Domani
tornerà l'alba tiepida con la diafana luce
e sarà come ieri e mai nulla accadrà.
L'uomo solo vorrebbe soltanto dormire.
Quando l'ultima stella si spegne nel cielo,
l'uomo adagio prepara la pipa e l'accende.

Morning Star over Calabria

The man alone rises when the sea is still dark
and the stars waver. A warmth like a breath
drifts up from the shore, where the sea has its bed,
and sweetens each breath. This is the hour when nothing
can happen. Even the pipe that hangs from his teeth
has gone out. At night, the sea's a soft splashing.
The man alone is burning a pile of branches
and watching it redden the ground. The sea too,
before long, will be like a flame — it will blaze.

Nothing's more bitter than the dawn of a day
in which nothing will happen. Nothing's more bitter
than uselessness. A pale greenish star
hanging tired in the sky, surprised by the dawn,
looks down on the still-dark sea and the spot of fire
where the man, to do something, is warming himself.
It looks, as it's falling asleep in its bed of snow
in the gloom of the mountains. The slowness of time,
for a man who knows nothing will happen, is brutal.

Is it worth the trouble for the sun to rise up
from the sea and begin the long day? Tomorrow
the warm dawn will return with its diaphanous light
and, just like yesterday, nothing will happen.
The man alone would like nothing more than to sleep.
When the last star has gone out in the sky,
the man slowly prepares his pipe and then lights it.

Part Three

Poems of
Disaffection

Frasi all'innamorata

Vado a spasso in silenzio con una bambina
abbordata per strada, lungo il viale, di sera,
il viale pieno d'alberi e di luci.
È il nostro terzo incontro.
La bambina è difficile nella scelta scabrosa:
al caffè non andiamo perché odiamo la folla,
al cinema neppure, perché la prima volta
siamo stati... perché... non dobbiamo piú farlo,
se tanto non ci amiamo.
                              Passeggiamo cosí,
fino a Po, fino al ponte, guarderemo i palazzi
di luce, che i lampioni fan nell'acqua.
La sazietà del terzo appuntamento.
So di lei tutto quanto può sapere un estraneo
che l'ha baciata e stretta in una sala buia,
dove altre coppie buie si stringevano
e l'orchestra—di un piano—suonava l'Aida.
Camminiamo nel viale, tra la gente.
Anche qui c'è un'orchestra che stride, che canta
ha un frastuono metallico come i tram che trabalzano.
Stringo a me la compagna e la guardo negli occhi:
ella mi guarda muta e mi sorride.
So di lei quanto ho sempre saputo di tutte,
che lavora, che è triste, e che, se le chiedessero
—«vuoi morire stanotte?»—direbbe di sí.
—«E la nostra avventura?»—«La nostra avventura è diversa,
ci lasceremo noi» (C'è un fidanzato in giro).

O mia bella bambina, stasera non sono il compagno
audace, che ti ha vinta, baciandoti per strada
sotto gli occhi di un vecchio signore stupito.
Questa sera cammino pensando tristezze,
come tu qualche volta pensi che vuoi morire.

Words for a Girlfriend

I walk without saying a word with a girl
I picked up on the street. It's evening,
the boulevard's lined with trees and with lights.
It's the third time we've met.
The girl makes the awkward decision more difficult:
cafés are ruled out since we can't stand the crowds,
the cinema, too, because of the first time
we went there... we shouldn't do that again,
if only because we aren't in love.
                              So let us keep walking
all the way to the Po, to the bridge, we'll look at the palaces
of light that the streetlamps make in the water.
The deadness of the third date.
I know of her all that can be known by a stranger
who has kissed and embraced her in a dark room
where other dark couples embraced,
where the orchestra—a single piano—played *Aida*.
We walk down the avenue, with everyone else.
Here too is an orchestra, screeching and singing,
a metallic commotion like the jolting of trams.
I pull her to me and look in her eyes:
she looks at me silent and smiling.
I know of her what I've always known about all girls:
that she works, that she's sad, and that, if I asked her,
"Do you want to die tonight?" she'd say yes.
"And our little affair?" "Our affair's something else,
it's only for now." (There's a boyfriend around.)

Oh beautiful girl, tonight I am not that boy,
audacious, who won you with a kiss on the street
in front of an old man who watched with astonishment.
This evening I walk with the saddest of thoughts,
like you when you say that you wish you could die.

Non ch'io voglia morire. È passato quel tempo
e, poi, «noi non ci amiamo». È la folla che passa
che mi preme e mi schiaccia, e anche tu sei la folla,
che, come tutti, mi cammini accanto.
Non ch'io t'odî, bambina—potresti pensarlo?—
ma sono solo e sempre sarò solo.

Ecco il Po.—«Com'è bello!... Stasera è un cristallo.
Le colonne di luce... e la curva del molo:
pare quasi, nel buio, la spiaggia del mare».
La compagna mi parla contenta e mi stringe:
dovrò anch'io abbracciarla piú stretto sul ponte.
Un'orchestra lontana c'insegue fin qui.
Le colline son buie.—«Verresti in collina?»
—«No, in collina. È lontano. Restiamo a guardare...»
Non desidero in fondo, stasera, nemmeno il tuo corpo,
o mia bella bambina, che pure sei viva
alla mano che cerca il tuo fianco.
So di te quanto ho sempre saputo di tutte:
che sei avida sotto la veste di seta azzurrina,
che lavori e sei triste e che un giorno sarai forse mia,
se vincerai—chi sa?—tutti gli scrupoli.
Ma in questo istante tacio e sono solo,
solo come sarò fino alla morte.
Non è orgoglio, bambina, da tempo ho scordato l'orgoglio,
ma non voglio, non voglio nessuno a stornarmi la vita.

—«Vuoi che andiamo un po' in barca, stasera?»—«Fa fresco, restiamo».
—«Ma no, staremo accanto»—«Ma è buio, si cade».
—«Cosa vuoi fare qui a guardare in aria?»
—«Ma qui è bello»—«Scendiamo. È piú bello dall'acqua.
Ci daranno il fanale». Le parlo, le stringo
la mano dolce e, goffo, le dò un bacio rapido
sulla guancia. Di sotto il caschetto di feltro mi fissa
e poi, quasi compunta, ripete—«Restiamo a guardare».

Not that I wish I could die. Those days have passed,
and besides, "we aren't in love." The crowd passes by,
pressing and crushing, and you too are the crowd,
like everyone else, you're walking beside me.
Not that I hate you — could you ever believe that? —
but I am alone, and I'll be alone always.

Here we are at the Po — "It's lovely — it's crystal this evening.
Columns of light... the curves of the dock:
it almost looks, in the dark, like the seashore."
She talks to me happily, holding me:
I should hold her more tightly, here on the bridge.
The distant orchestra has followed us here.
The hills are all dark. "Will you come to the hills?"
"Not to the hills, it's too far. Let's stay here and watch..."
I don't really desire even your body tonight,
my beautiful girl, even though you're alive
to my hand as it moves on your hip.
I know of you what I've always known about all girls:
that you're eager beneath the pale blue silk of your dress,
that you work and are sad and someday perhaps will be mine,
if you ever — and who knows? — abandon your scruples.
But I'm silent for now, and alone,
alone as I will be till death.
Nor is it pride, my girl, I've long since forgotten my pride,
it's just that I don't want anyone to turn me away from my life.

"How about a boat ride tonight?" "It's too cool, let's just stay here."
"No it's not, you'll be next to me." "But it's dark, we'll fall out."
"What do you want us to do here, staring off into space?"
"But it's beautiful here." "Come on. It's prettier still from the water.
They'll give us a lantern." I talk to her, holding
her sweet hand, and clumsily give her a peck
on the cheek. From beneath her felt hat she fixes me
and then, almost contritely, repeats: "Let's just stay here and watch."

Le maestrine

Le mie terre di vigne, di prugnoli e di castagneti
dove sono cresciute le frutta che ho sempre mangiato,
le mie belle colline—hanno un frutto migliore
che fantastico sempre e non ho morso mai.
Quando si hanno sei anni e si viene in campagna
solamente l'estate, è già molto riuscire
a scappar sulla strada e mangiar frutta acerba
coi ragazzotti scalzi, in pastura alle vacche.
Sotto il cielo d'estate, distesi nei prati,
si parlava di donne tra un gioco e una lite
e quegli altri sapevan misteri e misteri
sussurrati ghignando nell'ozio divino.
Sulla strada davanti alla villa si vedono ancora
—la domenica—parasolini passar dal paese;
ma è lontana la villa e non c'è piú ragazzi.

Mia sorella era allora ventenne. Venivano sempre
sul terrazzo a trovarci bei parasolini,
vesti chiare d'estate, parole ridenti:
maestrine. Parlavan magari di libri
imprestati tra loro—romanzi d'amore—
e di balli, di incontri. Io ascoltavo inquieto
e non pensavo ancora alle braccia scoperte,
ai capelli assolati. Il mio solo momento
era quando sceglievano me per guidare il gruppetto
a mangiare dell'uva e sedersi per terra.
Mi scherzavano insieme. Una volta mi chiesero
se non avevo già l'innamorata.
Fui seccato, piuttosto. Io stavo con loro
per distinguermi: come sapevo salire su un albero,
per trovare i bei grappoli e correre forte.

The Schoolmistresses

My land with its vineyards, its wild plums, its groves of chestnut,
where the fruits that I've eaten my whole life have grown,
my beautiful hills — they have a better fruit
that I always imagine and never have tasted.
When you're six and only come out to the country
in summertime, you're doing well if you manage
to get away from the house to eat sour fruit
with the barefoot kids in the cow pastures.
Under the summer sky, stretched out in the grass,
we talked about women between playing and fighting,
and the other kids knew all kinds of mysteries,
they whispered and sneered in our divine idleness.
On the road that runs past the summerhouse you can still see,
on Sundays, the little parasols passing from town;
but the summerhouse is far and the boys are long gone.

My sister was twenty. They always came out
onto the terrace to take up their parasols,
dressed in their summer whites, laughing their words:
the schoolmistresses. They might have been speaking of books
they'd loaned to each other — sentimental romances —
or of dances, or boys. I listened, vaguely disturbed,
but not thinking yet of their bare arms,
their shimmering hair. My single great moment
was when they would choose me to lead their small band
to eat grapes and sit on the ground.
They teased me, of course. One of them asked me
if I didn't already have a girlfriend.
I was annoyed. I stayed with them
so I could show off: how well I climbed trees
and found the best fruit, how fast I could run.

Una volta incontrai sulla Strada Ferrata
la piú schiva di queste ragazze, una faccia un po' assorta
ma bruciata di biondo e parlava italiano.
La chiamavano Flora. Io gettavo in quel mentre
sassi al disco dei treni. L'amica mi chiese
se sapevano a casa di quelle prodezze.
Io confuso. E la povera Flora mi prese con sé
perché andava—mi disse—a trovar mia sorella.
Era un gran pomeriggio dei primi d'estate
e per stare un po' all'ombra e arrivare piú presto
ci buttammo nei prati. Vicino a me Flora
mi chiedeva qualcosa che piú non ricordo.
Arrivammo a un ruscello ed io volli saltarlo:
finii mezzo nell'acqua, tra l'erba.
Dall'altra parte Flora rise forte,
poi si sedé e ordinò che non guardassi.
Ero tutto agitato. Sentivo sciacquare
la corrente, sciacquare e mi volsi improvviso.
Svelta com'era e forte nel corpo nascosto,
la mia amica scendeva la riva, le gambe scoperte,
abbagliante. (Era ricca Flora e non lavorava).
Mi rimproverò un poco coprendosi subito,
ma ridemmo alla fine e le porsi la mano.
Per la via del ritorno ero troppo felice.
Ma quando fummo a casa, niente busse.

Come Flora, a ventine ce n'è ai miei paesi.
Sono il frutto piú sano di quelle colline,
i parenti arricchiti le fanno studiare
e qualcuna ha mietuto nei campi. Hanno volti sicuri
che ti guardano seri e son tanto golosi:
signorine si vestono come in città.
Hanno nomi fantastici presi nei libri,
Flora, Lidia, Cordelia ed i grappoli d'uva,
i filari dei pioppi, non sono piú belli.
Me ne immagino sempre qualcuna che dica:

I once met, as I walked down the train tracks,
the shyest of these girls, who had a distracted air
and hair bleached by the sun. Her friends called her Flora,
and she didn't speak dialect. When I saw her,
I was throwing rocks at the train signal. She asked me
if my family was aware of this prowess of mine.
Confused me. Then poor Flora took me with her,
because she was headed, she said, to visit my sister.
It was a beautiful afternoon, early in summer,
and to have some shade and get there sooner
we cut through the fields. Close by my side,
Flora asked me a question I no longer remember.
We came to a stream I thought I could jump:
I landed half in the water, among weeds.
Flora laughed at me loudly from the bank,
then sat down and insisted I look away.
I was so nervous. When I heard the current
rinsing around her, I turned quickly toward her.
Graceful and strong in her hidden body,
she was descending the bank, her legs uncovered
and dazzling white. (She didn't work, she was rich.)
She scolded me briefly and covered up fast,
but soon we were laughing and I gave her my hand.
The rest of the way I was too happy.
And when we got to the house, no spanking.

There's a couple dozen like Flora in these parts.
They're the healthiest fruit of these hills,
with rich relatives who see that they study,
and a few even help in the fields. They look at you,
faces confident, serious, and full of desires:
they dress like the young city ladies.
They have fanciful names taken from books:
Flora, Lydia, Cordelia; and neither clusters of grapes
nor rows of poplars could be any lovelier.
I always imagine one of them saying:

Il mio sogno è di vivere fino a trent'anni
in una casa in cima a una collina
ben battuta dal vento e accudire soltanto
alle piante selvatiche spuntate lassú.
Sanno bene che cos'è la vita: alle scuole
passano in mezzo a tutte le miserie,
le bestialità aperte di piccoli bruti,
e sono sempre giovani. Da vecchie...
ma non voglio pensarle da vecchie, per me
le avrò sempre negli occhi, le mie maestrine,
col bel parasolino, vestite di chiaro,
—la collina un po' scabra e bruciata, per sfondo—
il *mio* frutto, il piú buono, che ogni anno rinnova.

My dream is to live until I'm thirty
in a house on the peak of a hill,
whipped by the wind, concerning myself
with only the plants that grow wild up there.
They know well what life is: at school
they pass among all possible miseries,
the frank brutalities of small beasts,
and they remain young. Once they are old…
but I can't stand to think of them old; for me,
in my mind's eye, they'll always be schoolmistresses,
with cute little parasols, dressed up in white —
the hill, rather rugged and scorched, as a backdrop —
my fruit, the best fruit, that each year returns.

Donne perdute

Hanno proprio ragione trattarle cosí.
E certo è meglio che compassionarle
col cuore e poi godersele nel letto.
«È un bisogno piú forte di tutta la vita»
di' piuttosto «e siam tutti dannati a quel passo;
ma se mai la ragazza mi facesse il mestiere
soffocherei di rabbia o saprei vendicarmi».

Sempre compassionare fu tempo perduto,
l'esistenza è tremenda e non muta per questo,
meglio stringere i denti e tacere.
                              Una sera
ho viaggiato su un treno che c'era una donna,
vesti sobrie, dipinta, serissima in faccia.
Fuori i lumi un po' pallidi e il verde un po' grigio
cancellavano il mondo. Eravamo isolati
nel vagone—una terza—la donna ed io giovane.
Non sapevo a quei tempi attaccare discorso
e piangevo pensando alle donne. Cosí
feci il viaggio osservando nervoso e quell'altra
mi guardò qualche volta e fumava. Non dissi,
non pensai certo nulla, ma ancora ho nel sangue
quello sguardo diretto, quel riso di un attimo
di chi ha ben lavorato ed ha preso la vita
come occorre, in silenzio.
                              Un amico, di quelli
che hanno in mente parole, vorrebbe salvare
una donna e asciugarle le lacrime e darle le gioie.
«No, è un bisogno piú forte di tutta la vita.
E noi, siamo dannati che han l'unica forza
in un'anima dura, che non serve a nulla».

Fallen Women

People are right to treat them like that.
It's certainly better than pitying them
in your heart before you enjoy them in bed.
"It's a need that's stronger than life itself,"
we should say, "a need that condemns us all;
but if my girl were ever to become one,
I'd choke with rage or else get my revenge."

Pity was always a waste of one's time.
Existence is terrible, pity won't change that.
It's better to keep quiet, jaws clenched.
                                    One evening
I was riding the train, a woman was next to me,
soberly dressed, made-up, a grave look on her face.
Outside the pale lights and the grayish green
erasing the world. Our compartment — third-class —
was an island, inhabited by only the two of us.
Back then I had no idea how to strike up talk
and I would cry to myself over women. And so,
on this trip, I nervously watched her, and she
glanced at me sometimes and smoked. I didn't say
or even think anything, but I can still feel in my blood
her frank gaze, that momentary laugh
of one who has known hard work and who takes life
as it comes, in silence.
                            A friend, one of those people
who know how to talk, would like to save
a woman and wipe her tears dry and give her some joy.
"No, it's a need that's stronger than life itself.
And we are condemned, we whose only strength
is a tough spirit, which doesn't do anyone good."

Le potete salvare a migliaia le donne
ma le tante che ho visto fumare e guardare
colla faccia sdegnosa o sorridere stanche
—le mie buone compagne—saran sempre vive
a soffrire in silenzio e pagare per tutti.

You could save thousands of women,
but all the ones I have seen smoking and gazing
with an indignant expression or a tired smile —
my dearest companions — they will always be there
to suffer in silence, paying for all of us.

Il Blues dei blues

Non c'è nulla di male a portare una bimba
nella propria stanza a sentire un gramofono.
Ma veniva il momento che i dischi morivano
soli e nessuno di noi due li ascoltava.
Si capisce—eravamo piú giovani ancora di loro
e quelle arie, quei suoni cantavano forte la vita.

Il male cominciò con me seduto
sul sofà e la ragazza che canterellando scendeva
a rimettere un disco dei soliti—un blues.
Erano cose gaie d'America, anche i blues
ma sentirli ripetere—sempre gli stessi—
e vederli ripetere, sempre, dalla medesima mano.

Ora—parlo soltanto di ieri—ma il giorno è venuto
che darei, darei tanto per tornare a vedere
la ragazza salirsene canterellando da me
e rimettere il disco d'un tempo—anche un blues.

The Blues Blues

There isn't anything wrong with bringing a girl
back to your room to listen to records.
But the moment would come when the records
died by themselves, neither one of us listening.
Understand — we were still younger than they were,
and those tunes, those sounds, were loud with life's power.

The bad part began with me on the sofa
and the girl, as she hummed, getting up
to replay the usual record — some blues.
Cheerful stuff from America, even the blues.
But hearing the same ones played and replayed,
and seeing them played, always, by the same hand —

This was just yesterday, but already today
I'd give quite a lot to go back to that time
when the girl would get up, humming to me,
and replay the old record — the usual blues.

Canzone

Le nuvole sono legate alla terra ed al vento.
Fin che ci saran nuvole sopra Torino
sarà bella la vita. Sollevo la testa
e un gran gioco si svolge lassú sotto il sole.
Masse bianche durissime e il vento vi circola
tutto azzurro—talvolta le disfa
e ne fa grandi veli impregnati di luce.
Sopra i tetti, a migliaia le nuvole bianche
copron tutto, la folla, le pietre e il frastuono.
Molte volte levandomi ho visto le nuvole
trasparire nell'acqua limpida di un catino.
Anche gli alberi uniscono il cielo alla terra.
Le città sterminate somiglian foreste
dove il cielo compare su su, tra le vie.
Come gli alberi vivi sul Po, nei torrenti
cosí vivono i mucchi di case nel sole.
Anche gli alberi soffrono e muoiono sotto le nubi
l'uomo sanguina e muore,—ma canta la gioia
tra la terra ed il cielo, la gran meraviglia
di città e di foreste. Avrò tempo domani
a rinchiudermi e stringere i denti. Ora tutta la vita
son le nubi le piante e le vie, perdute nel cielo.

Song

The clouds are bound to the earth and the wind.
As long as they gather high over Turin,
life will be good. I lift up my head
and watch the great game unfold in the sun.
Rock-hard white masses surrounded up there
by blue wind — at times it undoes them
and reshapes them into vast light-soaked sails.
Over the roofs, clouds by the thousand
cover all things: the crowds, the stones, the uproar.
Often I've risen and looked down to find
clouds gleaming in the basin's clear water.
Trees too bring together the sky and the earth.
And immense cities resemble the forests —
from down in the streets, we get glimpses of sky.
Like the vital trees on the banks of the Po,
heaps of houses live in torrents of sunlight.
Trees too suffer and die beneath clouds;
man bleeds, and he dies — but he sings his joy
between the earth and the sky, sings the great marvel
of cities and forests. Tomorrow there's time
to crawl into my shell, gritting my teeth. For now life's made
of clouds and of plants and of streets, all lost in the sky.

Il vino triste (1)

È un bel fatto che tutte le volte che siedo in un angolo
d'una tampa a sorbire il grappino, ci sia il pederasta
o i bambini che strillano o il disoccupato
o una bella ragazza che passa di fuori,
tutti a rompermi il filo del fumo. «È cosí, giovanotto,
ce lo dico davvero, lavoro a Lucento».
Ma la voce, la voce angosciata del vecchio
quarantenne — non so — che mi ha stretto la mano
nottetempo nel freddo e poi mi ha accompagnato
fino a casa, quel tono da vecchia cornetta,
non lo scordo, neanche se muoio.
Non diceva del vino, parlava con me
perché avevo studiato e fumavo la pipa.
«E chi fuma la pipa» esclamava tremando
«non può essere falso!» Approvai colla testa.

Ho trovato ragazze al ritorno, piú aperte, piú sane,
colle gambe scoperte — digiuno da mesi —
e mi sono sposato soltanto perché ero ubriaco
della loro freschezza — un amore senile.
Ho sposato la piú muscolosa e la piú impertinente
per sapere di nuovo la vita, per non piú morire
dietro un tavolo, dentro un ufficio, dinanzi ad estranei.
Ma anche Nella fu estranea per me e un allievo aviatore
me la vide una volta e ci mise le mani.
Ora è morto quel vile — quel povero giovane —
capotato nel cielo — no sono io il vile.
La mia Nella accudisce un bambino — non so se è mio figlio —
ed è tutta di casa e io sono un estraneo
che non sa accontentarla e non oso dir nulla
e anche Nella non parla, ma solo mi guarda.

Sad Wine (1)

It's a fine fact that whenever I sit in a tavern corner
sipping a grappa, the pederast's there, or the kids
with their screaming, or the unemployed guy,
or some beautiful girl outside — all breaking
the thread of my smoke. *That's how it is, kid,*
I'm telling it straight, I work at Lucento.
But that voice, the sorrowful voice of the old man
(forty-ish, maybe?) who shook my hand
one night in the cold and then walked with me back
to my house, that tone like an old cornet —
I'll never forget it, not even in death.
He said nothing of wine, but spoke to me then
because I had studied and was smoking a pipe.
"And pipe smokers," he declared, shaking a little,
"can always be trusted!" I nodded my head.

I came back to find the girls friendlier, healthier,
their skirts cut higher — this after months of hunger —
and I went and got married because I was drunk
on all their freshness — a senile love.
I married the sassiest, most muscular girl
so I'd taste life again, so I wouldn't die
behind a desk, in an office, surrounded by strangers.
But Nella too was a stranger to me, and a student pilot
saw her with me once, and later laid hands on her.
He's dead now, that coward — that poor kid —
spun out of the sky — I guess I'm the coward.
Now she's got her a baby — who knows if he's mine —
and she's home all the time and I'm just a stranger
who can't keep her happy. I don't dare say a word
and neither does Nella, she just looks at me.

E, il piú bello, piangeva quell'uomo a contarla,
come piange uno sbronzo, con tutto il suo corpo,
e mi cadeva addosso e diceva «Tra noi
sempre rispetto» ed io, a tremare nel freddo,
a cercare di andarmene, a dargli la mano.

Fa piacere sorbire il grappino, ma è un altro piacere
ascoltare gli sfoghi di un vecchio impotente
che è tornato dal fronte e vi chiede perdono.
Quali soddisfazioni ho mai io nella vita?
Ce lo dico davvero, lavoro a Lucento.
Quali soddisfazioni ho mai io nella vita?

It was beautiful how he cried as he told it,
the way a drunk cries, his whole body in it,
and he hung on my shoulder saying, *Between us,*
always respect, and there I was, shaking with cold,
wanting to leave, and helping him walk.

Sipping grappa is nice, but there's also a pleasure
in listening to the venting of an impotent old man
who's back from the front and asks your forgiveness.
What satisfaction will I ever have in this life?
I'm telling it straight, I work at Lucento.
What satisfaction will I ever have in this life?

Il ragazzo che era in me

Va' a sapere perché fossi là quella sera nei prati.
Forse mi ero lasciato cadere stremato di sole,
e fingevo l'indiano ferito. Il ragazzo a quei tempi
scollinava da solo cercando bisonti
e tirava le frecce dipinte e vibrava la lancia.
Quella sera ero tutto tatuato a colori di guerra.
Ora, l'aria era fresca e la medica pure
vellutata profonda, spruzzata dei fiori
rossogrigi e le nuvole e il cielo
s'accendevano in mezzo agli steli. Il ragazzo riverso
che alla villa sentiva lodarlo, fissava quel cielo.
Ma il tramonto stordiva. Era meglio socchiudere gli occhi
e godere l'abbraccio dell'erba. Avvolgeva come acqua.

Ad un tratto mi giunse una voce arrochita dal sole:
il padrone del prato, un nemico di casa,
che fermato a vedere la pozza dov'ero sommerso
mi conobbe per quel della villa e mi disse irritato
di guastar roba mia che potevo e lavarmi la faccia.
Saltai mezzo dall'erba. E rimasi, poggiato le mani,
a fissare tremando quel volto offuscato.

Oh la bella occasione di dare una freccia nel petto di un uomo!
Se il ragazzo non ne ebbe il coraggio, m'illudo a pensare
che sia stato per l'aria di duro comando che aveva quell'uomo.
Io che anche oggi mi illudo di agire impassibile e saldo
me ne andai quella sera in silenzio e stringevo le frecce
borbottando, gridando parole d'eroe moribondo.
Forse fu avvilimento dinanzi allo sguardo pesante
di che avrebbe potuto picchiarmi. O piuttosto vergogna
come quando si passa ridendo dinanzi a un facchino.
Ma ho il terrore che fosse paura. Fuggire, fuggii.
E, la notte, le lacrime e i morsi al guanciale
mi lasciarono in bocca sapore di sangue.

The Boy Who Was in Me

No telling why I was there in the fields that evening.
Maybe I'd dropped to the ground, worn out by the sun,
playing the wounded Indian. In those days the boy
roamed alone through the hills looking for buffalo,
shooting colorful arrows and shaking his spear.
That evening I was fully tattooed with war paint.
The air was fresh, the alfalfa as plush
as deep velvet, sprinkled with reddish gray flowers,
and the clouds and the sky caught fire
in the midst of those stalks. On his back, the boy stared
at that sky he'd so often heard praised at the summerhouse.
And the sunset astonished. I liked to half-close my eyes
and enjoy the embrace of the plants; they held me like water.

And then came a sudden and sun-roughened voice:
the alfalfa's owner, an old family nemesis,
had stopped at the pool where I lay submerged
and was telling me angrily to go ruin my own things,
since I could afford to, and to go wash my face.
I sprang halfway up. And froze, propped on my hands,
gaping and trembling at his shadow-dark face.

What a great chance to let fly an arrow into the chest of a man!
If the boy lacked courage, I like to pretend
it was only because of the man's cold air of authority.
I, who even today like to pretend to be cool and collected,
left with head bowed that evening, clutching my arrows
and muttering, shouting the words of a dying hero.
Dejected, perhaps, by the weight of the gaze
of a man who might thrash me. Or possibly shamed,
as when one happens to laugh in front of a beggar.
But I'm afraid it was fear. To escape, I escaped.
And that night, I cried and chewed hard on my pillow
and slept with the taste of blood in my mouth.

L'uomo è morto. La medica è stata divelta, erpicata
ma mi vedo chiarissimo il prato dinanzi
e, curioso, cammino e mi parlo, impassibile
come l'uomo alto e cotto dal sole parlò quella sera.

The man is now dead, the alfalfa long since harrowed up,
but that field is still vivid before me, and strangely
when I walk now and speak to myself, I'm as cold
as the tall sunbaked man who spoke on that evening to me.

Estate di San Martino

Le colline e le rive del Po sono un giallo bruciato
e noi siamo saliti quassú a maturarci nel sole.
Mi racconta costei—come fosse un amico—
Da domani abbandono Torino e non torno mai piú.
Sono stanca di vivere tutta la vita in prigione.
Si respira un sentore di terra e, di là dalle piante,
a Torino, a quest'ora, lavorano tutti in prigione.
Torno a casa dei miei dove almeno potrò stare sola
senza piangere e senza pensare alla gente che vive.
Là mi caccio un grembiale e mi sfogo in cattive risposte
ai parenti e per tutto l'inverno non esco mai piú.
Nei paesi novembre è un bel mese dell'anno:
c'è le foglie colore di terra e le nebbie al mattino,
poi c'è il sole che rompe le nebbie. Lo dico tra me
e respiro l'odore di freddo che ha il sole al mattino.
Me ne vado perché è troppo bella Torino a quest'ora:
a me piace girarci e vedere la gente
e mi tocca star chiusa finch'è tutto buio
e la sera soffrire da sola. Mi vuole vicino
come fossi un amico: quest'oggi ha saltato l'ufficio
per trovare un amico. *Ma posso star sola cosí?*
Giorno e notte—l'ufficio—le scale—la stanza da letto—
se alla sera esco a fare due passi non so dove andare
e ritorno cattiva e al mattino non voglio piú alzarmi.
Tanto bella sarebbe Torino—poterla godere—
solamente poter respirare. Le piazze e le strade
han lo stesso profumo di tiepido sole
che c'è qui tra le piante. Ritorni al paese.
Ma Torino è il piú bello di tutti i paesi.
Se trovassi un amico quest'oggi, starei sempre qui.

Indian Summer

The hills and banks of the Po are a burnt yellow,
and we've climbed here to get ripe in the sun.
This woman is telling me — as if we were friends —
Tomorrow I'm abandoning Turin, I'll never come back.
I'm tired of spending my whole life in a prison.
A faint scent of earth's in the air, as over the trees,
in Turin, right now, everyone labors in prison.
I'll go back to my parents', where I can at least be alone
without crying and thinking about people with lives.
I'll get me an apron and take comfort in being rude
to my family; I'll spend the whole winter indoors.
In the country, November's a beautiful month:
the earth-colored leaves, the fog in the morning
and the sun breaking through it. This to myself
as I breathe in the smell of the cold morning sun.
I'm leaving because Turin's too beautiful now:
I like wandering through it and watching the people,
but instead I'm cooped up until everything's dark,
to suffer the evenings alone. She wants me close by
as if we were friends: today she skipped work
to look for a friend. *Can I stay alone like that?*
Day and night — the office — the stairs — the bedroom.
If I go for a walk in the evening, there's nowhere to go,
I come home mean, the next day I don't want to get up.
Turin would be so beautiful — if you could enjoy it —
if you just had to breathe. The piazzas and streets
give off the same scent of warm sun
as these trees. You can go back to your town.
But Turin is the most beautiful of all towns.
If I were to find a friend today, I'd stay here forever.

Lavorare stanca (1)

I due, stesi sull'erba, vestiti, si guardano in faccia
tra gli steli sottili: la donna gli morde i capelli
e poi morde nell'erba. Sorride scomposta, tra l'erba.
L'uomo afferra la mano sottile e la morde
e s'addossa col corpo. La donna gli rotola via.
Mezza l'erba del prato è cosí scompigliata.
La ragazza, seduta, s'aggiusta i capelli
e non guarda il compagno, occhi aperti, disteso.

Tutti e due, a un tavolino, si guardano in faccia
nella sera, e i passanti non cessano mai.
Ogni tanto un colore piú gaio li distrae.
Ogni tanto lui pensa all'inutile giorno
di riposo, trascorso a inseguire costei,
che è felice di stargli vicina e guardarlo negli occhi.
Se le tocca col piede la gamba, sa bene
che si danno a vicenda uno sguardo sorpreso
e un sorriso, e la donna è felice. Altre donne che passano
non lo guardano in faccia, ma almeno si spogliano
con un uomo stanotte. O che forse ogni donna
ama solo chi perde il suo tempo per nulla.

Tutto il giorno si sono inseguiti e la donna è ancor rossa
alle guance, dal sole. Nel cuore ha per lui gratitudine.
Lei ricorda un baciozzo rabbioso scambiato in un bosco,
interrotto a un rumore di passi, e che ancora la brucia.
Stringe a sé il mazzo verde — raccolto sul sasso
di una grotta — di bel capelvenere e volge al compagno
un'occhiata struggente. Lui fissa il groviglio
degli steli nericci tra il verde tremante
e ripensa alla voglia di un altro groviglio,
presentito nel grembo dell'abito chiaro,
che la donna gli ignora. Nemmeno la furia

Work's Tiring (1)

Lying in grass, both dressed, they look at each other
through thin stalks: the woman bites his hair,
then a grass-blade. She smiles, disheveled, through grass.
The man takes hold of her thin hand and bites it,
then leans his body against her. She rolls away.
Half the grass in the field gets flattened like this.
The girl, sitting up, arranges her hair
without looking at him; he stares up at the sky.

They look at each other across a small table
in the evening, and people pass endlessly by.
Every so often a bright color distracts them.
Every so often he thinks of the wasted day
of rest, spent following a girl who's happy
just to be near him and look in his eyes.
If he touches her leg with his foot, he knows
they'll look at each other with wide-eyed surprise,
and smile, and then she'll be happy. Other women who pass
won't look in his eyes, but at least they'll undress
with a man tonight. Or perhaps every woman
loves only a man who'll waste his time for nothing.

They follow each other all day, and the woman is pink
in the cheeks from the sun. And grateful for him in her heart.
She recalls a rough, angry kiss exchanged in the woods,
interrupted by footsteps approaching, still burning her lips.
She clutches a green bunch of maidenhair, gathered
from stones down by the cave, and she gazes,
consumed, at her companion. He stares at the tangle
of dark stalks in the midst of the trembling green
and thinks again of his longing for a different tangling,
foreshadowed in the lap of her white frock,
a longing the woman ignores. Not even anger

non gli vale, perché la ragazza, che lo ama, riduce
ogni assalto in un bacio e gli prende le mani.

Ma stanotte, lasciatala, sa dove andrà:
tornerà a casa rotto di schiena e intontito,
ma assaporerà almeno nel corpo saziato
la dolcezza del sonno sul letto deserto.
Solamente, e quest'è la vendetta, s'immaginerà
che quel corpo di donna, che avrà come suo,
sia, senza pudori, in libidine, quello di lei.

avails him, because the girl, who loves him, reduces
every assault to a kiss and takes hold of his hands.

But tonight, having left her, he knows where he'll go.
He'll get home, his back aching and dazed,
but at least he will taste the sweetness of sleep
with a satisfied body, alone in his bed.
He will simply imagine, and this is his vengeance,
that the body of the woman he will make his
is, grown shameless and lustful, her body.

Gente non convinta

Questa pioggia che cade per piazze e per strade,
e in caserma e in collina, va tutta sprecata.
Domattina le piante saranno lavate,
lungo i viali, e il cortile in caserma bel molle,
da sfangarci al ginocchio: i lavori che fanno in città
sembran tutti quest'acqua che cade sui tetti.

> (Fuori, piova nel buio per tutte le strade,
> finirà che domani per terra c'è l'erba).

Si è veduto stasera venire giú l'acqua
per i fossi, in collina, e la terra ingiallita
dalle foglie e dal fango. Ma, sopra il sentore
della terra, uno sterile tanfo di fiori
che succhiavano l'acqua, e tra i fiori, le ville
che grondavano pioggia. Soltanto dall'altro versante,
arrivare sul vento un sentore di vigna.

> (Fuori, piova nel buio per piazze e per strade,
> non importa: c'è un vino che viene a scaldarci
> di un calore che ancora domani sapremo cos'è).

C'è un odore di pietra nel vento bagnato,
e per terra, soltanto rotaie. Le donne che passano
le conosce nessuno. Le donne in città
sono sempre diverse e non servono a niente.
Nel casino, là sí che gli odori son buoni
e le donne son brave. Ma vivono come in caserma
anche loro e il lavoro che fanno è una stupidità.

> (Non importa: le donne verranno a scaldarci
> di un calore che ancora domani sapremo cos'è).

The Unconvinced

This rain that falls on the streets and piazzas,
on the hills and the barracks, all of it's wasted.
In the morning the boulevards' bushes and trees
will be clean, and the barracks courtyard so wet
we'll have mud to our knees: the construction in town
is much like this water that falls on the roofs.

> (Outside, it rains in the dark on all the streets,
> we'll end up tomorrow with grass on the ground.)

The water's been seen coming down this evening
onto graves, onto hills, onto earth made yellow
by leaves and by mud. But over the scent
of the earth, the sterile stench of the flowers
that sucked up the water, and amid flowers the villas
that dripped with the rain. From over the hill,
the smell of a vineyard arrives on the wind.

> (Outside, it rains on the streets and piazzas —
> no matter: there's a wine that's coming to warm us
> with a heat that we'll still know tomorrow.)

There's the smell of stone on the wet wind,
nothing but rails on the ground. The women who pass,
nobody knows them. In the city, the women
are a different breed and not good for anything.
But a brothel, now there is a sweet-smelling place
where women are good. But they too are living
as if in a barracks, and their job is so stupid.

> (No matter: the women will be coming to warm us
> with a heat that we'll still know tomorrow.)

Fine della fantasia

Questo corpo mai piú ricomincia. A toccargli le occhiaie
uno sente che un mucchio di terra è piú vivo,
ché la terra, anche all'alba, non fa che tacere in se stessa.
Ma un cadavere è un resto di troppi risvegli.

Non abbiamo che questa virtú: cominciare
ogni giorno la vita—davanti alla terra,
sotto un cielo che tace—attendendo un risveglio.
Si stupisce qualcuno che l'alba sia tanta fatica;
di risveglio in risveglio un lavoro è compiuto.
Ma viviamo soltanto per dare in un brivido
al lavoro futuro e svegliare una volta la terra.
E talvolta ci accade. Poi torna a tacere con noi.

Se a sfiorare quel volto la mano non fosse malferma
—viva mano che sente la vita se tocca—
se davvero quel freddo non fosse che il freddo
della terra, nell'alba che gela la terra,
forse questo sarebbe un risveglio, e le cose che tacciono
sotto l'alba, direbbero ancora parole. Ma trema
la mia mano, e di tutte le cose somiglia alla mano
che non muove.
         Altre volte svegliarsi nell'alba
era un secco dolore, uno strappo di luce,
ma era pure una liberazione. L'avara parola
della terra era gaia, in un rapido istante,
e morire era ancora tornarci. Ora, il corpo che attende
è un avanzo di troppi risvegli e alla terra non torna.
Non lo dicon nemmeno, le labbra indurite.

Imagination's End

This body can never start over. Touching its eyelids
you'll know that a lump of clay's more alive,
since earth, even at dawn, merely turns inward in silence.
But a corpse is what's left after waking too often.

We have only this single virtue: to begin,
each morning, our life — in the face of the earth,
beneath a hushed sky — awaiting an awakening.
Some are amazed that dawn is such hard work;
from waking to waking a task is completed.
But we live merely to give with a shudder
to the future work and to wake up the earth once.
And sometimes it wakes. Then returns to our silence.

If the hand brushing that face were not so unsteady —
that living hand that feels life if it touches it —
if that cold were really nothing but the cold
of the earth, in the earth-freezing dawn, then perhaps
this would be an awakening, and all that's now silent
beneath dawn would again speak. But my hand
is shaking, and resembles of all things the hand
that is still.
              At other times, to awaken at dawn
was a sharp pain, a slashing of light,
but a liberation as well. The earth's stingy word
was happy for a moment, and to die was still to go back
to that place. Now, the body that's waiting is what's left
after waking too often, it won't return to the earth.
They can't even say it, the stiffening lips.

Gelosia (1)

Ci si siede di fronte e si vuotano i primi bicchieri
lentamente, fissando il rivale con l'occhio traverso.
Poi si aspetta che il vino gorgogli. Si guarda nel vuoto
canzonando. Se i muscoli tremano ancora
treman anche al rivale. Bisogna sforzarsi
per non bere di un fiato e sbronzarsi di colpo.

Oltre il bosco, si sente il ballabile e vedon lanterne
dondolanti—non sono restate che donne
sul palchetto. Lo schiaffo piantato alla bionda
ha portato via tutti a godersi lo scontro.
I rivali sentivano in bocca un sapore di rabbia
e di sangue; ora sentono il sapore del vino.
Per riempirsi di pugni bisogna esser soli
come a fare l'amore, ma c'è sempre la notte.

Sul palchetto i lampioni di carta e le donne
non stan fermi, nel fresco. La bionda, nervosa,
siede e cerca di ridere, ma s'immagina un prato
dove i due si dibattono e perdono sangue.
Li ha sentiti vociare di là dalle piante.
Malinconica, sopra il palchetto, una coppia di donne
gira in tondo; qualcuna fa cerchio alla bionda,
e s'informano se proprio le duole la faccia

Per riempirsi di pugni bisogna esser soli.
Tra i colleghi c'è sempre qualcuno che blatera
e fa fare le commedie. La gara del vino
non è mica uno sfogo: uno sente la rabbia
gorgogliare nel rutto e bruciare la gola.
Il rivale, piú calmo, dà mano al bicchiere
e lo vuota continuo. Ha finito il suo litro
e ne attacca un secondo. Il calore del sangue

Jealousy (1)

He sits out front and empties the first glasses
slowly, fixing his rival with an angled eye.
He waits for the wine to rumble. He looks into space
mockingly. If his muscles still tremble,
so do his rival's. He forces himself
not to gulp down his drinks and get instantly drunk.

Beyond the forest, he hears the dance music and sees
the swinging lanterns—there'd been only women
left on the platform. The slapping of the blonde
brought everyone else outside to enjoy the fight.
The rivals tasted the rage in their mouths
and blood; now they taste the flavor of wine.
To get their fill of punches they must be alone,
as you must for making love, but there's always the night.

On the platform, the paper lanterns and the women
are not still, in the coolness. The blonde, nervous,
is sitting and trying to laugh, but imagines a field
where the two rivals fight, each spilling blood.
She heard them shouting beyond the trees.
Gloomy, above the dance floor, a pair of women
turn in circles; one stands around the blonde,
asking if her face really hurts.

To fill up on punches you must be alone.
Among friends there's always someone who'll blab,
setting the dramas in motion. The wine competition
is not a release: he feels the rage
gurgling in a throat-burning belch.
The rival, now calmer, lays hands on his glass
and drains it. He's finished his liter
and starts in on another. The heat of his blood

manda in secco i bicchieri, come dentro una stufa.
I colleghi d'intorno hanno facce sbiancate
e oscillanti, le voci si sentono appena.
Il bicchiere, si cerca e non c'è. Per stanotte
—anche a vincere—la bionda torna a casa da sola.

leaves the glasses as dry as if they'd been in an oven.
The friends stand around, their faces white
and wavering, their voices just audible.
He looks for his glass. It's not there. For tonight,
the blonde, yet to be won, goes home by herself.

Il vino triste (II)

La fatica è sedersi senza farsi notare.
Tutto il resto poi viene da sé. Tre sorsate
e ritorna la voglia di pensarci da solo.
Si spalanca uno sfondo di lontani ronzii,
ogni cosa si sperde, e diventa un miracolo
esser nato e guardare il bicchiere. Il lavoro
(l'uomo solo non può non pensare al lavoro)
ridiventa l'antico destino che è bello soffrire
per poterci pensare. Poi gli occhi si fissano
a mezz'aria, dolenti, come fossero ciechi.

Se quest'uomo si rialza e va a casa a dormire,
pare un cieco che ha perso la strada. Chiunque
può sbucare da un angolo e pestarlo di colpi.
Può sbucare una donna e distendersi in strada,
bella e giovane, sotto un altr'uomo, gemendo
come un tempo una donna gemeva con lui.
Ma quest'uomo non vede. Va a casa a dormire
e la vita non è che un ronzio di silenzio.

A spogliarlo, quest'uomo, si trovano membra sfinite
e del pelo brutale, qua e là. Chi direbbe
che in quest'uomo trascorrono tiepide vene
dove un tempo la vita bruciava? Nessuno
crederebbe che un tempo una donna abbia fatto carezze
su quel corpo e baciato quel corpo, che trema,
e bagnato di lacrime, adesso che l'uomo,
giunto a casa a dormire, non riesce, ma geme.

Sad Wine (ii)

The hard thing's to sit without being noticed.
Everything else will come easy. Three sips
and the impulse returns to sit thinking alone.
Against the buzzing backdrop of noise
everything fades, and it's suddenly a miracle
to be born and to stare at a glass. And work
(a man who's alone can't not think of work)
becomes again the old fate that suffering's good
for focusing thought. And soon the eyes fix
on nothing particular, grieved, as if blind.

If this man gets up and goes home to sleep,
he'll look like a blind man who's lost. Anyone
could jump out of nowhere to brutally beat him.
A woman—beautiful, young—might appear,
and lie under a man in the street, and moan,
the way a woman once moaned under him.
But this man doesn't see. He heads home to sleep
and life becomes nothing but the buzzing of silence.

Undressing this man you'd find a body that's wasted
and, here and there, patches of fur. Who'd think,
to look at this man, that life once burned
in his lukewarm veins? No one would guess
that there was a woman, once, who gently touched
that body, who kissed that body, which shakes,
and wet it with tears, now that the man,
having come home to sleep, can't sleep, only moan.

Creazione

Sono vivo e ho sorpreso nell'alba le stelle.
La compagna continua a dormire e non sa.
Dormon tutti, i compagni. La chiara giornata
mi sta innanzi piú netta dei volti sommersi.

Passa un vecchio in distanza, che va a lavorare
o a godere il mattino. Non siamo diversi,
tutti e due respiriamo lo stesso chiarore
e fumiamo tranquilli a ingannare la fame.
Anche il corpo del vecchio dev'essere schietto
e vibrante—dovrebbe esser nudo davanti al mattino.

Stamattina la vita ci scorre sull'acqua
e nel sole: c'è intorno il fulgore dell'acqua
sempre giovane, i corpi di tutti saranno scoperti.
Ci sarà il grande sole e l'asprezza del largo
e la rude stanchezza che abbatte nel sole
e l'immobilità. Ci sarà la compagna
—un segreto di corpi. Ciascuno darà una sua voce.

Non c'è voce che rompe il silenzio dell'acqua
sotto l'alba. E nemmeno qualcosa trasale
sotto il cielo. C'è solo un tepore che scioglie le stelle.
Fa tremare sentire il mattino che vibra
tutto vergine, quasi nessuno di noi fosse sveglio.

Creation

I'm alive and at daybreak I've startled the stars.
My companion continues to sleep unaware.
All companions are sleeping. The day is a clear one
and stands sharper before me than faces in water.

In the distance an old man is walking to work
or enjoying the morning. We aren't so different,
we both breathe the same faint glimmer of light
as we casually smoke, beguiling our hunger.
The old man, too, must have a body that's pure
and vital—he ought to stand naked facing the morning.

Life this morning flows out over water
and in sunlight: around us the innocent splendor
of water, and all the bodies will soon be uncovered.
There'll be a bright sun and the sharpness of sea air
and the harsh exhaustion that beats down in sunlight
and stillness. And my companion will be here—
a shared secret of bodies, each with its own voice.

There's no voice to break the silence of water
at dawn. And neither is anything moving
beneath this sky. There's only a star-melting warmth.
One shudders to feel the morning trembling
so virginally, as if none of us here were awake.

La pace che regna

Il piacere del vecchio è sorprendere le ultime stelle
sotto l'alba, poi bere una volta e girare per strada.
Uno ha sempre saputo che il mondo finisce cosí:
ci si trova fra visi di gente inaudita,
e non basta guardarli e pensarci con calma.

Il mio vecchio comincia dall'alba a girare le strade
e nessuno s'accorge che guarda e ci pensa,
lui, che un tempo era giovane, com'è giovane il mondo.
Non c'è un cane che sappia com'è il corpo del vecchio,
nudo e debole, e come il mattino trascorra per lui,
mentre lui vede i corpi di giovani e donne
e di tutti conosce il vigore. Ma gli occhi dei giovani
che non badano al vecchio, trascorrono in strada
inquieti, e hanno tutti una vita che il vecchio non sa.

Certamente, le strade son sempre le stesse
e il mattino ha lo stesso splendore. Ma un giovane
che picchiasse e piombasse sui sassi il mio vecchio
non sarebbe che giusto. E il mio vecchio non sa,
benché pensi a ogni cosa, che questa è la sorte:
pensa ai giovani e ai vecchi che son tutta la vita.

Inquieto è anche il vecchio al pensiero che un giorno
saran vecchi anche questi, e nessuno saprà
con che sguardo gli ignoti urteranno le cose.
Ma un'occhiata sul mondo la stende chiunque
e al mattino ogni cosa si sveglia. Invecchiando,
sarà ancora un piacere sorprendere l'alba
e discendere in strada tra la folla vivente.

Reigning Peace

The old man likes to surprise the last of the stars
at dawn, then have a drink and stroll down the street.
Everyone knows that this is how the world ends:
you find yourself in a crowd of ridiculous people
and it's no good to stare or consider them calmly.

This old man begins strolling the streets at dawn
and no one's aware that he stares and considers,
he who was young once, as the world is young now.
Not even a dog knows what his body is like,
naked and weak, or how he spends his mornings,
watching the bodies of young men and women,
still knowing their vigor. But the young, whose eyes
don't notice the old man, wander the streets,
restless, each with a life he knows nothing about.

The streets remain as they were, of course,
and the mornings retain their splendor. But a youth
who decided to beat him or throw him on rocks
would be nothing but just. The old man doesn't know,
though he thinks about everything, that this is fate:
think of the young and the old that are all of our lives.

He's restless too at the thought that one day
even the young will grow old, and no one will know
with what gaze strangers will knock against things.
But a glance at the world will lay anyone out,
and everything wakes in the morning. Getting older,
he'll still take pleasure surprising the dawn
and walking down streets among throngs of the living.

Altri tempi

Anche il povero scemo che ha un occhio fiaccato
sanguinante, strizzandomi l'altro, rinvanga il suo sogno.

Occhi acuti, vedevano persino di notte;
e le spose, era inutile che spegnessero il lume.
Come un gatto. Gli uccelli passavano a volo
anche sopra le nubi, ma lui li arrivava
come noci sull'albero. Nei sereni d'inverno
sulla luna vedeva le montagne di ghiaccio.

Grandi muscoli aveva: portava il quintale
prima ancora dei baffi. Prendeva la pioggia
tutto un giorno d'inverno, che la pelle fumava,
e nemmeno tossiva. Le ragazze con lui
eran piú che contente: le lasciava per morte.
Nelle risse lasciava per morto il rivale:
le ragazze tornavano, ché godevano troppo
a morire in quel modo, ma un rivale abbattuto
non tornava. Per vivere ci vuole coraggio.
E per ogni rivale buttato sui sassi
c'è un bastardo di piú sotto il sole.
                              Ogni volta
le figliole le pensa piú belle e i figlioli piú grandi;
tutti han occhi da gatto. Se li sogna di notte.
Quello vero, che gira con lui, fa spavento:
non si passa l'estate a grattarsi i pidocchi
senza empirsi di croste. Si direbbe che mangiano
l'uno le ossa dell'altro. Anche il piccolo è guercio
ma capisce. Raccoglie le cicche e le fuma da sé.

Anche il povero scemo fumava, ai suoi tempi
quando aveva la vista e le donne. Mangiava
tutti i giorni, servito da una bella ragazza,

Other Days

Even the poor fool with one broken, bloody eye,
as he winks at me with the other, dredges up his dream.

Sharp eyes, they could see even in darkness;
it was pointless for brides to turn out the light.
Like a cat. And birds would fly overhead,
over clouds even, but he would reach up
and pluck them like fruit. Beneath winter's clear skies,
he could see the mountains of ice on the moon.

He was a muscular boy: he could carry a quintal
before he had whiskers. He worked in the rain
all day long one winter, skin steaming,
and never coughed once. The girls he went out with
were more than thrilled; he left them for dead.
In brawls he would leave his rivals for dead:
the girls would come back—they were too fond
of dying that way. But a rival, once beaten,
never came back. It takes courage to live.
And for every rival he left lying in gravel,
one bastard more walks the earth.
                         Each time
he thinks the daughters prettier and the sons bigger;
they all have cat eyes. If he dreams them at night.
His legitimate son—they're always together—is frightening:
you can't spend the whole summer scratching at lice
and not be covered with scabs. You might say
he didn't fall far from the tree. The little one's cross-eyed
but not dumb. He gathers up butts and smokes them.

Even the poor fool used to smoke, in his day,
when he had his sight and his women. He ate
every day, with a beautiful girl who served him his food

che gli dava anche il vino. Fin che un giorno s'accorse
di esser scemo e d'allora il ragazzo lo guida
sulla pubblica strada, di mattino in mattino.

and poured him his wine. Until one day he realized
he was stupid, and since then the boy guides him
through the public streets, morning after morning.

Poetica

Il ragazzo s'è accorto che l'albero vive.
Se le tenere foglie si schiudono a forza
una luce, rompendo spietate, la dura corteccia
deve troppo soffrire. Pure vive in silenzio.
Tutto il mondo è coperto di piante che soffrono
nella luce, e non s'ode nemmeno un sospiro.
È una tenera luce. Il ragazzo non sa
donde venga, è già sera; ma ogni tronco rileva
sopra un magico fondo. Dopo un attimo è buio.

Il ragazzo — qualcuno rimane ragazzo
troppo tempo — che aveva paura del buio,
va per strada e non bada alle case imbrunite
nel crepuscolo. Piega la testa in ascolto
di un ricordo remoto. Nelle strade deserte
come piazze, s'accumula un grave silenzio.
Il passante potrebbe esser solo in un bosco,
dove gli alberi fossero enormi. La luce
con un brivido corre i lampioni. Le case
abbagliate traspaiono nel vapore azzurrino,
e il ragazzo alza gli occhi. Quel silenzio remoto
che stringeva il respiro al passante, è fiorito
nella luce improvvisa. Sono gli alberi antichi
del ragazzo. E la luce è l'incanto d'allora.

E comincia, nel diafano cerchio, qualcuno
a passare in silenzio. Per la strada nessuno
mai rivela la pena che gli morde la vita.
Vanno svelti, ciascuno come assorto nel passo,
e grandi ombre barcollano. Hanno visi solcati
e le occhiaie dolenti, ma nessuno si lagna.
Tutta quanta la notte, nella luce azzurrina,
vanno come in un bosco, tra le case infinite.

Poetics

The boy is aware that the tree is alive.
If the tender leaves force themselves open,
bursting ruthlessly into the light, the hard bark
must suffer extremely. And it lives in silence.
The whole world is covered with plants that suffer
in light, not daring even to breathe.
A tender light, its source unknown to the boy.
It's evening already, but each trunk stands out
against a magical background. In a moment it's dark.

The boy — and some men remain boys
for too long — who once was afraid of the dark,
walks down the street, not minding the twilight
that darkens the houses. He listens, head bowed,
to a distant memory. In the emptied-out streets
that seem like piazzas, a grave silence gathers.
A person can feel he's alone in a forest
where the trees are enormous. The light
shudders through streetlamps. The houses
are dazzling, transparent in the bluish vapor,
and the boy raises his eyes. The distant silence
that can tighten a person's breath has flowered
in the sudden light. These are the boy's
ancient trees. And the light is the spell of that time.

And somebody now is walking silently past,
through the diaphanous circle. On the street, no one
ever reveals the pain that gnaws at their life.
They move quickly, as if absorbed in their stride,
their great shadows staggering. Their faces are furrowed,
their eyes full of grief, but no one complains.
And all through the night, in a bluish haze,
they move as if through a forest, among infinite houses.

Alter ego

Dal mattino alla sera vedevo il tatuaggio
sul suo petto setoso: una donna rossastra
fitta, come in un prato, nel pelo. Là sotto
mugge a volte un tumulto, che la donna sussulta.
La giornata passava in bestemmie e silenzî.
Se la donna non fosse un tatuaggio, ma viva
aggrappata sul petto peloso, quest'uomo
muggirebbe piú forte, nella piccola cella.

Occhi aperti, disteso sul letto taceva.
Un respiro profondo di mare saliva
dal suo corpo di grandi ossa salde: era steso
come sopra una tolda. Pesava sul letto
come chi s'è svegliato e potrebbe balzare.
Il suo corpo, salato di schiuma, grondava
un sudore solare. La piccola cella
non bastava all'ampiezza d'una sola sua occhiata.
A vedergli le mani si pensava alla donna.

Alter Ego

From morning till evening I'd watch the tattoo
on his bristly chest: a reddish woman,
planted, as if in a field, on his skin. From beneath
rose occasional noises, which startle the woman.
The day would pass in curses and silence.
If the woman were not a tattoo, but alive
and clinging to the hair on his chest, this man
would moan even louder in his little cell.

Eyes open, he'd lie on the bed in silence.
A deep ocean breath would rise up
from his solid-boned body: he'd stretch out
as if on a boat's deck. He sank in the bed
like one freshly woken who might suddenly rise.
His body, salty with spray, would drip
a sun-tinged sweat. His cell was too small
to contain even the slightest of the man's glances.
Seeing his hands, you'd think of the woman.

Abbozzo di paesaggio

Sulla strada camminano porci e ragazze
con un sacco sul capo; le stille di pioggia
vengon giú sbatacchiate dal vento. Sorride
ogni pozza, d'un grigio azzurrino, alle nubi.

Sulla piazza la gente non può litigare,
ma s'accolgono tutti con capre e maiali
contro i muri. Da un muro di cinta scrostato
s'erge saldo l'ammasso fiorito di un albero.

Sketch of a Landscape

The pigs and the girls with sacks on their heads
walk through the streets; droplets of rain
are whipped by the wind as they fall. Each puddle,
with its pale blue-gray face, smiles at the clouds.

In the piazza the people can't seem to argue,
they accommodate everyone, and goats and hogs,
along the town walls. Where mortar has crumbled,
there rises the solid flowering mass of a tree.

Ritorno di Deola

Torneremo per strada a fissare i passanti
e saremo passanti anche noi. Studieremo
come alzarci al mattino deponendo il disgusto
della notte e uscir fuori col passo di un tempo.
Piegheremo la testa al lavoro di un tempo.
Torneremo laggiú, contro il vetro, a fumare
intontiti. Ma gli occhi saranno gli stessi
e anche i gesti e anche il viso. Quel vano segreto
che c'indugia nel corpo e ci sperde lo sguardo
morirà lentamente nel ritmo del sangue
dove tutto scompare.

                  Usciremo un mattino,
non avremo piú casa, usciremo per via;
il disgusto notturno ci avrà abbandonati;
tremeremo a star soli. Ma vorremo star soli.
Fisseremo i passanti col morto sorriso
di chi è stato battuto, ma non odia e non grida
perché sa che da tempo remoto la sorte
—tutto quanto è già stato o sarà—è dentro il sangue,
nel sussurro del sangue. Piegheremo la fronte
soli, in mezzo alla strada, in ascolto di un'eco
dentro il sangue. E quest'eco non vibrerà piú.
Leveremo lo sguardo, fissando la strada.

Deola's Return

We'll watch in the street as people pass by
and we'll just be passing by, too. We'll learn
to get up in the morning, forgetting the bad taste
of night; we'll go out at a leisurely pace.
We'll go back, our head bowed, to our old job.
We'll go back and look out the window and smoke
in a daze. But our eyes will still be the same,
and our face, and our gestures. And the vain secret
that lingers in flesh and disperses a gaze
will gradually die to the rhythm of blood
where all things fade.

                      We'll go out some morning,
we won't have a house, we'll go into the street—
the bad taste of night will have finally left us—
we'll tremble at being alone. But we'll want it.
Anyone passing will meet the dead smile
of one who's been beaten, but won't hate or cry out,
knowing that ever since ancient times fate—
all that has been or will be—abides in the blood,
in the whisper of blood. We'll bow our head,
alone, in the street, to listen for echoes
in the blood. And the echoes then will be gone.
We'll lift our eyes, fixing our gaze on the street.

Abitudini

Sull'asfalto del viale la luna fa un lago
silenzioso e l'amico ricorda altri tempi.
Gli bastava in quei tempi un incontro improvviso
e non era piú solo. Guardando la luna,
respirava la notte. Ma piú fresco l'odore
della donna incontrata, della breve avventura
per le scale malcerte. La stanza tranquilla
e la rapida voglia di viverci sempre,
gli riempivano il cuore. Poi, sotto la luna,
a gran passi intontiti tornava, contento.

A quei tempi era un grande compagno di sé.
Si svegliava al mattino e saltava dal letto,
ritrovando il suo corpo e i suoi vecchi pensieri.
Gli piaceva uscir fuori prendendo la pioggia
o anche il sole, godeva a guardare le strade,
a parlare con gente improvvisa. Credeva
di saper cominciare cambiando mestiere
fino all'ultimo giorno, ogni nuovo mattino.
Dopo grandi fatiche sedeva fumando.
Il piacere piú forte era starsene solo.

È invecchiato l'amico e vorrebbe una casa
che gli fosse piú cara, e uscir fuori la notte
e fermarsi sul viale a guardare la luna,
ma trovare al ritorno una donna sommessa,
una donna tranquilla, in attesa paziente.
È invecchiato l'amico e non basta piú a sé.
I passanti son sempre gli stessi; la pioggia
e anche il sole, gli stessi; e il mattino, un deserto.
Faticare non vale la pena. E uscir fuori alla luna,
se nessuno l'aspetti, non vale la pena.

Habits

On the avenue's asphalt the moon makes a lake
of silence; my friend is recalling the past.
In those days, for him, a chance meeting sufficed
and he wouldn't be lonely. Watching the moon,
he'd breathe the night in. But fresher the scent
of the woman he'd met, of the brief romance
on precarious stairs. The comfortable room
and the sudden desire to live there forever—
they'd fatten his heart. Then, in the moonlight,
with great dazed strides he'd go home, contented.

In those days he kept himself company well.
He'd wake in the morning and jump out of bed,
finding his body still there and his thoughts.
He used to like going for walks in the rain
or the sun, enjoying the spectacle of streets
and talking to people he met. He believed
he could start, if he wanted, a new line of work
with every new morning, till the end of his days.
And after a hard day, he'd sit there and smoke.
His most powerful pleasure was being alone.

My friend's gotten older, he'd like for his house
to mean more than it does, he'd like to go out
and stop on the street to look at the moon,
and on the way back encounter a woman,
submissive and calm, patiently waiting.
My friend's gotten older, he isn't enough
for himself anymore. Always the same passersby,
the same rain, the same sun, and morning's a desert.
There's no point in working. And walking in moonlight,
if no one's waiting, there's no point in that.

Estate (II)

È riapparsa la donna dagli occhi socchiusi
e dal corpo raccolto, camminando per strada.
Ha guardato diritto tendendo la mano,
nell'immobile strada. Ogni cosa è riemersa.

Nell'immobile luce del giorno lontano
s'è spezzato il ricordo. La donna ha rialzato
la sua semplice fronte, e lo sguardo d'allora
è riapparso. La mano si è tesa alla mano
e la stretta angosciosa era quella d'allora.
Ogni cosa ha ripreso i colori e la vita
allo sguardo raccolto, alla bocca socchiusa.

È tornata l'angoscia dei giorni lontani
quando tutta un'immobile estate improvvisa
di colori e tepori emergeva, agli sguardi
di quegli occhi sommessi. È tornata l'angoscia
che nessuna dolcezza di labbra dischiuse
può lenire. Un immobile cielo s'accoglie
freddamente, in quegli occhi.
                              Era calmo il ricordo
alla luce sommessa del tempo, era un docile
moribondo cui già la finestra s'annebbia e scompare.
Si è spezzato il ricordo. La stretta angosciosa
della mano leggera ha riacceso i colori
e l'estate e i tepori sotto il vivido cielo.
Ma la bocca socchiusa e gli sguardi sommessi
non dan vita che a un duro inumano silenzio.

Summer (ii)

She's back, the woman with half-closed eyes
and reticent body, she appeared on the street.
She looked straight ahead and held out her hand
in the motionless street. Each detail resurfaced.

In the motionless light of that distant day
memory shattered. The woman raised up
her forehead a little, and that old simple look
reappeared. A hand stretching out toward a hand,
the old tensing anxiety. Everything
recovered its color and life in the presence
of that reticent glance, that half-closed mouth.

Again the anxiety of those distant days
when the whole of a motionless summer became
unexpectedly vivid and warm, in the gaze
of those subdued eyes. Again the anxiety
that not even the sweetness of half-open lips
can assuage. A motionless sky is gathering
coldly, in those eyes.
                          In time's subdued light
memory was calm, something docile and dying
whose window already was clouded and fading.
Memory shattered. The tensing anxiety
of her delicate hand has rekindled colors
and summer and warmth beneath the bright sky.
But the half-closed mouth and subdued glances
inspire nothing but a hard, inhuman silence.

Sogno

Ride ancora il tuo corpo all'acuta carezza
della mano o dell'aria, e ritrova nell'aria
qualche volta altri corpi? Ne ritornano tanti
da un tremore del sangue, da un nulla. Anche il corpo
che si stese al tuo fianco, ti ricerca in quel nulla.

Era un gioco leggero pensare che un giorno
la carezza dell'aria sarebbe riemersa
improvviso ricordo nel nulla. Il tuo corpo
si sarebbe svegliato un mattino, amoroso
del suo stesso tepore, sotto l'alba deserta.
Un acuto ricordo ti avrebbe percorsa
e un acuto sorriso. Quell'alba non torna?

Si sarebbe premuta al tuo corpo nell'aria
quella fresca carezza, nell'intimo sangue,
e tu avresti saputo che il tiepido istante
rispondeva nell'alba a un tremore diverso,
un tremore dal nulla. L'avresti saputo
come un giorno lontano sapevi che un corpo
era steso al tuo fianco.
                              Dormivi leggera
sotto un'aria ridente di labili corpi,
amorosa di un nulla. E l'acuto sorriso
ti percorse sbarrandoti gli occhi stupiti.
Non è piú ritornata, dal nulla, quell'alba?

Dream

Your body still laughs at the piercing caress
of a hand or the air—rediscovering perhaps
other bodies in that air? So many return
in a tremor of blood, in nothing. Even the body
lying beside you, seeks you in that nothing.

It was a frivolous game to think that someday
the gentle touch of the air would return—
a sudden memory of nothing. Your body
would have woken one morning, in love with
its own warmth, beneath a deserted dawn.
A memory would have pierced you right through,
a smile would have pierced. That dawn won't return?

That cool, gentle touch of the air would have pressed
into your body, into your intimate blood,
and you would have known that that tepid moment
was answering in the dawn a different tremor,
the tremor of nothing. You would have known
the way you once knew, long ago, that a body
was lying beside you.
                              In love with that nothing,
you slept lightly then, the air laughing above you
full of transient bodies. And the smile that pierces
right through you widens your eyes with amazement.
That dawn: didn't it ever return, out of nothing?

L'amico che dorme

Che diremo stanotte all'amico che dorme?
La parola piú tenue ci sale alle labbra
dalla pena piú atroce. Guarderemo l'amico,
le sue inutili labbra che non dicono nulla,
parleremo sommesso.
                    La notte avrà il volto
dell'antico dolore che riemerge ogni sera
impassibile e vivo. Il remoto silenzio
soffrirà come un'anima, muto, nel buio.
Parleremo alla notte che fiata sommessa.

Udiremo gli istanti stillare nel buio
al di là delle cose, nell'ansia dell'alba,
che verrà d'improvviso incidendo le cose
contro il morto silenzio. L'inutile luce
svelerà il volto assorto del giorno. Gli istanti
taceranno. E le cose parleranno sommesso.

Sleeping Friend

What will we say now to our sleeping friend?
The weakest of words will leap to our lips
from the deepest pain. We'll look at our friend,
his useless lips that say nothing at all,
we'll speak to him softly.
                              The face of the night
will be an old wound that reopens each evening,
impassive and living. The distant silence
will ache like a soul, mute, in the dark.
We'll speak to the night as it's whispering softly.

We'll hear each moment drip into darkness
beyond all things, in the anguish of dawn,
whose sudden appearance etches things into
dead silence. The useless light will reveal
the distracted face of the day. Each moment
will fall silent. And all things will speak softly.

Indifferenza

È sbocciato quest'odio come un vivido amore
dolorando, e contempla se stesso anelante.
Chiede un volto e una carne, come fosse un amore.

Sono morte la carne del mondo e le voci
che suonavano, un tremito ha colto le cose;
tutta quanta la vita è sospesa a una voce.
Sotto un'estasi amara trascorrono i giorni
alla triste carezza della voce che torna
scolorandoci il viso. Non senza dolcezza
questa voce al ricordo risuona spietata
e tremante: ha tremato una volta per noi.

Ma la carne non trema. Soltanto un amore
la potrebbe incendiare, e quest'odio la cerca.
Tutte quante le cose e la carne del mondo
e le voci, non valgono l'accesa carezza
di quel corpo e quegli occhi. Nell'estasi amara
che distrugge se stessa, quest'odio ritrova
ogni giorno uno sguardo, una rotta parola,
e li afferra, insaziabile, come fosse un amore.

Indifference

This hate, having bloomed with the brilliance
of love that suffers, regards itself gasping.
It seeks flesh and a face, as if it were love.

The flesh of the world, the sounds of its voices
are dead, everything seized by a chill;
the whole of life now hangs on a voice.
Suspended in bitter rapture the days pass
to the sad caress of the voice that returns
to drain blood from our face. Not without sweetness
this voice, resounding in memory ruthless
and trembling: at one time it trembled for us.

But the flesh doesn't tremble. Only a love
could set it on fire, and this hatred seeks flesh.
All things—all the flesh of the world,
all its voices—fall short of the burning caress
of that body, those eyes. This hatred,
in its bitter, self-ruining rapture, discovers
each day a particular look, a broken word,
and grabs hold of it, hungrily, as if it were love.

Gelosia (II)

L'uomo vecchio ha la terra di giorno, e di notte
ha una donna ch'è sua — ch'era sua fino a ieri.
Gli piaceva scoprirla, come aprire la terra,
e guardarsela a lungo, supina nell'ombra
attendendo. La donna sorrideva occhi chiusi.

L'uomo vecchio stanotte è seduto sul ciglio
del suo campo scoperto, ma non scruta la chiazza
della siepe lontana, non distende la mano
a divellere un'erba. Contempla fra i solchi
un pensiero rovente. La terra rivela
se qualcuno vi ha messo le mani e l'ha infranta:
lo rivela anche al buio. Ma non c'è donna viva
che conservi la traccia della stretta dell'uomo.

L'uomo vecchio si è accorto che la donna sorride
solamente occhi chiusi, attendendo supina,
e comprende improvviso che sul giovane corpo
passa in sogno la stretta di un altro ricordo.
L'uomo vecchio non vede piú il campo nell'ombra.
Si è buttato in ginocchio, stringendo la terra
come fosse una donna e sapesse parlare.
Ma la donna distesa nell'ombra, non parla.

Dov'è stesa occhi chiusi la donna non parla
né sorride, stanotte, dalla bocca piegata
alla livida spalla. Rivela sul corpo
finalmente la stretta di un uomo: la sola
che potesse segnarla, e le ha spento il sorriso.

Jealousy (11)

The old man, by day, has the land, and by night
a woman, his woman—his until yesterday.
He liked to discover her, like opening earth,
to watch her at length as she lay in the shadows
and waited. She would smile with closed eyes.

The old man tonight sits on the edge
of his wide-open field, ignoring the stain
of the hedge in the distance, not lifting a finger
to pluck a stray weed. He stares at the furrows,
a thought burning through him. Earth will reveal
where someone has touched it and broken it up,
even in darkness. But no woman alive
retains visible marks of a lover's embrace.

The old man noticed the woman would smile
only with closed eyes, stretched out and waiting,
but now for the first time he grasps that her body
dreamed of some other remembered embrace.
The old man no longer can see the dark field.
He falls to the ground, grabbing at dirt,
as if dirt were a woman and knew how to speak.
But the woman stretched out in the dark won't speak.

She's lying tonight with eyes closed, not speaking
or smiling, not now—her mouth angles down
toward her discolored shoulder. Her body reveals,
at last, the embrace of a man: the only embrace
that could have marked her, and it put out her smile.

Risveglio

Lo ripete anche l'aria che quel giorno non torna.
La finestra deserta s'imbeve di freddo
e di cielo. Non serve riaprire la gola
all'antico respiro, come chi si ritrovi
sbigottito ma vivo. È finita la notte
dei rimpianti e dei sogni. Ma quel giorno non torna.

Torna a vivere l'aria, con vigore inaudito,
l'aria immobile e fredda. La massa di piante
infuocata nell'oro dell'estate trascorsa
sbigottisce alla giovane forza del cielo.
Si dissolve al respiro dell'aria ogni forma
dell'estate e l'orrore notturno è svanito.
Nel ricordo notturno l'estate era un giorno
dolorante. Quel giorno è svanita, per noi.

Torna a vivere l'aria e la gola la beve
nella vaga ansietà di un sapore goduto
che non torna. E nemmeno non torna il rimpianto
ch'era nato stanotte. La breve finestra
beve il freddo sapore che ha dissolta l'estate.
Un vigore ci attende, sotto il cielo deserto.

Awakening

Even the air insists that that day won't return.
The deserted window drinks in the cold
and the sky. It's useless to open one's throat
to breathe the old way, as anyone knows
who's left stunned but alive. It's finished, the night
of dreams and regrets. But that day won't return.

The air that was cold and still, pulses again
with unheard-of energy. The profusion of plants,
aflame with the gold of the summer that's gone,
is amazed by the youthful strength of the sky.
Each shape of summer dissolves on breathing
this air, and the horror of night is over.
In night's memory, summer was a day
of suffering. A day that, for us, is now over.

The air pulses again and the throat drinks it in,
in the vague anxiety of a taste we've enjoyed
that will never return. Nor will the regret
that was born tonight. The brief window
drinks the cold taste that dissolved the summer.
New strength awaits us beneath the blank sky.

Paesaggio (ix)

Molte volte al mattino, sul gelo dell'acqua
una barca risale, di chiare sottane.
È ancor nuda la magra collina distesa
nella nebbia del sole e s'avvolge di verde
pubertà, come un velo. La barca inesperta
ha talvolta sussulti che schiumano bianco.

Le ragazze incrocicchiano le braccia allo sforzo
e si parlano a scatti. «Vedrai come il sole
annerisce». Hanno nude le schiene nell'aria.
La collina di ruggine sorride nel cielo.
Le ragazze la fissano a scatti. La terra
ha il colore che avranno al gran cielo d'agosto
spalle e fianchi nascosti nelle chiare sottane.

Nuvolette fiorite punteggiano i colli
sullo specchio dell'acqua. Le ragazze piegate
dànno un rapido sguardo ai capelli scomposti,
dentro l'acqua. Qualcuna sorride da sola
al suo volto. Qualcuna si terge di scatto
il sudore pungente che sa di rugiada.

A un sussulto piú forte, abbandonano i remi
e la barca gorgoglia. «Vedrai come il sole
annerisce». Ricadono le chiare sottane
dalle gambe. Qualcuna non distoglie piú gli occhi
dalla bella collina dove il sole vapora
la rugiada e tra poco empirà tutto il cielo.

Landscape (ix)

Often in the morning, a boat travels upstream
through ice-cold water, its clear skirts rippling.
Still naked, lying in the haze of the sun,
the thin hill is wrapping itself in a veil
of pubescent green. The clumsy boat
lunges occasionally, foaming the water.

The girls hook their arms together against the strain
and speak in quick bursts. "You'll see how the sun
will darken us." Their backs are exposed to the air.
Sometimes they look toward the rust-colored hill
that smiles in the sky. The earth is the color
that the wide skies of August will turn thighs
that are hiding for now beneath their pale skirts.

Cloudlets like flowers dot hills in the distance
over the mirror of water. The girls leaning over
glance at their disheveled hair reflected
in the water. One of them smiles at herself.
One of them quickly brushes away
the pungent sweat that must smell like the dew.

After a sharp lunge, they abandon the oars
and the boat just bobs. "You'll see how the sun
will darken us." The pale skirts fall back
over their legs. One of them can't take her eyes
from the beautiful hill where the sun burns off
the dew and prepares to fill the whole sky.

Due

Uomo e donna si guardano supini sul letto:
i due corpi si stendono grandi e spossati.
L'uomo è immobile, solo la donna respira piú a lungo
e ne palpita il molle costato. Le gambe distese
sono scarne e nodose, nell'uomo. Il bisbiglio
della strada coperta di sole è alle imposte.

L'aria pesa impalpabile nella grave penombra
e raggela le gocciole di vivo sudore
sulle labbra. Gli sguardi delle teste accostate
sono uguali, ma piú non ritrovano i corpi
come prima abbracciati. Si sfiorano appena.

Muove un poco le labbra la donna, che tace.
Il respiro che gonfia il costato si ferma
a uno sguardo piú lungo dell'uomo. La donna
volge il viso accostandogli la bocca alla bocca.
Ma lo sguardo dell'uomo non muta nell'ombra.

Gravi e immobili pesano gli occhi negli occhi
al tepore dell'alito che ravviva il sudore,
desolati. La donna non muove il suo corpo
molle e vivo. La bocca dell'uomo s'accosta.
Ma l'immobile sguardo non muta nell'ombra.

Two

Stretched out in bed, they look at each other:
their bodies, great and exhausted, sprawl.
The man isn't moving. The woman is taking deep breaths,
her soft ribcage pulsing. His outstretched legs
are knobby and lean. The sun-covered street
is only a whisper beyond the closed shutters.

The untouchable air sinks in grave shadows,
freezing the living droplets of sweat
on their lips. Their heads, side by side, still gaze
the same way, but no longer find their bodies
entwined as before. They barely touch now.

Her lips start moving a little, but say nothing.
The breath that was swelling her ribcage pauses
when she feels him staring at her. Her face
turns toward him, resting her mouth near his.
But his gaze doesn't change in that dark.

Their motionless, grave eyes are weighing each other,
in the warmth of the breath that reanimates sweat —
they're desolate eyes. Her body, unmoving,
is soft and alive. His mouth inches closer.
But his motionless gaze doesn't change in that dark.

La casa

L'uomo solo ascolta la voce calma
con lo sguardo socchiuso, quasi un respiro
gli alitasse sul volto, un respiro amico
che risale, incredibile, dal tempo andato.

L'uomo solo ascolta la voce antica
che i suoi padri, nei tempi, hanno udito, chiara
e raccolta, una voce che come il verde
degli stagni e dei colli incupisce a sera.

L'uomo solo conosce una voce d'ombra,
carezzante, che sgorga nei toni calmi
di una polla segreta: la beve intento,
occhi chiusi, e non pare che l'abbia accanto.

È la voce che un giorno ha fermato il padre
di suo padre, e ciascuno del sangue morto.
Una voce di donna che suona segreta
sulla soglia di casa, al cadere del buio.

The House

The man alone listens to the calm voice
with half-closed eyes, as if a breath
were blowing on his face, a friendly breath
rising—astonishing—from a lost time.

The man alone hears the ancient voice
that his fathers, in their day, heard, clear
and collected, a voice that, like the green
of ponds and hills, deepens with evening.

The man alone knows a shadow voice,
caressing, that rises up in the calm tones
of secret springs: he drinks it intently,
eyes closed. Its presence isn't apparent.

This is the voice that once stopped the father
of his father, and on back through dead blood.
The secretive voice of a woman that comes
from a doorway at the falling of dusk.

Part Four

Last Blues

Earth and Death

La terra e la morte

Terra rossa terra nera,
tu vieni dal mare,
dal verde riarso,
dove sono parole
antiche e fatica sanguigna
e gerani tra i sassi—
non sai quanto porti
di mare parole e fatica,
tu ricca come un ricordo,
come la brulla campagna,
tu dura e dolcissima
parola, antica per sangue
raccolto negli occhi;
giovane, come un frutto
che è ricordo e stagione—
il tuo fiato riposa
sotto il cielo d'agosto,
le olive del tuo sguardo
addolciscono il mare,
e tu vivi rivivi
senza stupire, certa
come la terra, buia
come la terra, frantoio
di stagioni e di sogni
che alla luna si scopre
antichissimo, come
le mani di tua madre,
la conca del braciere.

Red earth black earth
you come from the sea,
from the arid green,
place of ancient words
bloodred weariness
and geraniums among stones—
you bear more than you know
of sea and words and toil,
you, rich as a memory,
as the barren countryside,
you, hard and honeyed
word, old as the blood
gathered in your eyes;
and young, like a fruit
that is memory and season—
your breath rests
beneath the August sky,
the olives of your gaze
calm the sea, you live
and live again
as expected, certain
as the earth, dark
as the earth, grinder
of seasons and dreams
that moonlight reveals
to be ancient, like
the hands of your mother,
the hollow of the brazier.

Tu sei come una terra
che nessuno ha mai detto.
Tu non attendi nulla
se non la parola
che sgorgherà dal fondo
come un frutto tra i rami.
C'è un vento che ti giunge.
Cose secche e rimorte
t'ingombrano e vanno nel vento.
Membra e parole antiche.
Tu tremi nell'estate.

You are like a land
no one ever uttered.
You wait for nothing
if not for the word
that will burst from the deep
like a fruit among branches.
There's a wind that reaches you.
Dry and long-dead things
encumber you and leave on the wind.
Ancient words and limbs.
You shiver in the summer.

Anche tu sei collina
e sentiero di sassi
e gioco nei canneti,
e conosci la vigna
che di notte tace.
Tu non dici parole.

C'è una terra che tace
e non è terra tua.
C'è un silenzio che dura
sulle piante e sui colli.
Ci son acque e campagne.
Sei un chiuso silenzio
che non cede, sei labbra
e occhi bui. Sei la vigna.

È una terra che attende
e non dice parola.
Sono passati giorni
sotto cieli ardenti.
Tu hai giocato alle nubi.
È una terra cattiva —
la tua fronte lo sa.
Anche questo è la vigna.

Ritroverai le nubi
e il canneto, e le voci
come un'ombra di luna.
Ritroverai parole
oltre la vita breve
e notturna dei giochi,
oltre l'infanzia accesa.
Sarà dolce tacere.
Sei la terra e la vigna.
Un acceso silenzio
brucerà la campagna
come i falò la sera.

You are also hill
and stony path
and games in the canefields,
you know the vineyard
that at night hushes.
You utter no words.

There's a land that hushes
and it is not yours.
There's a silence that endures
over the plants and hills.
There are waters and countrysides.
You are a closed silence
that won't yield, you are lips,
dark eyes. You are the vineyard.

It's a land that waits
and doesn't say a word.
Days have gone by
under burning skies.
You have toyed with clouds.
It's a grudging land—
your forehead knows that.
This too is the vineyard.

You'll rediscover clouds
and the canefield, and voices
like a shadow in moonlight.
You'll rediscover words
beyond the brief
nocturnal life of games,
beyond the glow of childhood.
It will be sweet to grow quiet.
You're the land and the vineyard.
A bright silence
will burn the countryside
like bonfires in the evening.

Hai viso di pietra scolpita,
sangue di terra dura,
sei venuta dal mare.
Tutto accogli e scruti
e repudi da te
come il mare. Nel cuore
hai silenzio, hai parole
inghiottite. Sei buia.
Per te l'alba è silenzio.

E sei come le voci
della terra—l'urto
della secchia nel pozzo,
la canzone del fuoco,
il tonfo di una mela;
le parole rassegnate
e cupe sulle soglie,
il grido del bimbo—le cose
che non passano mai.
Tu non muti. Sei buia.
Sei la cantina chiusa,
dal battuto di terra,
dov'è entrato una volta
ch'era scalzo il bambino,
e ci ripensa sempre.
Sei la camera buia
cui si ripensa sempre,
come al cortile antico
dove s'apriva l'alba.

Your face is sculpted stone,
your blood hard earth,
you come from the sea.
You gather and examine
and push away all things
like the sea. In your heart
silence and swallowed words
abide. You are dark.
Dawn for you is silence.

And you're like the voices
of the earth—the crash
of the bucket in the well,
the song of fire,
the thud of an apple;
gloomy, resigned words
in door after door,
the cry of the child—
things that never pass.
You do not change. You are dark.
You are the closed cellar
with the hard earth floor,
which the child entered
once, his feet bare,
and will always remember.
You are the dark room
one always remembers,
like the ancient courtyard
where day would break.

Tu non sai le colline
dove si è sparso il sangue.
Tutti quanti fuggimmo
tutti quanti gettammo
l'arma e il nome. Una donna
ci guardava fuggire.
Uno solo di noi
si fermò a pugno chiuso,
vide il cielo vuoto,
chinò il capo e morí
sotto il muro, tacendo.
Ora è un cencio di sangue
e il suo nome. Una donna
ci aspetta alle colline.

You do not know the hills
where the blood flowed.
Each of us ran
each of us abandoned
weapon and name. A woman
watched us flee.
Only one among us
stopped with closed fists,
saw the empty sky,
bowed his head and died
beside the wall, silent.
He's now a bloody rag
and his name. A woman
awaits us in the hills.

Di salmastro e di terra
è il tuo sguardo. Un giorno
hai stillato di mare.
Ci sono state piante
al tuo fianco, calde,
sanno ancora di te.
L'agave e l'oleandro.
Tutto chiudi negli occhi.
Di salmastro e di terra
hai le vene, il fiato.

Bava di vento caldo,
ombra di solleone —
tutto chiudi in te.
Sei la voce roca
della campagna, il grido
della quaglia nascosta,
il tepore del sasso.
La campagna è fatica,
la campagna è dolore.
Con la notte il gesto
del contadino tace.
Sei la grande fatica
e la notte che sazia.

Come la roccia e l'erba,
come terra, sei chiusa;
ti sbatti come il mare.
La parola non c'è
che ti può possedere
o fermare. Cogli
come la terra gli urti,
e ne fai vita, fiato
che carezza, silenzio.
Sei riarsa come il mare,

Your gaze is brine and earth.
One day you dripped
from the sea. There were
plants alongside you,
warm ones, they are
marked by you still.
Agave and oleander.
Your eyes enclose everything.
Your veins, your breath
are brine and earth.

Froth of hot wind,
dog day shadows—
you contain all things.
You are the raspy voice
of the countryside, the cry
of the hidden quail,
the warmth of the stone.
The land is weariness,
the land is sorrow.
At night, the gesture
of the peasant is stilled.
You are the great strain
and the satiating night.

Like rock and grass,
like earth, you are closed;
you churn like the sea.
No word can possess you
or stand in your way.
You gather wounds
as the earth does
and make of them life, breath
that caresses, silence.
You are parched like the sea,

come un frutto di scoglio,
e non dici parole
e nessuno ti parla.

like a clam on a reef,
and you don't say a word
and no one speaks to you.

Sempre vieni dal mare
e ne hai la voce roca,
sempre hai occhi segreti
d'acqua viva tra i rovi,
e fronte bassa, come
cielo basso di nubi.
Ogni volta rivivi
come una cosa antica
e selvaggia, che il cuore
già sapeva e si serra.

Ogni volta è uno strappo,
ogni volta è la morte.
Noi sempre combattemmo.
Chi si risolve all'urto
ha gustato la morte
e la porta nel sangue.
Come buoni nemici
che non s'odiano più
noi abbiamo una stessa
voce, una stessa pena
e viviamo affrontati
sotto povero cielo.
Tra noi non insidie,
non inutili cose—
combatteremo sempre.
Combatteremo ancora,
combatteremo sempre,
perché cerchiamo il sonno
della morte affiancati,
e abbiamo voce roca,
fronte bassa e selvaggia
e un identico cielo.
Fummo fatti per questo.
Se tu od io cede all'urto,
segue una notte lunga

You always come from the sea,
you speak with its hoarse voice.
You always have secret eyes
of living water in the brambles,
and a low forehead, like
a sky heavy with clouds.
Each time you live again
like something ancient
and savage that the heart
already knew and encloses.

Each time it's wrenching,
each time it's death.
We have always fought.
Whoever chooses conflict
has savored death
and carries it in the blood.
Like good enemies
who've given up their hate
we share a single voice
and a single pain,
we live face-to-face
under a meager sky.
No treachery between us,
no useless things—
we will always fight.
We will fight again,
we will always fight,
because we seek the sleep
of death together,
and we have a hoarse voice
a low and savage forehead
and a matching sky.
We were made for this.
If you or I yield to conflict
a long night will follow

che non è pace o tregua
e non è morte vera.
Tu non sei piú. Le braccia
si dibattono invano.

Fin che ci trema il cuore.
Hanno detto un tuo nome.
Ricomincia la morte.
Cosa ignota e selvaggia
sei rinata dal mare.

that isn't peace or truce
and isn't truly death.
You are no longer. Arms
struggle in vain.

As long as our heart trembles.
They spoke a name of yours.
Death begins again.
Savage, unknown creature,
you are reborn from the sea.

E allora noi vili
che amavamo la sera
bisbigliante, le case,
i sentieri sul fiume,
le luci rosse e sporche
di quei luoghi, il dolore
addolcito e taciuto—
noi tendemmo le mani
alla viva catena
e tacemmo, ma il cuore
ci sussultò di sangue,
e non fu piú dolcezza,
non fu piú abbandonarsi
al sentiero sul fiume—
non piú servi, sapemmo
di essere soli e vivi.

And then we cowards
who loved the whispering
evening, the houses,
the paths by the river,
the dirty red lights
of those places, the sweet
soundless sorrow—
we reached our hands out
toward the living chain
in silence, but our heart
startled us with blood,
and no more sweetness then,
no more losing ourselves
on the path by the river—
no longer slaves, we knew
we were alone and alive.

Sei la terra e la morte.
La tua stagione è il buio
e il silenzio. Non vive
cosa che piú di te
sia remota dall'alba.

Quando sembri destarti
sei soltanto dolore,
l'hai negli occhi e nel sangue
ma tu non senti. Vivi
come vive una pietra,
come la terra dura.
E ti vestono sogni
movimenti singulti
che tu ignori. Il dolore
come l'acqua di un lago
trepida e ti circonda.
Sono cerchi sull'acqua.
Tu li lasci svanire.
Sei la terra e la morte.

You are earth and death.
Your season is darkness
and silence. Nothing alive
is more distant than you
from the dawn.

When you seem to wake
you are nothing but grief,
it's in your eyes, your blood,
but you do not feel it.
You live like a stone lives,
like the enduring earth.
And you are dressed in
dreams gestures agonies
that you ignore. Grief
like the water of a lake
trembles and encircles you.
There are rings on the water.
You allow them to vanish.
You are earth and death.

Two Poems for T.

Due poesie a T.

Le piante del lago
ti hanno vista un mattino.
I sassi le capre il sudore
sono fuori dei giorni,
come l'acqua del lago.
Il dolore e il tumulto dei giorni
non scalfiscono il lago.
Passeranno i mattini,
passeranno le angosce,
altri sassi e sudore
ti morderanno il sangue
—non sarà cosí sempre.
Ritroverai qualcosa.
Ritornerà un mattino
che, di là dal tumulto,
sarai sola sul lago.

The plants of the lake
saw you one morning.
The stones the goats the sweat
exist outside of days
like the water of the lake.
The lake remains unmarked
by the days' pain and clamor.
The mornings will pass,
the anguish will pass,
other stones and sweat
will bite into your blood —
it won't always be like this.
You'll rediscover something.
Another morning will come
when, beyond the clamor,
you'll be alone on the lake.

Anche tu sei l'amore.
Sei di sangue e di terra
come gli altri. Cammini
come chi non si stacca
dalla porta di casa.
Guardi come chi attende
e non vede. Sei terra
che dolora e che tace.
Hai sussulti e stanchezze,
hai parole—cammini
in attesa. L'amore
è il tuo sangue—non altro.

You also are love.
Made of blood and earth
like the others. You walk
like one who won't stray far
from your own front door.
You watch like one who waits
and doesn't see. You are earth
that aches and keeps silent.
You have bursts and lapses,
you have words—you walk
and wait. Your blood
is love—that's all.

Death Will Come and
Will Have Your Eyes

Verrà la morte e avrà i tuoi occhi

To C. from C.*

You,
dappled smile
on frozen snows —
wind of March,
ballet of boughs
sprung on the snow,
moaning and glowing
your little "ohs" —
white-limbed doe,
gracious,
would I could know
yet
the gliding grace
of all your days,
the foam-like lace
of all your ways —
to-morrow is frozen
down on the plain —
you dappled smile,
you glowing laughter.

*originally in English

In the morning you always come back

Lo spiraglio dell'alba
respira con la tua bocca
in fondo alle vie vuote.
Luce grigia i tuoi occhi,
dolci gocce dell'alba
sulle colline scure.
Il tuo passo e il tuo fiato
come il vento dell'alba
sommergono le case.
La città abbrividisce,
odorano le pietre —
sei la vita, il risveglio.

Stella sperduta
nella luce dell'alba,
cigolío della brezza,
tepore, respiro —
è finita la notte.

Sei la luce e il mattino.

In the Morning You Always Come Back

The glimmer of dawn
breathes with your mouth
at the end of empty streets.
The gray light of your eyes—
sweet drops of dawn
on the dark hills.
Your step and your breath
flood over the houses
like wind at daybreak.
The city quivers,
stones scent the air—
you are life, renewal.

A star eclipsed
by the light of dawn,
a creaking breeze,
warmth, breath—
the night is finished.

You are light and morning.

Hai un sangue, un respiro.
Sei fatta di carne
di capelli di sguardi
anche tu. Terra e piante,
cielo di marzo, luce,
vibrano e ti somigliano —
il tuo riso e il tuo passo
come acque che sussultano —
la tua ruga fra gli occhi
come nubi raccolte —
il tuo tenero corpo
una zolla nel sole.

Hai un sangue, un respiro.
Vivi su questa terra.
Ne conosci i sapori
le stagioni i risvegli,
hai giocato nel sole,
hai parlato con noi.
Acqua chiara, virgulto
primaverile, terra,
germogliante silenzio,
tu hai giocato bambina
sotto un cielo diverso,
ne hai negli occhi il silenzio,
una nube, che sgorga
come polla dal fondo.
Ora ridi e sussulti
sopra questo silenzio.
Dolce frutto che vivi
sotto il cielo chiaro,
che respiri e vivi
questa nostra stagione,
nel tuo chiuso silenzio
è la tua forza. Come
erba viva nell'aria

You have a blood, a breath.
You are made of flesh,
of strands of hair, of gazes,
even you. Earth and plants,
the March sky, light,
they vibrate and resemble you—
your laugh and your step
like trembling waters—
the wrinkle between your eyes
like gathered clouds—
your tender body
a lump of soil in the sun.

You have a blood, a breath.
You live on this land.
You know its flavors
its seasons its renewals,
you've played in the sun,
you've spoken with us.
New shoot of spring,
clear water, earth,
burgeoning silence,
as a child you played
under a different sky,
your eyes contain its silence,
a cloud, rising like
a spring from the depths.
You laugh now and leap
above this silence.
Sweet fruit living
beneath a clear sky,
breathing and living
this season of ours,
in your closed silence
is your strength. Like grass
alive in the air,

rabbrividisci e ridi,
ma tu, tu sei terra.
Sei radice feroce.
Sei la terra che aspetta.

Verrà la morte e avrà i tuoi occhi—
questa morte che ci accompagna
dal mattino alla sera, insonne,
sorda, come un vecchio rimorso
o un vizio assurdo. I tuoi occhi
saranno una vana parola,
un grido taciuto, un silenzio.
Cosí li vedi ogni mattina
quando su te sola ti pieghi
nello specchio. O cara speranza,
quel giorno sapremo anche noi
che sei la vita e sei il nulla.

Per tutti la morte ha uno sguardo.
Verrà la morte e avrà i tuoi occhi.
Sarà come smettere un vizio,
come vedere nello specchio
riemergere un viso morto,
come ascoltare un labbro chiuso.
Scenderemo nel gorgo muti.

Death will come and will have your eyes—
this death that accompanies us
from morning till evening, unsleeping,
deaf, like an old remorse
or an absurd vice. Your eyes
will be a useless word,
a suppressed cry, a silence.
That's what you see each morning
when alone with yourself you lean
toward the mirror. O precious hope,
that day we too will know
that you are life and you are nothingness.

Death has a look for everyone.
Death will come and will have your eyes.
It will be like renouncing a vice,
like seeing a dead face
reappear in the mirror,
like listening to a lip that's shut.
We'll go down into the maelstrom mute.

You, wind of March

Sei la vita e la morte.
Sei venuta di marzo
sulla terra nuda —
il tuo brivido dura.
Sangue di primavera
— anemone o nube —
il tuo passo leggero
ha violato la terra.
Ricomincia il dolore.

Il tuo passo leggero
ha riaperto il dolore.
Era fredda la terra
sotto povero cielo,
era immobile e chiusa
in un torpido sogno,
come chi piú non soffre.
Anche il gelo era dolce
dentro il cuore profondo.
Tra la vita e la morte
la speranza taceva.

Ora ha una voce e un sangue
ogni cosa che vive.
Ora la terra e il cielo
sono un brivido forte,
la speranza li torce,
li sconvolge il mattino,
li sommerge il tuo passo,
il tuo fiato d'aurora.
Sangue di primavera,
tutta la terra trema
di un antico tremore.

You, Wind of March

You are life and death.
In March you arrived
on the naked earth—
your shudder endures.
Blood of springtime—
anemone or cloud—
your light step
has violated the earth.
The pain begins again.

Your light step
reopened the wound.
The earth was cold
beneath a meager sky,
immobile and closed
like the sluggish dream
of one beyond suffering.
Even the frost was sweet
in the deep of the heart.
Between life and death
hope was hushed.

Now each living thing
has a voice and a blood.
Now the earth and sky
are a forceful shudder,
hope contorts them,
morning overwhelms them,
your step covers them,
your breath of daybreak.
Blood of springtime,
the entire earth trembles
from an ancient tremor.

Hai riaperto il dolore.
Sei la vita e la morte.
Sopra la terra nuda
sei passata leggera
come rondine o nube,
e il torrente del cuore

si è ridestato e irrompe
e si specchia nel cielo
e rispecchia le cose —
e le cose, nel cielo e nel cuore,
soffrono e si contorcono
nell'attesa di te.
È il mattino, è l'aurora,
sangue di primavera,
tu hai violato la terra.

La speranza si torce,
e ti attende ti chiama.
Sei la vita e la morte.
Il tuo passo è leggero.

You reopened the wound.
You are life and death.
You passed lightly
over the naked earth
like a swallow or cloud,
and the heart's torrent
awakes and erupts
and is mirrored in the sky
and itself mirrors things
in the sky and heart
that suffer and writhe
while waiting for you.
It is morning, dawn,
blood of springtime,
you have violated the earth.

Hope becomes contorted,
and waits for you calls you.
You are life and death.
Your step is light.

Passerò per Piazza di Spagna

Sarà un cielo chiaro.
S'apriranno le strade
sul colle di pini e di pietra.
Il tumulto delle strade
non muterà quell'aria ferma.
I fiori spruzzati
di colori alle fontane,
occhieggeranno come donne
divertite. Le scale
le terrazze le rondini
canteranno nel sole.
S'aprirà quella strada,
le pietre canteranno,
il cuore batterà sussultando
come l'acqua nelle fontane—
sarà questa la voce
che salirà le tue scale.
Le finestre sapranno
l'odore della pietra e dell'aria
mattutina. S'aprirà una porta.
Il tumulto delle strade
sarà il tumulto del cuore
nella luce smarrita.

Sarai tu—ferma e chiara.

I Will Pass through Piazza di Spagna

There will be a clear sky.
The streets will open up
onto hills of pine and stone.
The clamor in the streets
will not alter that still air.
The color-splashed flowers
around the fountain
will cast glances like women
amused. The flights of steps
the terraces the swallows
will sing in the sun.
That street will open,
the stones will sing,
my heart will pound, leaping
like the water in the fountain—
this will be the voice
that climbs your stairs.
The windows will know
the smell of morning air
and stone. A door will open.
The clamor of the streets
will be my heart's own clamor
in the vanished light.

It will be you—still and clear.

I mattini passano chiari
e deserti. Cosí i tuoi occhi
s'aprivano un tempo. Il mattino
trascorreva lento, era un gorgo
d'immobile luce. Taceva.
Tu viva tacevi; le cose
vivevano sotto i tuoi occhi
(non pena non febbre non ombra)
come un mare al mattino, chiaro.

Dove sei tu, luce, è il mattino.
Tu eri la vita e le cose.
In te desti respiravamo
sotto il cielo che ancora è in noi.
Non pena non febbre allora,
non quest'ombra greve del giorno
affollato e diverso. O luce,
chiarezza lontana, respiro
affannoso, rivolgi gli occhi
immobili e chiari su noi.
È buio il mattino che passa
senza la luce dei tuoi occhi.

The mornings pass clear
and deserted. Your eyes
used to open like that. Morning
crept by, a motionless
maelstrom of light, silent.
You lived in silence, life
right before your eyes
(no pain no fever no shadow)
like a morning sea, clear.

Where you are, light, is morning.
You were life and all things.
Awake in you, we breathed
beneath a sky that's still within us.
Not sorrow not fever then,
not this leaden shadow of day,
crowded and different. O light,
distant clarity, difficult
breath, turn again your clear
and motionless eyes to us.
With no light from your eyes
morning is dark.

The night you slept

Anche la notte ti somiglia,
la notte remota che piange
muta, dentro il cuore profondo,
e le stelle passano stanche.
Una guancia tocca una guancia—
è un brivido freddo, qualcuno
si dibatte e t'implora, solo,
sperduto in te, nella tua febbre.

La notte soffre e anela l'alba,
povero cuore che sussulti.
O viso chiuso, buia angoscia,
febbre che rattristi le stelle,
c'è chi come te attende l'alba
scrutando il tuo viso in silenzio.
Sei distesa sotto la notte
come un chiuso orizzonte morto.
Povero cuore che sussulti,
un giorno lontano eri l'alba.

The Night You Slept

Even the night resembles you,
the distant night whose tears
fall mutely in the heart's core,
and the stars pass wearied.
A cheek touches a cheek—
a cold shudder, someone
struggles and implores you, alone,
lost in you, in your fever.

Night suffers and craves the dawn,
wretched heart that moves for you.
O closed face, dark anguish,
fever that grieves the stars,
like you another waits for dawn
examining your face in silence.
You stretch out beneath the night
like a closed and dead horizon.
Wretched heart that moves for you,
one distant day you were dawn.

The cats will know

Ancora cadrà la pioggia
sui tuoi dolci selciati,
una pioggia leggera
come un alito o un passo.
Ancora la brezza e l'alba
fioriranno leggere
come sotto il tuo passo,
quando tu rientrerai.
Tra fiori e davanzali
i gatti lo sapranno.

Ci saranno altri giorni,
ci saranno altre voci.
Sorriderai da sola.
I gatti lo sapranno.
Udrai parole antiche,
parole stanche e vane
come i costumi smessi
delle feste di ieri.

Farai gesti anche tu.
Risponderai parole—
viso di primavera,
farai gesti anche tu.

I gatti lo sapranno,
viso di primavera;
e la pioggia leggera,
l'alba color giacinto,
che dilaniano il cuore
di chi piú non ti spera,
sono il triste sorriso
che sorridi da sola.

The Cats Will Know

Rain will fall again
on your smooth pavement,
a light rain like
a breath or a step.
The breeze and the dawn
will flourish again
when you return,
as if beneath your step.
Between flowers and sills
the cats will know.

There will be other days,
there will be other voices.
You will smile alone.
The cats will know.
You will hear words
old and spent and useless
like costumes left over
from yesterday's parties.

You too will make gestures.
You'll answer with words—
face of springtime,
you too will make gestures.

The cats will know,
face of springtime;
and the light rain
and the hyacinth dawn
that wrench the heart of him
who hopes no more for you—
they are the sad smile
you smile by yourself.

Ci saranno altri giorni,
altre voci e risvegli.
Soffriremo nell'alba,
viso di primavera.

There will be other days,
other voices and renewals.
Face of springtime,
we will suffer at daybreak.

Last Blues, to Be Read Some Day*

'Twas only a flirt
you sure did know —
some one was hurt
long time ago.

All is the same
time has gone by —
some day you came
some day you'll die.

Some one has died
long time ago —
some one who tried
but didn't know.

originally in English

Notes on the Text

I have, for the most part, followed the organizing principles set out by Mariarosa Masoero in her excellent edition of Pavese's poetry (*Le Poesie,* Einaudi 1998). Also, where there are textual differences between the Masoero edition and earlier editions, I have generally followed Masoero.

PART I: WORK'S TIRING (1936)

This section contains, in their original order, all the poems that appeared in the first edition of *Lavorare stanca* (*Work's Tiring*), published in 1936 by Solaria. It also includes four poems ("Dina Thinking," "The Billy-Goat God," "Ballet," and "Fatherhood (1)") that Pavese intended to include but that were deleted by Fascist censors on "moral" grounds; these poems have been restored to their originally intended positions, as indicated by a precensor version of the table of contents.

PART II: WORK'S TIRING (1943)

This section contains the poems Pavese added to *Work's Tiring* for the Einaudi edition of 1943. That edition also included all the earlier poems except for seven ("Street Song," "Idleness," "Landholders," "Dina Thinking," "Betrayal," "Bad Company," and "Ancient Discipline"). Since the poems from the 1936 edition are not, following Masoero, included in this section, there is little reason to maintain the thematic divisions that Pavese introduced in the 1943 edition. I have, however, maintained the original order of these additional poems.

PART III: POEMS OF DISAFFECTION

This section contains all of Pavese's poems from 1930 through 1940 that were not included in either edition of *Work's Tiring.* Among the strongest are eleven that Pavese grouped together under the heading "Poesie del disamore" ("Poems of Disaffection"): "Sad Wine (II),"

"Creation," "Deola's Return," "Habits," "Summer (ii)," "Dream," "Sleeping Friend," "Indifference," "Jealousy (ii)," "Awakening," and "Two." *Poesie del disamore* also became the title of a posthumous volume, edited by Italo Calvino, that included nearly all of the poems contained in parts three and four of this volume. The poems in this section are, following Masoero, presented in chronological order.

PART IV: LAST BLUES

This section contains the poems Pavese wrote during the last five years of his life. In 1951, the year following his suicide, the two long sequences were published together in a slim volume, *Verrà la morte e avrà i tuoi occhi (Death Will Come and Will Have Your Eyes)*, that has remained among his most popular works. Davide Lajolo's biography of Pavese, *Il vizio assurdo (The Absurd Vice)*, takes its title from line five of the title poem of that collection.

About the Author

Cesare Pavese—poet, novelist, diarist, essayist—is among the essential Italian writers of the twentieth century. Born in 1908 near Turin, he first rose to prominence as a translator and critic of American literature. In 1936, he published the first of two editions of *Work's Tiring* (*Lavorare stanca*), an extraordinary collection of narrative poems, or "poem-stories" as he called them, and then turned most of his energy toward fiction. By 1950 he had published nine short novels that Italo Calvino called "the most dense, dramatic, and homogeneous narrative cycle of modern Italy." Pavese returned to poetry near the end of his life, and his late lyrics provide a haunting coda to his career. He killed himself in August of 1950, a few weeks after receiving the Premio Strega, Italy's most prestigious literary prize.

About the Translator

Geoffrey Brock received the Academy of American Poets' Raiziss / de Palchi Translation Fellowship for his work on Pavese's poetry. His own poems have appeared widely in journals including *The Hudson Review, New England Review, The Paris Review,* and *Poetry.* Currently a Stegner Fellow at Stanford University, he lives in San Francisco.

Index of English Titles

Affairs, 143
Afterwards, 185
Agony, 175
Alter Ego, 279
Ancestors, 25
Ancient Civilization, 93
Ancient Discipline, 105
"And then we cowards," 327
Atavism, 141
Atlantic Oil, 77
August Moon, 147
Awakening, 297
Bad Company, 97
Ballet, 101
Betrayal, 61
Billy-Goat God, The, 67
Blues Blues, The, 241
Boatman's Wife, The, 199
Boy Who Was in Me, The, 249
Burnt Lands, 149
Cats Will Know, The, 359
City in the Country, 81
Country Whore, The, 181
Creation, 269
"Death will come and will have your
   eyes," 347
Deola Thinking, 35
Deola's Return, 283
Dina Thinking, 59
Discipline, 111
Displaced People, 33
Dream, 289
Drunk Old Woman, The, 203
Fallen Women, 237
Fatherhood (I), 103
Fatherhood (II), 221
Generation, A, 137
Grappa in September, 75
Green Wood, 113
Habits, 285
House, The, 303

House under Construction, 89
I Will Pass through Piazza
   di Spagna, 353
Idleness, 43
Imagination's End, 261
In the Morning You Always Come
   Back, 341
Indian Summer, 253
Indifference, 293
Indiscipline, 107
Instinct, 219
Jealousy (I), 263
Jealousy (II), 295
Landholders, 47
Landscape (I), 29
Landscape (II), 51
Landscape (III), 53
Landscape (IV), 133
Landscape (V), 109
Landscape (VI), 153
Landscape (VII), 177
Landscape (VIII), 205
Landscape (IX), 299
Last Blues, to Be Read Some Day, 363
Mediterraneans, 125
Meeting, 165
Memory, A, 195
Morning, 169
Morning Star over Calabria, 223
Motherhood, 135
Myth, 213
Night, The, 163
Night You Slept, The, 357
Nocturnal Pleasures, 99
Nocturne, 173
Other Days, 273
Outside, 117
Paradise above the Roofs, 215
Passion for Solitude, 65
Passionate Women, 145
People Who Don't Understand, 85

People Who've Been There, 161
Poetics, 277
Poggio Reale, 151
Portrait of the Author, 121
"Red earth black earth," 309
Reigning Peace, 271
Revelation, 167
Revolt, 115
Sad Supper, 129
Sad Wine (I), 245
Sad Wine (II), 267
Sand-Diggers' Twilight, 189
Schoolmistresses, The, 231
Season, A, 55
Simplicity, 217
Sketch of a Landscape, 281
Sleeping Friend, 291
Smokers of Paper, 207
Song, 243
South Seas, 17
Street Song, 39
Summer (I), 171
Summer (II), 287
"The mornings pass clear," 355
"The plants of the lake," 333

Time Passes, 71
To C. from C., 339
Tolerance, 179
Two, 301
Two Cigarettes, 41
Ulysses, 139
Unconvinced, The, 259
Voice, The, 197
Wagoner, The, 193
Widow's Son, The, 157
Words for a Girlfriend, 227
Words from Confinement, 211
Work's Tiring (I), 255
Work's Tiring (II), 119
"You also are love," 335
"You always come from the sea," 323
"You are also hill," 313
"You are earth and death," 329
"You are like a land," 311
"You do not know the hills," 317
"You have a blood, a breath," 343
"You, Wind of March," 349
"Your face is sculpted stone," 315
"Your gaze is brine and earth," 319

Index of Italian Titles

Abbozzo di paesaggio, 280
Abitudini, 284
Agonia, 174
Alter ego, 278
Altri tempi, 272
«Anche tu sei collina,» 312
«Anche tu sei l'amore,» 336
Antenati, 24
Atavismo, 140
Atlantic Oil, 76
Avventure, 142
Balletto, 100
Canzone, 242
Canzone di strada, 38
Casa in costruzione, 88
Cattive compagnie, 96
Città in campagna, 80
Civiltà antica, 92
Creazione, 268
Crepuscolo di sabbiatori, 188
«Di salmastro e di terra,» 318
Disciplina, 110
Disciplina antica, 104
Donne appassionate, 144
Donne perdute , 236
Dopo, 184
Due, 300
Due sigarette, 40
«E allora noi vili,» 328
Estate (I), 170
Estate (II), 286
Estate di San Martino, 252
Esterno, 116
Fine della fantasia, 260
Frasi all'innamorata, 226
Fumatori di carta, 206
Gelosia (I), 262
Gelosia (II), 294
Gente che c'è stata, 160
Gente che non capisce, 84
Gente non convinta, 258

Gente spaesata, 32
Grappa a settembre, 74
«Hai un sangue, un respiro,» 342
«Hai viso di pietra scolpita,» 314
I mari del Sud, 16
«I mattini passano chiari,» 354
Il Blues dei blues, 240
Il carrettiere, 192
Il dio-caprone, 66
Il figlio della vedova, 156
Il paradiso sui tetti, 214
Il ragazzo che era in me, 248
Il tempo passa, 70
Il vino triste (I), 244
Il vino triste (II), 266
In the morning you always come
    back, 340
Incontro, 164
Indifferenza, 292
Indisciplina, 106
L'amico che dorme, 290
L'istinto, 218
La casa, 302
La cena triste, 128
La moglie del barcaiolo, 198
La notte, 162
La pace che regna, 270
La puttana contadina, 180
La vecchia ubriaca, 202
La voce, 196
Last Blues, to Be Read Some Day, 363
Lavorare stanca (I), 254
Lavorare stanca (II), 118
Le maestrine, 230
«Le piante del lago,» 332
Legna verde, 112
Lo steddazzu, 222
Luna d'agosto, 146
Mania di solitudine, 64
Maternità, 134
Mattino, 168

Mediterranea, 124

Mito, 212

Notturno, 172

Ozio, 42

Paesaggio (i), 28

Paesaggio (ii), 50

Paesaggio (iii), 52

Paesaggio (iv), 132

Paesaggio (v), 108

Paesaggio (vi), 152

Paesaggio (vii), 176

Paesaggio (viii), 204

Paesaggio (ix), 298

Parole del politico, 210

Passerò per Piazza di Spagna, 352

Paternità (i), 102

Paternità (ii), 220

Pensieri di Deola, 34

Pensieri di Dina, 58

Piaceri notturni, 98

Poetica, 276

Poggio Reale, 150

Proprietari, 46

Risveglio, 296

Ritorno di Deola, 282

Ritratto d'autore, 120

Rivelazione, 166

Rivolta, 114

«Sei la terra e la morte,» 328

Semplicità, 216

«Sempre vieni dal mare,» 322

Sogno, 288

«Terra rossa terra nera,» 308

Terre bruciate, 148

The cats will know, 358

The night you slept, 356

To C. from C., 339

Tolleranza, 178

Tradimento, 60

«Tu non sai le colline,» 316

«Tu sei come una terra,» 310

Ulisse, 138

Un ricordo, 194

Una generazio, 136

Una stagione, 54

«Verrà la morte e avrà i tuoi
occhi,» 346

You, wind of March, 348

Copper Canyon Press wishes to acknowledge the support of
Lannan Foundation in funding the publication and distribution
of exceptional literary works.

LANNAN LITERARY SELECTIONS 2002

Cesare Pavese, *Disaffections: Complete Poems 1930–1950*,
translated by Geoffrey Brock

Kenneth Rexroth, *The Complete Poems of Kenneth Rexroth*,
edited by Sam Hamill and Bradford Morrow

Alberto Ríos, *The Smallest Muscle in the Human Body*

Ruth Stone, *In the Next Galaxy*

C.D. Wright, *Steal Away: Selected and New Poems*

LANNAN LITERARY SELECTIONS 2001

Hayden Carruth, *Doctor Jazz*

Norman Dubie, *The Mercy Seat: Collected & New Poems, 1967–2001*

Theodore Roethke, *On Poetry & Craft*

Ann Stanford, *Holding Our Own: The Selected Poems of Ann Stanford*,
edited by Maxine Scates and David Trinidad

Reversible Monuments: Contemporary Mexican Poetry,
edited by Mónica de la Torre and Michael Wiegers

LANNAN LITERARY SELECTIONS 2000

John Balaban, *Spring Essence: The Poetry of Hồ Xuân Hương*

Sascha Feinstein, *Misterioso*

Jim Harrison, *The Shape of the Journey: New and Collected Poems*

Maxine Kumin, *Always Beginning: Essays on a Life in Poetry*

W.S. Merwin, *The First Four Books of Poems*

The Chinese character for poetry is made up of two parts: "word" and "temple." It also serves as pressmark for Copper Canyon Press.

Founded in 1972, Copper Canyon Press remains dedicated to publishing poetry exclusively, from Nobel laureates to new and emerging authors. The Press thrives with the generous patronage of readers, writers, booksellers, librarians, teachers, students, and funders — everyone who shares the conviction that poetry invigorates the language and sharpens our appreciation of the world.

PUBLISHERS' CIRCLE
The Allen Foundation for the Arts
Lannan Foundation
Lila Wallace-Reader's Digest Fund
National Endowment for the Arts

EDITORS' CIRCLE
Thatcher Bailey
The Breneman Jaech Foundation
Cynthia Hartwig and Tom Booster
Port Townsend Paper Company
Target Stores
Emily Warn and Daj Oberg
Washington State Arts Commission

For information and catalogs:

COPPER CANYON PRESS
Post Office Box 271
Port Townsend, Washington 98368
360/385-4925
www.coppercanyonpress.org

The text is set in Dante, designed by Giovanni Mardersteig in 1954. Mardersteig was a fine printer and type designer who left his native Germany and eventually made his home in Verona, where he directed the Officina Bodoni and the Stamperia Valdonega. The titles are set in ITC Tyfa, designed by Czech Josef Týfa in 1959. Book design and composition by Valerie Brewster, Scribe Typography. Printed on archival-quality Glatfelter Author's Text by McNaughton & Gunn.